MANAGING THE SUCCESSFUL SCHOOL LIBRARY

MANAGING THE SUCCESSFUL SCHOOL LIBRARY

STRATEGIC PLANNING AND REFLECTIVE PRACTICE

LESLEY S. J. FARMER

Neal-Schuman

An imprint of the American Library Association

Chicago | 2017

Dr. Lesley Farmer is a professor at California State University, Long Beach (CSULB), where she coordinates the Librarianship Program. She earned her MS in library science at the University of North Carolina, Chapel Hill, and received her doctorate in adult education from Temple University. Farmer has worked as a librarian in K–12 school settings, as well as in public, special, and academic libraries. She chairs the International Federation of Library Associations and Institutions' School Libraries Section and is a Fulbright Scholar. Dr. Farmer received the American Library Association's Beta Phi Mu Award for distinguished service to library education, as well as several other professional association awards and national and international grants. Her research interests include information literacy, assessment, and educational technology, especially digital citizenship. A frequent presenter and writer for the profession, Farmer has published over thirty professional books and more than a hundred professional book chapters and articles.

ISBNs
978-0-8389-1494-6 (paper)
978-0-8389-1515-8 (PDF)
978-0-8389-1516-5 (ePub)
978-0-8389-1517-2 (Kindle)

Library of Congress Cataloging-in-Publication Data
Names: Farmer, Lesley S. J., author.
Title: Managing the successful school library : strategic planning and reflective practice / Dr. Lesley S.J. Farmer.
Description: Chicago : ALA Neal-Schuman, an imprint of the American Library Association, 2017. | Includes bibliographical references and index.
Identifiers: LCCN 2016031059 | ISBN 9780838914946 (pbk. : alk. paper)
Subjects: LCSH: School libraries—Administration. | School libraries—United States—Administration.
Classification: LCC Z675.S3 F23727 2016 | DDC 025.1/978—dc23 LC record available at https://lccn.loc.gov/2016031059

Cover design by T. J. Johnson. Cover image © Shutterstock, Inc.

♾ This paper meets the requirements of ANSI/NISO Z39.48–1992 (Permanence of Paper).

Printed in the United States of America

21 20 19 18 17   5 4 3 2 1

CONTENTS

Preface ix

1 Introduction...1

A Few Definitions *4*
Managing School Library Programs *6*
Management Principles and Theories *7*
Management Roles *10*
Bringing It Down to You *11*
References *11*

2 Ideal School Library Programs.....13

Guidelines and Standards for School Libraries *14*
Making Ideal School Library Programs Concrete *17*
REAL School Library Programs *19*
Impact on Management *21*
Bringing It Down to You *22*
References *23*

3 The School Library's Context.........25

The School as an Organization or System *26*
School Vision and Mission *27*
School Curriculum *29*
School Resources *34*
Facilities and Utilities *34*
Material *36*
School Culture *37*
Factors That Impact the School *40*
Bringing It Down to You *42*
References *43*

4 Starting with Yourself 45
   What's Your Vision? *45*
   Another Growth Spurt *46*
   Looking from the Inside Out *47*
   What Is Your Role as a Manager? *48*
   What Do You Bring to the Role? *51*
   How Do You Decide? *52*
   What Is Your Management Style? *53*
   Issues in Personal Management *56*
   Bringing It Down to You *58*
   References *58*

5 Planning 61
   Why Plan? *61*
   Types of Plans *62*
   Steps in Planning *63*
   A Few Words about Change *75*
   Bringing It Down to You *77*
   References *78*

6 Managing Resources........................81
   The Role of Resources and Resource Management *81*
   Analyzing the School Community *83*
   Analyzing the Library's Resources *86*
   Selection *92*
   Collection Development Policies and Procedures *95*
   Acquisitions *96*
   Processing *98*
   Cataloging Issues *99*
   Access *100*
   Circulation *101*
   Maintenance and Repair *104*
   Deselection *107*
   Green Resource Management *108*
   Bringing It Down to You *109*
   References *109*

7 Managing Facilities 111

The Impact of Space on Learning *111*
Learning Theories and Space *112*
Learning Spaces and School Libraries *113*
Functional Areas of the School Library *114*
Access Issues *117*
Furniture Issues *120*
Technology Facilities Issues *122*
A Word about Maintenance *123*
Making Adjustments *123*
Moving *126*
Thinking Green *127*
Renovations and New Facilities *128*
Virtual Spaces *130*
Disaster Planning *131*
Bringing It Down to You *133*
References *133*

8 Managing Funding 135

The Hidden Cost and Funding of School Library Programs *135*
Budget Basics *137*
Ways to Optimize Fiscal Management *142*
Finding Alternative Funding Sources *145*
Administering Grants *148*
Bringing It Down to You *149*
References *149*

9 Managing People 151

What Needs to Be Done? *152*
Matching Functions with Personnel *155*
Staffing from the Start *157*
Training *160*
Using Volunteers *162*
Supervision, Performance Evaluation, and Improvement *168*
Interpersonal Issues *172*
Bringing It Down to You *177*
References *178*

10 Managing Services.......................... 181

A Systems Approach to Library Services *181*
Optimizing Services through Management *185*
Managing Specific Library Services *188*
Bringing It Down to You *192*
References *193*

11 Managing Communication............ 195

A Communication Model *196*
Marketing *210*
Advocacy *215*
From Communication to Relationships *218*
Policies and Procedures *222*
Bringing It Down to You *225*
References *226*

12 From Manager to Leader............. 227

Who Are Leaders? *227*
Leadership Skills and Characteristics *229*
Conditions for Leadership *230*
Student-Centered Leadership *232*
Representative Leadership Styles *233*
Making the Change *235*
Leadership for Results *236*
Bringing It Down to You *237*
References *238*

Bibliography 241

Index 247

PREFACE

HOW DO YOU MANAGE THE SCHOOL LIBRARY PROGRAM ON A PRO-fessional level?

Several good books are available to describe basic operations: how to shelve, how to conduct story hours, how to keep the place organized. As valuable as these functions are, they do not address the professional decisions that school librarians must make on a daily business.

Other books cover strategic planning, but few deal with the realities of school libraries as they need to align with school mission statements and policies, as well as negotiating for budgets alongside other departments.

A couple of years ago a former student and I coauthored *Technology Management Handbook for School Library Media Centers* (2010, Neal-Schuman), which dealt with management issues through a technology lens. It provided both specific tips on topics such as RSS feeds and creating equipment databases, and addressed broader management issues, including selection policies and assessment. However, it didn't address the big picture of management.

In the new American Association of School Librarians standards for school library media programs, the issue of leadership has become more important. School librarians must not only manage the library, but also serve as educational leaders. The question arose: are management skills still needed? Yes!

This book takes a deeper, more professional look at management, its theories, and principles, and explains how school library programs must be systematically planned in light of standards and school community needs. Managers now must be both responsive and proactive. This book links management with leadership, differentiates the two, and shows how the school librarian can carry out both roles.

Chapter one introduces the concept of school library programs, and provides an overview of school library program management. It then discusses management principles and theories.

Chapter two imagines ideal school library programs. It examines professional and legislated standards, focusing on management issues. How those standards are implemented at the local level depends on the school librarian's ability to interpret the school community's vision while following these professional standards.

Just as information gains meaning within a context, the school library program gains meaning and significance within the context of the school community. Chapter three provides tips for conducting an environmental scan that will outline how to manage responsively.

Before managing the library program as a whole, your role as a school librarian will require you to manage yourself. Chapter four looks from the inside out to examine the skills, knowledge, and approaches that you bring to the management table.

By implementing ideas about ideal school library programs, doing a reality check on available resources, and identifying responsibilities, as the school librarian, you can start developing an effective management strategy to bridge the gap between the current and ideal situation. Both short-term and long-term goals are discussed in chapter five. This chapter also provides step-by-step guidelines for connecting process and product to provide a top-quality, effective school library program.

School communities continue to think of the library as consisting of its books and other material resources. Therefore, chapter six explains how to manage those resources in order to meet others' expectations. It overviews the expanding scope of resources in terms of both collections and access. It also discusses how these resources are selected, acquired, organized, stored, and maintained for effective retrieval and use.

Chapter seven examines the spatial elements of resources and services, taking into account their physical interaction and how they are used for the intellectual, social, and emotional development of the school community.

Chapter eight explains how to develop and work with budgets, obtain additional funding, and collaborate with other entities to support the school library program.

Chapter nine gives concrete guidelines for hiring, training, supervising, assessing, and recognizing library workers and other library team members (e.g., advisory boards). Although collaboration and partnering are not management function per se, their support and sustenance do depend on management skills. What management conditions support beneficial interactions? How can partnerships lead to resource allocation and management?

Chapter ten discussed how to manage services. Strategic planning and ongoing assessment must drive services in order for the school library to influence the school most effectively.

Because school librarianship is basically a service profession, effective communication is a core activity. Chapter eleven provides tools to help you manage the communication function for the best results.

Chapter twelve defines leadership, and discusses the conditions for leadership that go beyond management skills and transcend the school library program. The chapter also provides guidelines to help you transition from competent manager to inspiring leader.

I hope that you gain important insights about school library programs and their management—and about yourself as a manager and leader.

1

Introduction

F LIBRARIES HAD NOT ALREADY BEEN INVENTED, THEY WOULD NEED TO be created now. Why?

- All people need information. Some information is required by everyone, but most information needs depend on interests, personal and professional situations, demographics, psychographics, income, literacy factors, culture, physical characteristics, and other variables.
- Information must be accurate, relevant, and appropriate. This requires someone who can select it knowledgeably.
- Access to information should be convenient. This depends on locale, transportation, income, personal attributes (e.g., language), and available forms of access.
- People want to share information. At some point, people may want to share information in real time in mutual physical space. That space must be safe, dependable, and accessible.
- People need help with their information tasks. Someone must know how to meet these needs.
- For society to function, equitable access to information is needed. Some kind of legal, public entity must oversee information access. Therefore, some physical space needs to be established conveniently within the community with access to needed information, managed by a knowledgeable librarian.

This logical argument can be extended to school libraries in terms of convenience (just-in-time learning), safety, unique user focus, and instructional mission.

When asked, "What is the first thing that comes to mind when you think about a library?" people are most likely to say "books" or "resources" or perhaps "information." In short, resources are the key aspect of school libraries. Many also think of the library as a place that houses these resources and enables people to use them. These two aspects do in fact represent the core idea of a library: to help people generate knowledge. The librarian facilitates this process through resource management and, to a degree, instruction or guidance.

School librarians are quick to refute the first assertion—that school libraries are not necessary—on several counts. (The second issue will be discussed later.)

- Not everything is available online. The vast majority of information exists in other formats: print, video, images, sound files. A collection of these alternative resources should be made available, and convenient to access. Public libraries serve the entire community, so their collections might not satisfy the academic needs of the entire school; nor are public libraries located close to every school.
- Not everything online is free. For instance, access to periodicals is usually limited to one week (for newspapers) or another designated time frame,

 Food for Thought

Suppose the school principal says one day: "You can find everything online. The classroom becomes the place for learning, and common areas are used for cross-curricular discussion. Teachers provide the guidance. And there's always the public library to support students' reading. In these tight financial times, we really can't afford a school library, and certainly not a school librarian."

The negative implication of such a mindset is the potential devaluation and extermination of school libraries. Generally, bookstores cannot replace libraries for two reasons: limited resources and cost. However, if information resources can be found for free online, in the convenience of a classroom or home, then a case could be made that the school library is not necessary. How would you counter this opinion?

Let's say that you convince the principal that the library is needed. Maybe it's mandated by the state education code. When you bring up the importance of managing the library, the principal says, "Well, there are several options: parent volunteers, an office clerk, the textbook lady, maybe teachers can take turns during their prep period." How would you respond?

or only to sample articles that require the user to pay for each document every time it is accessed. Subscriptions to fee-based information are most effectively managed centrally.

- Not everyone has equitable access to digital resources. A supervised site with Internet-connective hardware is required for all-day access. Even with computer carts, someone needs to manage the equipment fairly (i.e., sharing among classes) and equitably (i.e., ensuring access for all students, including those with disabilities). The public library provides free Internet access, but its location might not be convenient for students; furthermore, the rest of the community also vie for access to the same computers.
- Not everyone is comfortable using digital resources, and some users may not know how to access them. School librarians are trained in this process, and know how to teach others.
- Not everything online (or elsewhere) is relevant, developmentally appropriate, or of high quality. Resources need to be evaluated, and not everyone knows how to select critically and knowledgeably—or has the time. For that reason, some schools limit online access, and some teachers stick to textbooks and other sources that they already use rather than letting students explore other resources. School librarians, on the other hand, are trained in selecting materials, and because they know all about the curriculum and school community, they can be sure that materials support the school curriculum.
- Copyright law must be followed. Interlibrary loan (which is strictly a library function) limits the number of items that can be borrowed. Even fair use has its limits; teachers, for instance, cannot use the same movie year after year without permission.
- Classroom collections, although convenient for the teacher, are not cost-effective. Few classroom teachers can afford to buy rich collections that match each student's needs and reading abilities, and teachers seldom exchange resources with each other. Resource inequities emerge because of budget constraints and teacher perspectives. A centralized library results in more cost-effective collections, less duplication of efforts and resources, more equitable access, and better management.
- A school library is not confined to a physical space. Collections can be both digital and virtual, and should be selected and managed as carefully as physical collections. Furthermore, access to information is now just as important as ownership of material resources, and access to digital resources must be managed efficiently. School librarians create and follow management principles that encompass all aspects of resources, their organization, and effective use.

In short, school library programs serve as valuable, cost-effective learning centers. A good case can be made that strong school library programs are needed now more than ever because of the greater need for information and technological literacies, growing economic pressures, and increased diversity in the school community and the world at large.

A Few Definitions

In daily parlance, the term "library" usually refers to a physical place with resources, services, and professional staff. The California Education Code defines a school library as "a library that is established to support the curriculum-related research and instructional reading needs of pupils and teachers and provides the collections, related equipment, and instructional services of a staff for an elementary or secondary school" (EC 18810, Article 2). The code also stipulates that only a credentialed teacher librarian can provide library instruction. The law further requires that any library must have:

1. An explicit written mission statement and service objectives
2. A fixed location in California
3. Established hours of service
4. An organized collection of information and materials accessible for use by its primary clientele
5. Designated, on-site, paid staff for library services, one of which must have a master's degree in library/information science or a California credentialed teacher librarian.

The federal government's definition of a public library, according to the Institute of Education Statistics (2005), echoes California's criteria:

A public library is an entity that is established under state enabling laws or regulations to serve a community, district, or region, and that provides at least the following:

1. An organized collection of printed or other library materials, or a combination thereof
2. Paid staff
3. An established schedule in which services of the staff are available to the public
4. The facilities necessary to support such a collection, staff, and schedule
5. Is supported in whole or in part with public funds.

The National Center for Education Statistics (1998, 13) defined library media centers as "an organized collection of printed and/or audiovisual and/or computer resources which [a] is administered as a unit, [b] is located in a designated place or places, and [c] makes resources and services available to students, teachers, and administrators. It is this definition, not the name, that is important; it could be called a library, media center, resource center, information center, instructional materials center, learning resource center, or some other name."

The latter definition raises the issue of terminology. Besides the terms above, school libraries have been called instructional media centers, media centers, information centers, information commons, iCenters, learning labs, learning commons, digital libraries, and cybraries. For the purposes of this book, the term "school library" will be used. Although the term "information commons" is becoming more popular, it has a different connotation in higher education. The hope is that the school community will see how school librarians redefine school libraries in the digital age.

The term "school library (media) program" also needs to be defined. According to the American Association of School Librarian's 1988 publication *Information Power* (AASL 1998, 1), the mission of the library media program "is to ensure that students and staff are effective users of ideas and information. This mission is accomplished through physical and intellectual access to materials, instruction, and collaboration." Thus, the school library program includes the library's resources and services, supported by qualified library staff. In public library settings, a library program is usually associated with an event, but in the school library arena a program is considered to be a full range of material and intellectual offerings that should be planned systematically to support the school's mission. The emphasis is on action rather than on static conditions.

Library staff implement the school library program. The school librarian is considered as the program's manager or administrator. It requires that the professional be credentialed by the state, and sometimes requires a master's degree in library or information studies. Each state determines the basis for certification or licensure; the school librarian usually has to hold a teaching credential as well. As with the terms "library" and "library program," several alternative terms for "school librarian" exist: teacher librarian, library teacher, (school) library media specialist, library media teacher, cybrarian, information navigator, information specialist, information professional, and even information scientist. The 2009 AASL mission statement operationalizes this position (it is called "school library media specialist") in terms of that person's function "[to] empower students to be critical thinkers, enthusiastic readers, skillful researchers, and ethical users of information" (8) through collaborative instructional design, access to materials, and educational leadership. Since issuing that statement, AASL reconfirmed "school librarian" as the preferred term, in the hope that these professionals will reconceptualize their position to reflect current practice.

The bottom line? School libraries and their programs, managed by school librarians, exist in terms of their mission: to serve their communities. Although one of the core criteria of a library is a fixed location, it does not stipulate that the location should be limited to a physical location. Rather, the core function of libraries is to provide information collections that their clientele can physically and digitally access. The central business of libraries is transmitting information that helps their clientele generate knowledge. The school library is distinguished from other libraries by its target population, its explicit instructional charge; and its existence within, and support of, its school system.

Managing School Library Programs

School library program management remains a core function of school librarians. Recently, management has gotten a bad rap, sometimes connoting staid, status quo supervision. However, lack of management is certainly considered a negative. If material and human resources are not well organized and supervised, then the school community will have a harder time using them. Another way to approach the concept of management is to think of it in terms of providing a value-added program that optimizes available resources to support the school's mission.

Basically, the school librarian is responsible for planning, organizing, leading, implementing, controlling, and assessing the school library program. These activities are all managerial (Fayol 1916). The school librarian has to develop and maintain resources, oversee the physical facilities, handle finances, manage people, coordinate and monitor services, oversee and leverage communications, and address policies and procedures. Management provides the conditions for school library programs (SLPs) to be effective and to contribute to the school's overall mission.

The term "administration" may also be used to describe these functions. It usually refers to decision making and planning, and organizing resources and staff so they can achieve certain goals. Management implements those plans and policies by running the operation and working with and through people. In some quarters, management is considered a subset of administration. Sometimes policy-making and service delivery are kept far apart, when in the best case, they should be intertwined. A case can be made that the school librarian administers the school library program, but still has to report to the school's administration. Therefore, the model of a middle management reflects the library's situation more accurately. (It should be noted that this book deals with administrative issues of planning, policy, and finances, but they are addressed within the context of the school site as a whole.) Furthermore, as distributed leadership gains a hold in education, the SLP manager as leader has earned more credence.

Why is the management of school library programs so crucial? Each entity in the school community should contribute to student achievement and the school's overall mission. On a concrete level, the school library program reflects a sizable investment of resources and funding. The athletic department and library have the largest inventories and the most generous budgets of any school entity. The school library is also the largest contained area that provides all-day flexible access to classes and individuals. The school library also provides the individualized, customized instruction at the same time that it serves every student and staff member. In sum, the school library program is a highly visible part of the school, and requires professional management. Because effectiveness depends on substantive collaboration, as the school librarian you must demonstrate your ability to handle your job expertly. You must know how to leverage the school library's resources to maximize student learning, and create the conditions for optimum learning by providing a top-quality, engaging learning environment. Furthermore, as an effective manager, you demonstrate that you have the potential to manage other programs, such as schoolwide literacy initiatives.

Management Principles and Theories

Defining organizations is a good way to start thinking about management. Basically, an organization is a complex group of people that is deliberately formed in order to achieve common goals that cannot be achieved individually. An organization may also be considered a managed system of interdependent parts. As the system receives inputs (e.g., students and resources), it acts upon those inputs and transforms them into outputs (e.g., winning teams and prepared graduates).

Organizations are configured to optimize their systems to achieve their goals. Their structure defines how resources will be allocated and how tasks will be performed using those resources. The organizational structure involves division of labor, rules of authority and responsibility, integration of resources and efforts, monitoring and regulation, and norms of behavior. Within this system, managers are responsible for functions that advance the organization.

Almost a hundred years ago, industrial executive Henri Fayol (1916) posited the five functions mentioned above, as well as fourteen principles of management, several of which still resonate today:

- division of labor into specialized tasks and responsibilities to optimize efficiency
- authority and responsibility, with power to reward and penalize
- discipline and respect for organizational rules
- unity of command so that each person reports to a single supervisor
- unity of direction to standardize operations
- subordination of individual interests to the greater good of the organization
- remuneration to reward effort
- centralization of authority balanced with delegation
- hierarchical line of authority and communication
- order to support the organization's goals
- equity and fairness for staff
- stability of staff
- support of initiative
- esprit de corps

Of these principles, the ones that have changed the most include those of unity, hierarchy, and division of labor. Additionally, in some entrepreneurial situations, discipline may seem less valued, but social norms may replace bureaucratic rules.

Throughout the twentieth century, different management theories have emerged (Barbour 2006; Stuart and Moran 2007):

- In the early 1900s scientific management applied empirical methods to ascertain the most efficient way to perform tasks, which led to standardization.
- In the 1920s sociological and psychological approaches focused on harmonious human relationships and creative problem solving.
- In the 1930s the Hawthorne Effect demonstrated how employees' self-perception of their importance to the organization impacted their productivity. Research also revealed how social codes and conventions impacted work relationships. Social systems theory grew, noting the importance of environmental and social goals, and emphasizing the need for leaders to maintain a stable system of communication. Management operated within a network of interactions and social relationships.
- In the 1940s operations research emerged, which used scientific methods to manage issue such as logistics. At the same time, humanist Abraham Maslow put forth his hierarchical model of human needs, which examined human needs and motivation.

- In the 1950s Douglas McGregor introduced his Theory X and Theory Y of management style, the former reflecting traditional patriarchal assumptions and the latter proposing a more participatory model. Ludwig von Bertalanffy's Open Systems school of management posited organizations as interactive systems that needed to reconcile commercial and human demands.
- In the 1960s Frederick Herzberg built on Maslow's model, identifying contextual maintenance factors (e.g., salary and job security) that, if absent, led to employee dissatisfaction. Content theory emphasized that motivating or growth factors (e.g., recognition and responsibility) were needed for employees to be satisfied and fulfilled. During that same decade, the Social Action school of thought analyzed organizations from the individual employee's perspective, and asserted that organizations had competing factions and that managers had limited power.
- Although it had its roots in the 1920s, the Total Quality Management (TQM) model resurfaced in 1969, emphasizing the need for all employees to be involved in company-wide quality control. TQM became more popular in the 1980s and 1990s. During this time, the contingency approach to management also emerged; it asserted that no single best management style exists, except in the context of the situation.
- In the 1990s, chaos theory was applied to management by asserting that as organizations become increasingly complex and more volatile, more energy is needed to maintain their stability. A balance between stagnation and chaos is needed, with the "edge of chaos" serving as the sweet spot for continuous creativity. This management theory also emphasized how complex systems are linked synergistically. In the same decade, critical management theory examined hegemony and power, and encouraged management for critical action.
- Spanning the end of the twentieth century and the start of the twenty-first century, management of change became more popular. Managers needed to examine the dynamics of systems, particularly in light of cyberspace; align stakeholders' expectations; and train for change. As another way to deal with change, the idea of the learning community, set forth by Peter Senge, gained attention. This approach emphasized a flat hierarchy, open communication, and decentralized decision making.

At the very least, management has evolved from a top-down, standardized process of control to a dynamic complex system that should involve all stakeholders actively both in terms of productivity as well as socialization. Technology and globalization are driving emerging management theories. Each of the theories address at least one aspect of management, and as a cluster of theories, demonstrate management's many facets. As such, you will likely experience a variety of management theories that are played out in education, and will need to negotiate them as you try to function as an effective SLP manager.

Management Roles

Collins (1993) identified managerial roles that apply to school librarians:

- Interpersonal roles: figurehead who carries out symbolic duties, leader of people, liaison with external information networks
- Informational roles: information monitor, information disseminators, spokesperson who transmits information to outsiders
- Decisional roles: entrepreneurial change agent, disturbance handler, resources allocator, and negotiator

These roles are performed at three levels:

- Operational: supervising nonmanagement personnel, and producing products and services
- Tactical: translating school goals into specific library program objectives and activities, and coordinating resources
- Strategic: managing interactions with the external environment

Collins also noted that these roles can only be effective if the manager self-reflects and improves his or her own behavior.

Think about your own managerial roles. Which ones do you practice? How often? You might try an experiment by creating a grid wherein each column is one role, and each row is a unit of time, be it hour or day. The easiest way to document your role is to take a few moments at the end of each day, and check each role that you played. Of course, it would be more accurate to do this check each hour, but it probably would be more distracting than helpful. How well did you perform each role? You can give yourself a plus, minus, or dash to indicate relative quality. By the end of the month, you can get a fairly good idea of the frequency and quality of each role, which you can then use as a start for self-improvement.

Bringing It Down to You

What are your thoughts about management? Think about your perceptions of managers. Draw upon your own experiences as an employee or client, what you have read or observed, maybe even from movies about managers (e.g., http://images.businessweek.com/slideshows/20110711/top-30-must-see-movies-for-business-students/).

1. Write your own definition of a manager.
2. Describe the perfect manager.
3. Describe the worst manager.
4. What distinguishes the effective manager from an ineffective one?
5. How can those management principles be applied to the SLP?

Next, think about yourself as a manager. Usually people become school librarians because they like people, reading, the research process, libraries, and education (Farmer 2008). Few people mention management. However, when asked why they think they would be a good school librarian, "being organized" is a common response, which is an aspect of management. Ask yourself these questions:

1. Do I see myself as a manager?
2. What managerial functions have I done in my life?
3. In what ways have I been a successful manager? Why?
4. What knowledge, skills, and dispositions do I bring to the SLP table?
5. What other knowledge and skills do I want to acquire as an SLP manager?

The rest of the book provides you with details about different aspects of SLP management. You are encouraged to observe effective managers and to try out some of these practices in your own setting.

References

Barbour, J. 2006. "Management Theories." In *Encyclopedia of Educational Leadership and Administration,* edited by K. English, 635–39. Thousand Oaks, CA: SAGE.

Collins, R. 1993. *Effective Management.* Chicago, IL: Commerce Clearing House.

Farmer, L. 2008. "Predictors for Success: Experiences of Beginning and Expert Teacher Librarians." In *Educational Media and Technology Annual,* edited by V. J. McClendon. 157–84. Westport, CT: Libraries Unlimited.

Fayol, H. 1916. *Administration industrielle et general.* Paris, France: Dunod.

National Center for Education Statistics. 1998. *Evaluation of Definitions and Analysis of Comparative Data for the School Library Statistics Program.* Washington, DC: National Center for Education Statistics.

Stuart, R., and B. Moran. 2007. *Library and Information Center Management.* Westport, CT: Libraries Unlimited.

2

Ideal School Library Programs

" I CAN'T WAIT TO BECOME A SCHOOL LIBRARIAN, AND HAVE THE PER-
fect school library!" Such enthusiasm is laudatory, and reflects enthusiasm
and commitment, but it also requires solid grounding.

What is the ideal school library? How do you imagine it? Cozy? Vibrant?
Contemplative? Buzzing? Rich with books? Digitally advanced? Take
a moment to jot down your thoughts about—maybe draw a picture of—your
school ideal library. Your response probably says a lot about you: your past
library experiences, your academic training, your sense of space, your attitudes about people, your sense of service, and so on. Is there a perfect school
library? Very unlikely, because the library is contextualized by the school, its
community, available resources, and the surrounding cultures. Each person has
a unique vision of *the* ideal school library, which is informed by his or her own
background and experiences, so one of your challenges will be to try to optimize
the school library and its program in light of varying expectations, needs, and
wants.

Although the specifics may differ, several overarching standards do exist to
guide school library programs. This chapter examines professional and legislated standards, focusing on management issues. How those standards are
implemented at the local level depends on your management ability to interpret
the school community's vision to comply with these professional standards.

Guidelines and Standards for School Libraries

As noted above, no perfect school library exists, and no single school library is likely to meet the needs of all school communities. Nevertheless, guidelines and standards for school libraries do exist, which reflect best practices that lead to effective users of information and users. At this point, dozens of studies have demonstrated that school library programs impact students' academic success, helping to make them effective users of information and ideas. In a meta-analysis of studies examining the school library program conditions that lead to student success, Farmer (2008) identified these factors: staffing; the library facility itself as a physical learning environment; library collections; instruction, collaboration, reading-related and other services; and program administration. More specifically, the following variables were identified as necessary conditions for a high-quality school library program (SLP):

- one full-time teacher librarian
- one full-time paraprofessional
- an integrated library management system (cataloging and circulation), including an online public access catalog
- Internet access for students
- the library is open thirty-six hours or more per week
- at least some flexible scheduling
- a library web page or portal
- adequate facilities, that is, space and seating for one class and additional individuals as well as for the collection
- a minimum of ten computers at the elementary level; fifteen computers at the middle school level; and twenty-five computers at the high school level)
- at least two online subscription databases (one video/image-based and at least one periodicals aggregator); the model baseline for text databases is one for elementary, two for middle school, and three for high school
- regular planning with at least one grade or department of teachers (20 percent or more)
- ongoing services, including readers' advisory/guidance, information literacy instruction, and Internet and database instruction
- a current set of policies and procedures and a yearly strategic plan that includes assessment of program goals

These findings formed the basis for California's model school library standards.

Because education is largely a local issue, each state and regional accreditation agency has its own SLP standards, which may vary from a single catch-all sentence to quantitative measures along several dimensions. Several states refer to the American Association of School Librarians (AASL) standards. Some states also have library curriculum standards. Some SLP standards have legislative weight (e.g., those stipulated in state codes), while others are recommendations of professional associations, which are not legally binding. The websites Resources for School Librarians (www.sldirectory.com/libsf/resf/evaluate.html) and National Association of State Educational Media Professionals (http://nastemp.wiki spaces.com) maintain lists of school library standards.

AASL's 2009 guidelines for school library media programs focuses on actions that school librarians should take. To support teaching for learning, the school library program should:

- Promote collaborative partnerships.
- Promote reading.
- Provide instruction that addresses multiple literacies.
- Model an inquiry-based learning approach and information searching process.
- Assess students learning regularly as part of SLP assessment.
- Model best practice and leadership within the school community.

In terms of building an effective learning environment, the SLP should:

- Build on a strategic plan that supports the school's mission, goals, and objectives.
- Include an advocacy plan.
- Be staffed by at least one full-time credentialed school librarian, and supported by qualified staff.
- Provide flexible and equitable access to well-developed resource collections in various formats that support the school curriculum and learner needs.
- Have sufficient funding to support and improve the SLP.
- Have policies and procedures.
- Support professional development.

The National Council for Accreditation of Teacher Education (NCATE) serves as the national accreditation agency for school librarian preparation programs. Under this umbrella, the American Library Association (ALA) and AASL (2010) specified the knowledge, skills, and dispositions of entering school librarian professionals (designated as "candidates"). Management aspects are indicated by italics.

- Standard 1: Teaching for learning. Candidates are effective teachers who demonstrate knowledge of learners and learning and who model and *promote collaborative planning,* instruction in multiple literacies, and inquiry-based learning, enabling members of the learning community to become effective users and creators of ideas and information. Candidates *design and implement instruction* that engages students' interests and develops their ability to inquire, think critically, gain, and share knowledge (1).
- Standard 2: Literacy and reading. Candidates *promote reading* for learning, personal growth, and enjoyment. Candidates are aware of major trends in children's and young adult literature and select reading materials in multiple formats to support reading for information, reading for pleasure, and reading for lifelong learning. Candidates use a variety of strategies to *reinforce classroom reading instruction* to address the diverse needs and interests of all readers (6).
- Standard 3: Information and knowledge. Candidates *model and promote ethical, equitable access to and use of physical, digital, and virtual collections* of resources. Candidates demonstrate knowledge of a variety of information sources and services that support the needs of the diverse learning community. Candidates demonstrate the *use of a variety of research strategies to generate knowledge to improve practice* (10).
- Standard 4: Advocacy and leadership. Candidates *advocate* for dynamic school library programs and positive learning environments that focus on student learning and achievement by collaborating and connecting with teachers, administrators, librarians, and the community. Candidates are *committed to continuous learning and professional growth* and *lead professional development* activities for other educators. Candidates *provide leadership by articulating ways in which school libraries contribute* to student achievement (14).

The National Board for Professional Teaching Standards stipulates the standards for accomplished school librarians and other educators. The standards are based on five core propositions:

1. Teachers are committed to students and their learning.
2. Teachers know the subjects they teach and how to teach those subjects to students.
3. Teachers are responsible for managing and monitoring student learning.
4. Teachers think systematically about their practice.
5. Teachers are members of learning communities.

Their specific standards that apply to school librarians (National Board for Professional Teaching Standards 2012, 22–23) are quoted below. Again, management aspects are indicated by italics.

- Understand the academic, personal, and social characteristics of students and *relate* them to learning.
- Understand and apply the principles of library and information studies to support student learning and to *create an effective, integrated library media program.*
- Are *visionary leaders* in their schools and in the profession.
- Use a range of strategies and techniques to manage and administer effective library media programs.
- Use *technologies effectively and creatively to support student learning and library media program administration.*
- *Provide access, ensure equity,* and embrace diversity.
- *Uphold and promote professional ethics and ethical information behavior.*
- Promote the library media program through *outreach and the development of advocates.*
- Engage in *reflective practice* to improve student learning.

The bases for these school library standards vary; some build on research, such as California's, but most seem to reflect professionals' consensus of best practice.

Making Ideal School Library Programs Concrete

When imagining the ideal school library program at the local level, people tend to operationalize their ideal in concrete terms: what the library looks like and what happens therein. Each stakeholder is likely to think in terms of his or her own reality and needs. For instance, an elementary student may envision a library that has toys and a swimming pool and "tons" of computers. A middle school teacher might include a production area with endless supplies for students to use. A high school administrator might imagine a quiet center for intellectual study. A parent might imagine a safe and cozy haven for reading and story hours. These ideas may draw upon childhood memories, generalizations from other types of libraries, or observations of current library practice. People are likely to start with their personal concept of a library, and then extrapolate to the school and their own needs. Less often does the school community start with existing SLP standards, or dig more deeply into the concept of information needs in general. On the other hand, understanding such perspectives helps you as the school librarian to understand the stance of stakeholders, and reminds you how impactful library experiences can be! For instance, a library's musty smell can remain in someone's memory for a long time—as can a helpful librarian who "saved" a student's research paper. Emotionally powerful memories can be easily triggered, and negative impressions can be difficult to overcome.

Nevertheless, the school community can benefit from learning about of an effective SLP's potential.

- The following video can stimulate lively discussion about imagining school libraries: www.youtube.com/watch?v = w0F0vR4WGIg and http://vimeo.com/11807471.
- Construct a survey based on SLP standards, and disseminate it to key stakeholders and decision-makers. Ask respondents to what degree they value those standards and to whether they think the current SLP meets those standards. If both the library staff and the respondents think that the library meets the standard, then everyone agrees that the SLP is on the right track. If both parties do not think that the library meets the standard, but should, then a supported plan of action can be forthcoming. If perceptions disagree, then the respondent needs to be educated about the issue—which is a good conversation starter.
- Share the best practices of publicly recognized school library programs. Professional associations such as AASL and state groups often award high-quality SLPs and school librarians. The California School Library Association, for instance, produces an annual "Good Ideas" publication (www.csla.net/index.php/publications/good-ideas) that features effective collaborative learning activities—and outstanding administrators who support SLPs. In addition, periodicals in the field feature the efforts of successful school librarians.
- Find out if any effective school libraries are located near you, and check them out. Find out what kind of administrative support exists at such sites, and if administrators would be willing to chat with your site administration staff. A visit or web conference can make ideas into concrete realities.
- Compare your SLP, its resources, and its services with other sites. States usually maintain statistics about school libraries, and the Institute of Education Statistics gathers statistics about school libraries (http://nces .ed.gov/surveys/libraries/school.asp). Library Research Services (www .lrs.org/school) conducts research on school libraries, and links to other government sources of school library statistics. AASL has collected data about school libraries since 2007, and also maintains links to other data sources (www.ala.org/aasl/researchandstatistics/researchandstatistics). *School Library Journal* routinely surveys school libraries about budgets and other data. You can share these sources directly, or create infographics comparing SLPs. However, this can be a double-edged sword. First,

you must be able to gather your own statistics and then analyze them (which will be covered in the chapter on planning). You also have to look carefully at the numbers to make sure that they support your arguments; for instance, if the library collection is large but old, the administrator might just stop at the number of volumes per student and conclude that the library doesn't need to buy any more books.

• If you serve a high school population, invite librarians and teaching faculty from the local post-secondary institution to talk about the academic needs of their students. How can the high school and its SLP ensure that their graduates will be college-ready? What resources and instruction should the SLP provide?

This latter approach speaks to the need to identify student exit learning outcomes. Because the SLP should align with, and support, the school's mission, to approach the idea of a site-based ideal SLP, it makes sense to examine the conditions that ensure that students meet those outcomes. This process is detailed in the following chapter. The underlying idea is that each person sees the library in terms of its benefit to him or her. For example, students should be able to read fluently. Reading specialists diagnose students' reading issues, and select interventions that can help students read successfully. For reading specialists to be effective, they require assessment tools and instructional materials on hand, as well as a rich collection of reading material, and they must keep current in the field. The SLP can provide a rich collection of student and professional reading, and the school librarian can monitor new developments in the field. Reading specialists may have other wishes, which the SLP might address. In any case, this kind of conversation among school community members and library staff frames the concept of the ideal SLP to appeal to each stakeholder while emphasizing the school's bottom line: student success. It also transcends prior conceptions to afford a fresh look at SLP possibilities.

REAL School Library Programs

In any case, each person's perspective about the ideal SLP is unique, just as the ultimate SLP is a unique reflection of each school community. For instance, the needs of new Americans from rural Central America differ from those of inner-city African-Americans. Elementary schools differ from high schools. Schools configured as career path academies differ from comprehensive K–12 settings. Different regions of the United States reflect different expectations. For each setting and population, the SLP must provide appropriate and relevant resources and services.

Now that everyone's perspective and visions are on the table, they can be considered when creating the best possible SLP for that site. Note the term "possible": what material and human resources are available now—or potentially—to make the ideal a reality? Additionally, different people's wishes may conflict with one another. For instance, if even a quarter of all classroom teachers wanted to use the library every day, it would not be possible to accommodate them all. Nevertheless, the input provides a starting point for prioritizing wishes, distinguishing between wants and needs, and aligning ideas with the school mission. Furthermore, if enough constituents demand a specific SLP resource or service that the library does not currently provide, such as a professional reading collection or digital citizenship instruction, then a solid case may be made to administrators to allocate funds for such initiatives.

Notice too that this process actively involves the school community. People want to be recognized for their ideas, and appreciate when those ideas are acted upon. Indeed, if you don't want to follow up on their comments, think carefully about asking for their help. On the other hand, when you do acknowledge and build on community needs in concert with the community, then the SLP's sphere of influence grows. Furthermore, the community gains a greater sense of ownership, and is more likely to support library efforts.

Food for Thought

As part of your plan to involve the middle school community in working towards the ideal SLP for the site, you decide to brainstorm with some of the teachers. The art teacher volunteers her plan for students to draw pictures of the ideal school library. At the time, you think that's a great idea, and believe that it will engage the preteens and spark some good ideas. The results of the plan are mixed, but largely disheartening. Some students clearly didn't care, and made goofy stick drawings and crude book covers. Others drew the library as a Star Trek interior, a beach resort, a TV studio, a Hogwarts spin-off, and a prison. Others portrayed very conventional ideas of a library with students reading and sitting at computers surrounded by book shelves. One disturbing image showed kids in an arcade burning books in the corner. A couple were rather clever: cloud areas for different functions, a homey image with a fireplace and storyteller, a shopping mall motif. While you flip through the drawings during lunch, the gym teacher walks by and spots an image of kids tossing books through a basket hoop. "Yeh, I could see that; we need to fix the gym before spending a lot of effort on the library." How do you respond to the gym teacher and the art teacher? How do the drawings inform you? What do you take away from these inputs?

The preceding scenario demonstrates that input must be analyzed. Input is only as good as its interpretation. Surveys should be followed up with stakeholder focus groups and a few strategic interviews. Furthermore, you should remember that the SLP is just one part of the school, so other priorities might compete, which you will have to investigate and negotiate.

Impact on Management

For the ideal SLP to become a reality, effective management is required. From the moment that you begin to search for SLP standards to the time you assess the resultant action plan and identify all the people skills involved in these processes, you are displaying managerial skills.

As with school library standards, guidelines also exist for managing SLPs. Although teaching and leadership require management skills, the obvious role that pertains to management in the AASL 2009 guidelines is program administration. An effective SLP "requires the collaborative development of the program mission, strategic plan, and policies as well as the effective management of staff, the program subject, and the physical and visual spaces" (American Association of School Librarians 2009, 18). The school librarian has to provide access to needed resources, collaborate with stakeholders and relevant organizations, and address broader educational issues.

Management skills are required for the aspects of the SLP designated by AASL (2009).

Teaching for learning:

- promoting collaboration among the school community through interpersonal skills
- promoting reading through coordinating and overseeing implementing reading promotional activities
- providing instruction, which requires assessment, planning, collaboration, scheduling, organization, facilities management, and general supervision skills
- assessing students, which requires resource evaluation and management, interpersonal skills, and analysis skills

Building the learning environment:

- developing and implementing a long-term strategic plan for the SLP
- recruiting, selecting, hiring, training, and supervising library staff and volunteers

- providing flexible and equitable access through facilities management, collaboration, and resource management
- developing and managing collections, which requires financial expertise, analytical skills, facilities management, organization, and supervision
- seeking, locating, and managing funds
- creating, complying with, and monitoring policies and procedures
- creating and implementing an SLP advocacy plan through communication and interpersonal skills
- supporting professional development, which requires human resource management, interpersonal skills, and communication skills
- providing leadership, which requires assessment, planning, analysis, decision-making, communication, interpersonal skills, collaboration, organization, resource management, and supervision skills

In short, SLP management standards encompasses more than following policies and procedures, maintaining collections, taking care of the library facility, handling money, dealing with people, and communicating.

Bringing It Down to You

Now you can explore the "vision thing" relative to your concept of ideal SLP management. You read about this idea a bit in the first chapter. As you imagine the ideal SLP, particularly as it could leverage other factors at your school, think about how you could ideally manage it. If you already manage the SLP, imagine how you might redesign that management function.

- What would your day look like?
- How long a day would it be, and what would be your ideal hours?
- How much of the day would you like to spend on managing?
- What kinds of management activities would you be doing? Who would help you in this endeavor—and what would they do?
- Would you like to do the visioning and let other people handle the details, or are you a hands-on type of person?
- Do you see yourself behind a desk, or moving around a lot?
- How much time would you spend in the library and elsewhere?
- How would you make decisions?
- What would be your ideal management style?
- How would you like to feel as a manager?
- Who would you talk with—and to what end?

- How would you relate to other people in management positions?
- Do you see yourself as responding to change, or making change happen?

In short, what do you want out of the SLP management job? You might want to jot down some of your thoughts now, and then review them after finishing this book and working a while in the library to see if your ideas—and ideals—have changed. There's nothing like a reality check to test your assumptions about ideal management.

References

American Association of School Librarians. 2009. *Empowering Learners: Guidelines for Library Media Programs.* Chicago, IL: American Library Association.

American Association of School Librarians and Association of Educational Communications and Technology. 1988. *Information Power.* Chicago, IL: American Library Association.

American Library Association and American Association of School Librarians. 2010. *ALA/AASL Standards for Initial Preparation of School Librarians.* Chicago, IL: American Library Association.

Farmer, L. 2008. "Predictors for Success: Experiences of Beginning and Expert Teacher Librarians." In *Educational Media and Technology Annual,* edited by V. J. McClendon, 157 – 84. Westport, CT: Libraries Unlimited.

National Board for Professional Teaching Standards. 2012. *Library Media Standards,* 2nd ed. Arlington, VA: National Board for Professional Teaching Standards.

National Center for Education Statistics. 1998. *Evaluation of Definitions and Analysis of Comparative Data for the School Library Statistics Program.* Washington, DC: National Center for Education Statistics.

3

The School Library's Context

JUST AS INFORMATION GAINS MEANING WHEN IT IS IN CONTEXT, so too does the school library program gain meaning and significance within the context of the school community. Although standards and ideals are useful and inspiring, the reality is that the school library exists within the context of the school district where it is located, and its management should ensure that the library aligns with the district's mission and vision. Student success is usually the chief goal, and the primary means to achieve that goal are the curriculum and supporting resources (material and human). Teacher librarians need to identify school resources that they can use to support the library's program, just as they manage library resources to improve overall school impact on student success. The school culture, with its norms and expectations, shape the direction and implementation of the entire enterprise, so school librarians must assess that culture in order to determine what managerial approaches will be the most effective for carrying out the library program. Additionally, the entire school depends on district, state, and federal resources and expectations. Therefore, management of the school library is also accountable to all of these entities. This chapter provides tips for conducting an environmental scan in order to manage responsively.

The School as an Organization or System

A school may be considered as a large, complex group of individuals who interact and share some commonality (e.g., people involved in neighborhood elementary education), who usually share a common goal or purpose, that is, its mission. A group has an identity that differentiates it from the "outside," but the individuals within the group may have unique roles. Groups may be measured on their functional and social dimensions. Do they support and accomplish goals, such as graduating prepared students? Do the members of the group socialize with each other? Groups change over time, but sustainable groups have enough cohesiveness to endure changes in personnel.

More accurately, then, this complex group constitutes an organization, which includes several groups; each has its unique goals, but they share an overarching mission and work interdependently. Organizations exist as a means to bring people together, and to allocate resources so that identified goals can be achieved that would be impossible to carry out individually or in small groups. The whole is greater than the sum of its parts.

Alternatively, a school may be considered as a managed system that processes inputs that then result in outputs. Policies and procedures guide these transformations, which are enforced through a system of rewards and penalties. Sometimes schools are called loosely coupled systems because groups within the system can operate fairly independently and use a variety of means to meet a goal. For example, the school librarian may have great latitude in how to manage the library, and other entities in the school may have similar functions, such as collection development (of textbooks, science supplies, athletic supplies, etc.), instruction, and event planning. Schools may also be called open systems because they deal with their surrounding environment, taking in and transforming resources based on assessment and feedback processes. In terms of the school library program (SLP), school librarians may connect with other librarians for various purposes: homework support, interlibrary loan, reference help, program coordination. As a result of these interactions, the school librarian might add materials to the collection or talk with classroom teachers about assignments.

More specifically, a school's input products include:

- Facilities: land, buildings, utilities, furniture
- Material resources: equipment, software, textbooks, library collection, supplies
- Fiscal resources: school/district/state/national funding, grants, awards, donations, sales, tuition, fees

- Human resources: staff, students, volunteers, friends, families, consultants
- Intellectual resources: experience, academic preparation, expertise, policies, and procedures

The SLP often has substantial input products: library space, collections, technologies, supplies, a variety of funding sources (government, parents, friends, donations, grants), staff, and volunteers.

Human resources then process and use these inputs: teaching, managing, communicating, assessing, advising, providing specialized services such as nursing and counseling, providing operational services, maintaining facilities, ensuring safety. Likewise, the SLP actively uses resources: managing facilities, collections in the broadest definition, funding, and personnel, largely dependent on available intellectual resources.

The results constitute outcome products: student and staff work, student and staff assessment results, facilities status (wear and improvement), student and staff retention or departure, awards and other public recognition, and revenue. These outcomes are the result of output processes: school and community behaviors and attitudes, which may be impacted by health, personal issues, and social situations. These processes apply to library personnel as well.

Because schools are open systems, they are also influenced by external factors: natural and man-made disasters, community expectations and activities, government policies and legislation, and other socioeconomic concerns. Libraries, for instance, can flood, may be impacted by state budget shortfalls due to bad economic times, or might be mandated to merge with a public library.

School Vision and Mission

A good place to start thinking about the SLP's role is to consider the school's own ideal. Its vision statement talks about the school's future, and communicates the school's values and purpose. A vision statement might focus on

- teaching students how to learn
- imparting culture to students
- helping students find self-fulfillment
- preparing students to become productive citizens and change the social order
- giving students tools needed to master subjects

You can see how these statements reflect philosophies about education in general, and may well reflect the ideologies of the community.

Likewise, the mission links the present with the future, identifying the school's goals. A school mission may be considered its "brand," and should reflect deep and broad-based discussion. The school mission should also be reviewed regularly to make sure that all the groups within the school organization align with and support the mission. Everyone should be moving in the same direction, even if they take slightly different paths (which reflects loose coupling).

Schools are more likely to have a mission statement than a vision statement, possibly because goals need not be long-term or future-oriented, and a school might be more comfortable maintaining the status quo rather than changing. If it is mandated from outside the organization (e.g., as a requirement for accreditation), and not "owned" by the organization, then the mission statement's usefulness is limited, or it may languish on the principal's shelf. An interesting exercise is to go to a school's public documents, such as its website, and locate its mission statement—it is startling how few you will see.

Here are examples of mission statements:

- Kitty Hawk Elementary School seeks to create a challenging learning environment that encourages high expectations for success through development-appropriate instruction that allows for individual differences and learning styles. Our school promotes a safe, orderly, caring, and supportive environment. Each student's self-esteem is fostered by positive relationships with students and staff. We strive to have our parents, teachers, and community members actively involved on our students' learning.
- The [Princeton Academy of the Sacred Heart's] mission is to develop young men with active and creative minds, a sense of understanding and compassion for others, and the courage to act on their beliefs. We stress the total development of each child: spiritual, moral, intellectual, social, emotional, and physical.
- The Tamalpais Union High School District is dedicated to the development of creative, passionate, and self-motivated learners. Upon graduation, students will be prepared for engaged citizenship and able to contribute individually and collaboratively in order to address the challenges of a dynamic and diverse world. To these ends, all students will demonstrate mastery of core competencies and will be offered meaningful learning experiences to enable them to access and critically analyze information, pose substantive questions, and communicate effectively.

You should always examine the school's mission carefully.

- How easy is it to locate?
- How many people can recite and explain it?
- How is it communicated—and for what reason?
- How was it developed?
- How is it implemented day-to-day?
- How do decisions reflect the school's mission?
- How does resource allocation align with the mission?
- How does the library's mission statement (if it has one) align with the school's?

If the school's mission drives decisions, then the SLP should align with it. If the mission is moribund, or if the school's efforts conflict with the mission, then the school librarian needs to dig deeper to uncover the *real* mission of the school— or at least the basis for decision making and resource allocation. In either case, the SLP either should reflect the mission or the school's tacit values—or the ideal SLP could inspire the school to adopt a new, improved mission.

School Curriculum

Curriculum may be defined as the knowledge and skills that schools are supposed to help students master. Curriculum can be considered as subject matter, as a plan, as a series of experiences, and in terms of outcomes.

The official description of programs, courses, and objectives constitute the explicit curriculum, but other curricula also exist:

- implicit or hidden curriculum as reflected in the school's "atmosphere" or norms (e.g., a "jock" school, a technical school, a competitive school, a culture of creativity), or exhibited in the ways the teachers present subject matter (e.g., inquiry-based, ideological bents, rote)
- null, or what is *not* taught (e.g., technical training, parenting, dance)
- extracurricular or co-curricular, usually offered through clubs and other student activities
- integrated, which mixes concepts and skills across subject areas, as is most often seen in career academies

The school's mission should drive curriculum, but enough ambiguity exists in most mission statements that other drivers (generally from the outside) usually take up most of the curriculum "road":

- federal mandates (e.g., the Every Student Succeeds Act, federal funding qualifications)
- state standards and mandates
- standardized testing
- professional association standards (e.g., National Council of Teachers of Mathematics, National Association of Independent Schools)
- business and nonprofit organizations (e.g., The Partnership for 21st Century Skills, foundations)
- accreditation agencies
- state college and university admissions requirements
- social issues and public opinion (e.g., fear of pandemics, obesity, globalization, economic competitiveness)
- educational publishing, especially textbooks
- local school boards
- parents

Local education, in particular, seems to have many masters. By the time that each influencer gives its list of "musts," school districts and local schools have little wiggle room for major curricular differences.

Nevertheless, student need and demographics comprise the other main basis of curriculum decision making. For instance, if most students are English language learners, then remedial, bilingual, or enrichment courses are needed. If the site serves as a magnet school for students with severe special needs, then curriculum and instruction needs to address these differences. A quick look at socioeconomic neighborhood profiles often gives an idea of the kind of curriculum that may be offered at the local school: college-preparatory versus career and technical education—or career pathways.

Curriculum development involves several steps, as detailed below (Wiles 2005). Where does the school library program fit into curriculum development? Theoretically, it should constitute an integral part of the entire process, from philosophy through lesson planning. In the following, possible SLP involvement and impact at each step are indicated by italics. If you can't be involved throughout the process, at least be aware of the process and the decisions because they *will* impact the SLP and its management.

Philosophy. The vision statement tends to be best at capturing educational philosophy. It expresses the decision makers' values and priorities, and sets expectations about subject matter, instruction, and students' roles. For example, an idealistic philosophy focuses on enduring truths; schools try to sharpen students' minds through lectures and discussions. In contrast, an experimental philosophy believes that reality is ever-changing and relative; learning focuses on active group problem solving. *Information literacy, a core principle in library science, takes on different guises depending on the school's philosophy. For instance, in an idealistic philosophy, students might memorize a research process model, while an experimental philosophy would support a more inquiry-based approach to information literacy.*

Program concept. The philosophy, in turn, frames the program's conception. How will the school community be involved? How will classrooms be configured? How will knowledge be organized? What will be the staffing pattern? How will governance be handled? What teaching strategies will be used? What will be the school's climate? *In a school that focuses on project-based learning, the SLP can serve as a learning laboratory with resources and tools for student use to produce projects; the school librarian might co-teach classes. If the school has a very hierarchical structure, the school librarian might find it hard to pinpoint his or her status in the organization; the SLP will probably be considered a support service along with technology, special education, and health services.*

Broad goals. Goals represent intended results or outcomes, which are based on the program's framework. Goals can also be expressed in terms of belief statements that define a core value, such as "all students can learn" or "the role of the teacher is a facilitator for student learning." In today's educational climate, the Common Core State Standards might well serve as one "leg" of the school's goals. *In such a climate, the school librarian should show how the SLP supports Common Core, such as the American Association of School Librarians' (AASL) crosswalk between their twenty-first-century learning skills and Common Core* (www.ala.org/ aasl/guidelinesandstandards/commoncorecrosswalk/). *School librarians should also bring their goals, such as AASL's standards and position statements, to the table at this point.*

Objectives. Goals are concretized into specific measurable objectives. The AASL twenty-first-century learning skills include useful objectives that can be woven into the school's curriculum.

Program design. At this point, the general approach to the curriculum is developed, for example, career academies, magnet schools, or schools that use an interdisciplinary approach. This framework then guides instructional design and cross-curricular consistency. *At this point, the SLP curriculum starts to take shape. For instance, in an academy design, the school librarian can serve as one of the core faculty, and integrate library-related learning processes into the mix. In a subject-centered magnet program, the SLP should make sure that the collection reflects that focus, and that library-related activities have a subject-specific spin.*

Evaluative standards. How well should students perform in order to advance to the next course or level? Standards provide the measure of competency. *Most library-related curriculum leads to authentic performance standards, such as the traditional ability to write a research report or evaluate information.*

Needs assessments. What must be in place for learning experiences to be designed and taught so students can meet standards: facilities, resources, time, staffing? What prerequisite skills and knowledge are needed when students begin a course? As noted above, students' existing knowledge and skills should be assessed in order to determine what curriculum is appropriate for them. *The school librarian needs to be front and center at this point because resource allocation decisions are made at this juncture. The library collection, be it physical or virtual, serves as an effective organization for schoolwide information resources. Technology access should be considered, such as infrastructure to support library, classroom, and home access to library-organized resources. For example, for students to meet Common Core State Standards, the school librarian can partner with classroom teachers to teach learning processes; therefore, the school's schedule should include time for joint planning and teaching—and the school library staffing to support such activities.*

Curriculum alignment. Typically, a program matrix is developed that determines in which course each objective will be addressed. Then the courses are articulated to build upon prior learning. A scope-and-sequence chart provides both a grade-level and subject-based look at instruction. *As part of the curriculum mapping, library-related curriculum or learning standards should be integrated. Table 3.1 shows a sample matrix.*

The school may decide that stand-alone courses, such as information and digital literacy, should be taught by the school librarian. Alternatively, library-related curriculum might be embedded into certain courses, or crafted as a unit linked to designated courses.

Course frameworks. Courses are often developed in light of a state's course framework, which provide blueprints for designing instruction. The framework determines the sequence and pacing of content to be addressed. In some disciplines, such as mathematics, concepts build upon each other. In others, a spiral design might be used to dig deeper into strands of knowledge throughout the course—or among courses. Modular course design, with separate units (e.g., on different social issues), is another framework. *School librarians need to plan with each subject or grade level group to integrate library-related curriculum or learning standards. The Common Core, especially as it relates to library standards, facilitates such linkages. Where the SLP offers separate courses, the school librarian can design the framework relatively independently; however, collaboration with other course designers improves student transfer of learning and further legitimizes and contextualizes the library standards.*

Lesson planning. The basic building block of curriculum is lesson planning: setting the stage for the learning activity (activation), presentation of content, student engagement with the content, student learning/integration of the content, and possible application of the new learning. Assessment throughout the process is built into the instructional design. *As with course design, lesson planning may be done independently or in collaboration with classroom teachers, depending on the school's program design. In any case, the school librarian should serve as a consultant in lesson planning, if for no other reason than to identify appropriate resources and help teach relevant processes.*

Table 3.1
Learning Skills Curriculum Map

	Language Arts	Social Studies	Math	Science	Arts	Health and PE	Other
Gain knowledge							
Seek knowledge using an inquiry-based process	I-search paper	Social issue debate	Develop an algo-rithm	Science experi-ment	Mix paint	Health plan	Plan a trip to Spain
Show persistence in seeking information							
Comply with copyright law							
Ask for help if needed							
Apply and generate knowledge							
Share knowledge							
Pursue personal growth							

(Based on AASL 2007.)

Food for Thought

As you see, effective schools align their curriculum efforts from their overarching philosophy down to specific learning activities. Nevertheless, as noted above, schools often act as loosely coupled organizations; as such, groups within the school may act semi-independently and even have conflicting agendas. Whatever the case, the SLP should support the school's values and priorities. What happens when the school librarian's philosophy about SLPs conflicts with the school's? How do you deal with a program concept that seems to contradict current practice of SLPs? What stance should you take? How forcefully should you state your case? With whom will you align your efforts? How will you deal with inconsistencies as you manage the SLP? Do you think it matters?

The preceding scenario happens more frequently than might be anticipated. It is further amplified when the school community's perception about school libraries and their management contradicts your own philosophy and professional best practice. Something has to change—a concept that will be developed in the last chapter of the book. Briefly, though, either the school's philosophy has to change, which involves modifying the mindset and culture of many people; you have to change, or at least mitigate, your practice; or you can leave the situation. Sometimes the philosophy and direction depend largely upon the principal. In that case, you might be able to change that one person's mind, which can trigger top-down changes; this option happens most often in very hierarchical or paternalistic settings. Although these alternatives seem rather harsh, they serve as a cautionary tale when you are interviewing for a job. What is the school's philosophy? What is its curriculum, and how is it developed? If your own philosophy clashes with the school's, you might want to think twice about accepting a job where you will have to deal with these realities.

School Resources

The school can implement its vision and achieve its goals only to the extent of its resources: material, fiscal, human, and time. Within that universe, the SLP represents a significant investment of resources, and decision makers keep a very keen eye on the returns on those allocations. Likewise, the SLP operates in light of the school community's resources overall, so school librarians need to be aware of what is available, and determine how to share and align with those resources in order to maximize the SLP's impact.

Money reflects values; if you want to know what is important, follow the money trail. This adage applies to school settings. The picture that unfolds is that the school community values people. According to the American Association of School Administrators (2012), about two-thirds of school budgets are allocated to instruction and instruction-related expenses (which include library services), and of that amount about 90 percent goes to salaries and benefits; instructional supplies make up just under 5 percent. Other major budget categories include transportation, facilities, energy, food services, and school leadership.

Facilities and Utilities

Any householder knows how expensive facilities can be. Basic maintenance, utilities, and taxes can be costly—and those costs never go away. Besides capital outlay and reoccurring expenses, repairs and other unanticipated expenses such as flooding or property damage require socking away some reserve funds for those rainy days. Furthermore, schools get rough handling because hundreds of bodies are using them constantly throughout the year. Libraries in particular require upkeep because traffic moves through them all day, and unlike classrooms, that ever-shifting population is less likely to feel any ownership of and responsibility to the space because they do not inhabit it with the same regularity as a classroom.

Because of their size, libraries sometimes function as meeting and testing places, which can jeopardize routine class and individual access. In fact, when classes overflow, they may end up in the library space, which then impacts access by the rest of the school community. School libraries sometimes have to share the same spaces, such as multipurpose or eating areas, at different times during the day. Such facility sharing can physically harm library resources as well as compromise equitable library service.

Technology adds another dimension to the resource issue because the infrastructure must accommodate changing technologies. Some school buildings still lack a sufficient number of power outlets, and those may not be grounded. Even power sources and surge protectors might be insufficient as classrooms and the library add more technologies. With Wi-Fi becoming the norm, sites might have to rethink hard-wired connections. Schools also have to comply with OSHA safety standards. Often school libraries spearhead technology initiatives so facilities have to accommodate physically storing and securing the hardware, software, and the furniture needed to support the technologies. In some cases, the library might manage a class set of computers or share a lab facility; in either case, human and material resources are required to support these technology spaces. Furthermore, with online resources, not only physical space but also cyberspace issues need to be addressed. Can existing bandwidth handle streaming data? What kinds of security and authentication should be added if remote access to digital resources is planned? Note that while technology support is not a material resource, humans are needed to utilize technology. Remember that behind every great technology program is a great person. Develop positive working relationships with the tech support people.

What happens when schools are renovated? What role does the school library play? Again, changes in one part of a campus can impact another part, especially during construction (another case when the library may be repurposed as a temporary classroom). If infrastructures change, then the school librarian should be at the table discussing library implications if only because of access and security issues. If classrooms get more connectivity, for instance, will users be able to access library resources and connect with the librarian via web conferencing? If the school starts a one-to-one laptop program, will facilities, including the library, be able to support the additional power and the increased need for outlets?

Material

Furniture constitutes a major capital outlay. The library uses both generic school furniture such as chairs and desks as well as special fixtures like magazine stands and carrels. Depending on local budgets and available inventory of furniture, the school library may have to make do with repurposed pieces, and, for example, use old typing tables for desktop stations.

Instructional materials, especially textbooks, constitute the greatest proportion of portable resources. In some states, such as California, schools are required to provide both classroom sets of textbooks as well as copies for student to take home. Some school libraries keep one copy of each textbook for in-library use.

When the same materials budget covers both textbooks and library books, the library may get short shrift unless the school librarian (SL) negotiates effectively with classroom teachers. In primary grades, the classroom may have its own book collection, which could compete for the same book budget dollars as the library. In such cases, the librarian might convince teachers that a rotating collection from the library would serve the same purpose, and enable students to access a greater variety of materials. Furthermore, some teachers do not manage textbooks—and other book collections—as closely as librarians, and might not collect fees for damaged or lost books; occasionally a department may ask for additional funds to replace damaged textbooks, which further diminishes funding that could be allocated for library books. In some cases, the SL manages textbooks as well as library collections, thus doubling the responsibility.

Increasingly, schools are exploring open textbook initiatives that use open-source materials, preferably in digital formats. Such initiatives usually require public-private partnerships. Ideally, these materials will save taxpayers millions of dollars in acquisitions and maintenance costs. The cost of a laptop is less than the total cost of print materials. If resources are downloaded onto laptops or accessed from remote servers, space and weight problems are avoided. Nevertheless, some issues remain: textbook quality and currency, installation and authentication processes, bandwidth load, Internet connectivity, laptop maintenance and loss, and interoperability on different storage devices. The library staff might be involved in these digital initiatives, which can be time-consuming, especially at the start; librarians will need to determine the return on investment in terms of the library's value and role within the school community.

Nonprint instructional materials complement print materials. Some DVDs, posters, and realia are still purchased, but most audiovisual materials exist in digital format, and are accessed through school, district, or remote vendor services. Many of these resources are accessed rather than owned by the school, and made available through yearly subscriptions. Software programs constitute the most likely stand-alone nonprint purchases, which could be managed by any or all of the following personnel: the classroom teacher, the subject department (e.g., science), the computer teacher, the technician, or the library staff. In any case, the SL should participate in the school's acquisition plans and processes to ensure cost-effective use of funds. For instance, it might make sense for the library to manage all digital subscriptions and licenses in order to maximize access and management. Site licenses for software might also make more financial and access sense than departmental licenses, especially for productivity tools. Open source productivity suites such as OpenOffice and Google Docs solve access and cost issues, although they may also test school filtering practices.

In order to access these digital resources, hardware is required. Most classroom teachers have some kind of computer and a projection system, although the latter might be shared with other classrooms. Although many schools have a computer lab, they might use COWS (a class set of Computers On Wheeled carts) instead of, or as a supplement to, lab access. Schools increasingly find one-to-one laptop programs and BYOD (Bring Your Own Device) programs to be cost-effective, especially in terms of inventory and maintenance. On the other hand, issues of equity and interoperability loom. Library staff often manage the circulation of computer sets, and may also circulate other equipment such as class sets of portable response systems (e.g., clickers) or camcorders. In any case, library resources must run on the school's equipment, so platform and system requirements should be considered when acquiring digital material. Authentication processes will also need to be addressed, especially if resources are accessed remotely. Furthermore, equipment requires maintenance and service, which entails decisions about technical support and its costs. Because technical materials involve so many issues, librarians should participate actively in these decisions and accompanying policies.

Even consumables can eat up budgets: student workbooks, art supplies, and so on. Library budgets may have to stretch to encompass copy and printer supplies, along with the supplies needed to process books and other materials. Sometimes other entities such as parents' organization or student body will underwrite printing costs. Furthermore, as students can download digital resource and submit work online, printing demands may decline.

School Culture

Not only should the school library program align with, and support, the school's mission, but it should also reflect the school's culture—or at least address that culture. What are the shared beliefs and values as they are manifested in the school? Culture may be defined as "the customary beliefs, social forms, and material traits of a racial, religious, or social group" and "the set of shared

attitudes, values, goals, and practices that characterizes an institution or organization" (*Webster's Collegiate Dictionary*, 11th edition). School culture may be
manifested in artifacts (e.g., sports trophies, school newspaper, classroom fur-
nishings), explicit beliefs and values (e.g., collaborative learning, pluralism, a
union shop), and unconscious assumptions (e.g., parents should read to their
children, students should come to school prepared, all students should be prepared to go to college) (Velasquez 2013). In librarianship, cultural issues apply
to the clientele, the librarian, the setting, and the library program in general
(e.g., resources and services).

In some cases, the school's mission may conflict with its culture. For instance,
the mission might tout individual self-fulfillment, but the classroom arrangement might be rows of students, and teaching might consist of lectures and rote
learning. As you look at the role of the school library program within the school,
you will need to identify school culture indicators, and determine their impact
on the library. At the very least, you should find out how much the school community values the library.

Food for Thought

Take the pulse of the school and of the library cultures. How do
they compare? What might you change?

- What are the demographics of the school community (students, staff,
  parents): socioeconomic, political, religious, ethnic, age? How do the
  library staff demographics reflect the school's?
- What is the general sense of people's behavior? What is the typical noise
  level? What is the typical traffic flow? What are the typical body language
  and gestures? What is the typical walking pace? How do people seem to
  treat one another and interact with each other? What behaviors occur in
  the library?
- What is the overall physical impression of the school? Is the site open to
  the public or heavily gated? How clean and organized is it? What symbols
  decorate the school (e.g., mascots, college flags, student work, graduation pictures, fine art, graffiti, announcement bulletin boards, school
  rules, trophies, athletic banners)? How are rooms arranged? What is the
  technology presence? Where is the library situated physically relative to
  the rest of the school? Is it a space (physical and virtual) that the school
  community takes pride in and uses?
- What is the school's governance structure? How are decisions made?
  How broad-based is the decision process? Who has power—and why?
  Who has responsibility, and who has authority? How does the power

structure compare with the organizational structure? How are library staff involved in governance?

- How do people work together? What is the basis of their relationships: by grade, subject expertise, personality, age? Do they work collaboratively or competitively? To what degree do they share expertise? How autonomously do they work? How much authority are they given? What are the library staff's working patterns among themselves and with the rest of the staff?

- How does the school community socialize? Do cliques exist—on what basis are they formed? Where does socializing occur—and how often? What are the social norms, and to what degree are outliers tolerated or supported? What are the library staff's social patterns among themselves and with the rest of the staff?

- How does the school community communicate? What communications channels do they use: website, e-mail, social media, telephone, newsletters, flyers, print documents, student publications, meetings? What is the frequency of their communication? What is the content of their communication: announcements, policies, events, accomplishments, requests for input?

- How is the school's revenue allocated? Who decides? What percentage of the budget is allocated to the library—or supports the library program?

- How does the curriculum reflect the school's culture? What is taught, and what is omitted? What is the cocurriculum (e.g., clubs, student activities)? How is curriculum developed? How are students advised? Do different tracks or pathways exist—and who is eligible? What is the library's role in developing curriculum?

- What are the teaching norms? How do people, both adults and students, learn? How is learning valued? What is the typical learning climate—and how much does it vary throughout the school? To what degree do library program practices reflect the norms of the rest of the school?

- What is the role of assessment? What is assessed—and how is it done? How are people accountable for their actions, and how are rules enforced? What are the consequences of assessment? How is the library assessed, and what actions are taken as a result?

To answer several of these questions, you may have to visit and interact with these entities. Take the opportunity to attend department or grade meetings, parent-teacher association meetings, school board meetings, local service groups such as the Chamber of Commerce or Junior League. Introduce yourself and share your vision; find out about their missions and goals. These groups will welcome your presence, and will appreciate that you are there because you are interested in them. By establishing a positive working relationship with these community stakeholders, you will have credibility when you ask to present to them—or request their support.

As noted previously, if the library staff and the school library program align with the school culture, then less negotiation will probably be required. If they conflict or clash, then serious analysis and communication are required. Something has to change—or you may want to leave rather than remain frustrated. Perhaps the school's culture seems foreign to you; think of this as an anthropological adventure, and as an opportunity to hone cross-cultural competence. Kalyanpur and Harry (1999) offer some benchmarks in becoming cultural competent.

1. Get to know the school's culture—and subcultures. What are their characteristics, behaviors, and values? What is the history of these cultures?
2. Keep an open mind and remain flexible as you relate to people of different cultures.
3. Avoid assigning relative values to differences in cultures while still recognizing cultural similarities and differences.
4. Develop a congruent set of behaviors, attitudes, and policies that help you interact with people who are different from yourself.

However, your own cultural competence does not suffice; the entire library staff must be culturally competent. Why? Because the school library program must provide resources and services that meet the needs of the entire school community's cultures. Furthermore, the library staff must promote an inclusive learning environment.

Factors That Impact the School

Schools are not closed systems. More than ever, schools have external pressures and demands put on them, and they are increasingly held accountable for their efforts and results. For instance, in addition to the traditional expectations of preparing students academically, schools often have to shoulder the responsibility for teaching cultural traditions such as nursery rhymes and other cultural references (e.g., folktale motifs, Biblical references, proverbs), manners, character education, nutrition, healthy life choices, sex education, digital safety, citizenship, and career exploration.

Many socioeconomic realities impact a school's curriculum and service choices, such as increased mobility, poverty, unemployment, increased competition for jobs, the digital divide, conflicting values, complex family configurations, unstable neighborhoods, socially transmitted diseases, availability of drugs, and social inequality. Increased globalization has led to more cross-cultural opportunities and conflicts as well as an increasing push for global economic competitiveness. Technology has increased access to resources, but also requires additional technical and evaluative skills.

Even within education itself, several factors impact school practice: state and national content standards, federal mandates such as Every Student Succeeds Act, high-stakes standardized testing, more rigorous graduation requirements, greater emphasis on preparing students for college and careers, at the same time that federal and state funding for schools has decreased.

School library programs may have resources and expertise that can help address these factors:

- a rich collection of current information that support the school's mission, which is available in a variety of formats
- a welcoming and student-centered learning environment that supports formal and informal education and socialization
- tech-savvy library staff and supporting technologies
- school librarians who can teach lifelong learning skills and promote positive reading habits
- just-in-time instruction and guidance that is responsive to the user
- inquiry-based and collaborative learning activities that cross the curriculum
- opportunities for school community engagement, growth, and leadership
- community-involved library staff

In some cases, these assets may require more support, but in other cases, library staff will only need to communicate more effectively about these assets. In either case, library staff should promote themselves as team players who can help deal with these external factors and improve the school's responsiveness and effectiveness.

The SLP should serve as the heartbeat of the school community. To that end, you as the manager must make sure that the library program's "blood"—its resources and services—reach the farthest ends of that school community, circulating widely from one part of the school to the other. For that flow to work efficiently, library staff must understand how the school itself functions, and how the library interacts with each aspect of the organization, just as the heart and blood perform different functions in the foot than they do in the eye.

As the SLP manager, you must identify each entity: its personnel, resources, and services. You must see how resources flow: from the needs assessment to the decision-making process to the resource allocations and accountability, the school library program should participate—and benefit—at each step. Furthermore, you have to understand and work with the overall school culture and its subgroups in order to facilitate acceptance and effective interaction.

No entity within the school can manage independently. Certainly the school library program must work with other members of the school community to share resources, services, and expertise. Having common goals and mutually agreeable strategies make the work flow more efficiently and effectively. Continuing with the heart and blood metaphor, blood clots and other obstacles in the bloodstream, as well as stresses to the heart, have to be identified and addressed efficiently. The school "body" has to take care of the heart as much as the heart has to support it. School library program management helps regulate the heart and circulation system in consort with the rest of the body system— and together the entire school body can deal with the external factors, and hopefully thrive.

Bringing It Down to You

If the school is conceptualized as a body (maybe the body politic as well), what is the school library program? If the school community is the brain and soul of the school body, what is your role as the library program manager relative to those functions? What is the symbiotic relationship between the school library program management and the management of the school as a whole? Consider all the preceding contexts in which the school library program operates.

- How does the SLP's mission support the school's mission?
- How does the SLP support the school's curriculum? Where does the SLP's curriculum fit into the picture?
- What school resources does the SLP need to function effectively? What SLP resources benefit the rest of the school community?
- How is SLP management engaged in the school's operations and decision-making?
- How does the SLP culture compare with the rest of the school's?
- How does the SLP benefit the rest of the school—and vice versa?

In sum, is the school library program and its management in or out of the school's loop? Are you even aware of the school's loop? Do you create the school's loop, or are you creating a separate library loop altogether?

References

American Association of School Administrators. 2012. *School Budgets 101*. Alexandria, VA: American Association of School Administrators.

American Association of School Librarians. 2009. *Empowering Learners*. Chicago, IL: American Library Association.

American Association of School Librarians. 2007. *Standards for the 21st Century Learner*. Chicago, IL: American Library Association.

Kalyanpur, M., and Harry, B. 1999. *Culture in Special Education*. Baltimore, MD: Paul Brookes.

Velasquez, D., ed. 2013. *Library Management 101*. Chicago, IL: American Library Association.

Wiles, J. 2005. *Curriculum Essentials*. New York, NY: Pearson.

4

Starting with Yourself

BEFORE MANAGING THE LIBRARY PROGRAM AS A WHOLE, YOU AS a school librarian (SL) should be able to manage yourself. What is your vision of the school library program (SLP)? What role does management play in carrying out that vision? What do you bring to the table? Self-confidence and personal management success builds a reputation that encourages others to work with you. What are your learning style and motivation, and how can they help you improve your management skills? What is your management style? This chapter includes a management self-assessment tool.

What's Your Vision?

In chapter two, you had an opportunity to envision the ideal school library program and your management role within that ideal. In chapter three, you saw how that ideal has to exist within the very real context of the rest of the school. Did that change your vision of being a manager? The essential role of the manager—implementing plans and policies, running the program and working with people—remains the same. How that role is carried out depends on the resources—material, human, and time—and the context of the school community.

The question then becomes: how can your management optimally improve the school library program progress from its present status to its best possible outcome? To answer that question requires you to evaluate current management practice—and even more profoundly, assess your personal effectiveness. Only then can you build a strategy that improves management impact on the school library program to make it more influential in the school.

Another Growth Spurt

As an SLP manager, you acquire skills beyond academic preparation, and perhaps beyond prior work experience. You may feel that you know how a school library operates, and you may be an experienced classroom teacher as well. However, just as school administration requires a different skill set from classroom teaching, so does library management require specialized expertise—the one needed for beyond collection development, instruction, and day-to-day service. If you are new to the management role, you may find yourself feeling uncomfortably incompetent.

Fortunately, most school librarians are lifelong learners and like to take intellectual risks. They tend to believe that intelligence is not a fixed entity but rather can grow through effort and persistence. Additionally, most school librarians achieved professional success prior to assuming the management role, so they know what success feels like—and know that they can learn the skills needed for this new position. Drawing upon an established repertoire of skills and experiences, they can develop schema to help them apply their skills in new situations and make situational decisions quickly. SLs also draw upon the expertise of their peers, pursue professional development opportunities, and join professional associations as ways to gain leadership skills.

These managerial skills take time to master. It normally requires over 10,000 hours, or about five years, to optimize your experiences in different situations and gain true domain-specific expertise that is manifested in easily identifying trends and solving problems efficiently. However, if school librarians focus on performance alone, they may well settle for competence rather than display exemplary performance. Dall'Alba and Sandberg (2006) echoed this possibility, defining two dimensions of professional development: improved skills (the competency level) and embodied understanding of practice (the "big picture"); beginners tend to focus on the former, but as they practice they may shift to the other perspective. So be kind to, and patient with, yourself.

Hopefully, you feel that you can perceive and assess your own skills realistically, and feel that you can self-initiate personal growth. When your feel self-confident and optimistic about yourself, you are more likely to cope well with the challenges of management and find effective ways to produce long-term results for the school library program.

Looking from the Inside Out

Collins (1993) conceptualized management from the inside out, using the individual effectiveness model described below.

The model's innermost circle focuses on self-perception of your beliefs and values, and examines your self-image and self-esteem. These factors form the central lens for viewing the world, and shape how you interact with others. Personal effectiveness depends on self-knowledge, self-respect and confidence, a sense of purpose, emotional independence, the ability to prioritize, and a willingness to take risks. With these characteristics, you are more likely to communicate openly, listen actively, and reach out and accept others. On the other hand, if your self-image is self-defeating or self-delusional, you will probably be self-defensive and narrow-minded. Try writing down your key values by completing the phrase "I am . . ." ten times, and prioritizing those ten characteristics. In the final analysis, it is important to be true to yourself so that you can deal with others more effectively, whether they are like you or not.

The second circle focuses on self-management. How well do you manage time and stress? How well do you maintain personal health and energy? Do you consciously try to improve yourself? Probably the most telling issue is pressure. What are your pressure points: self, family, peers, students, supervisors? How do you deal with those pressures? A certain amount of stress can energize and stimulate you. However, too much stress can hurt you physically and mentally. Here are some ways to look after yourself: keep physically fit, maintain a balanced diet, relax, laugh, treat yourself, share with others. You can also determine how much stress is avoidable, in which case you can address the issue; if the stress is unavoidable, either you or the situation needs to change. Besides being kind to yourself, defining clear goals can help balance your life.

Think about how you spend your time during the week: what percentage of your time do you spend on work, professional development, family, friends, self? How does your allocation of time reflect—or conflict—with your inner values? If you spend less than ten percent of your time on yourself, you might want to rebalance your life, which can also help you manage stress and change in the workplace. As for time management, several practices can help:

- Maintain short-term and long-term checklist and "to do" lists.
- Use scheduling tools.
- Prioritize tasks based on their relative worth.
- Focus on building relationships.
- Recognize opportunities.
- Focus on significant roles.

The third circle focuses on relationships. Management requires relating to, and communicating with, others. Workplace relationships involve supporting others, including giving meaningful feedback and rewarding exemplary performance. As a manager, you must influence others in order to achieve results, and you will have to negotiate with others to resolve conflict as well as to empower others to use their full potential to optimize school library programs. The circle of self-management also applies to this third circle in that one way to manage your time effectively is to delegate tasks to others as appropriate. This approach to management can build good interdependent working relationships and empower others. This latter fact is important: those delegated tasks should entail authority as well as responsibility; otherwise, those people doing the task will feel "put upon" rather than empowered.

The outer circle focuses on being effective in group settings. To this end, you will need to effectively lead others, build strong networks, and plan strategically. This is the point when you should share your vision with your staff, and help them make it their own as well—and motivate them to help make that vision real. You should also consider what each staff member and stakeholder can contribute to that vision.

What Is Your Role as a Manager?

What makes for an effective manager? Burgoyne and Stuart (1976) proposed basic knowledge and personal qualities that relate to school library management:

- facts about the school, its community, and the library's role within that setting
- relevant technical knowledge
- management knowledge
- analytical problem-solving skills
- interpersonal skills
- sensitivity to people and situations
- ability to work well under stress
- ability to respond to current situations with a long term consequences mindset
- creativity
- mental flexibility
- abstract and concrete thinking
- self-knowledge

Food for Thought

As a way to concretize these circles of management, you can create your own circles, labeling each circle with your current activity—and what you think needs improvement. In this way, you can literally target your management efforts.

Targeting Individual Effectiveness as a Manager

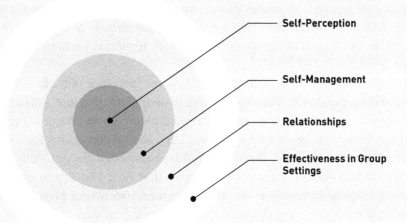

In examining the four circles of management, you may find that you lack some competencies. Self-assessment and self-recognition are the first steps to self-improvement. Similarly, changing behavior requires reexamining core beliefs and values about how you manage. Only then can you change behaviors and form more productive habits. One way to proceed is to designate a "day of difference": a day to starting doing something different, no matter how small. Perhaps it means getting up ten minutes earlier to take a brisk walk, or perhaps you can start a to-do list and review it at the end of the day. Try the new habit for thirty days, and journal your efforts daily. Describe your behavior, noting what helped you change and what difficulties you encountered; how you addressed change, and what you learned. This metacognitive activity helps reinforce personal improvement that will result in improved management.

As a manager, you need technical skills, interpersonal and communication skills, and conceptual and decision-making skills, that is, the ability to work with things, with people, and with ideas. Specific management competence includes two clusters of skills:

1. Planning, organizing, directing, controlling
2. Team management skills such as motivating, training and coaching, and empowering and involving workers

The first cluster focuses on goal-setting; identifying available and needed resources; setting a direction to achieve the goals; organizing people and materials within a predictable structure; creating the climate to carry out the needed tasks; evaluating all of the elements; and making adjustments to optimize efforts and results.

The second cluster of skills recognizes the importance of human relationships and interdependence. Managers have to negotiate the fine balance between being part of the team (i.e., as an accepted member) and supervising the team. As the library program manager, you have the responsibility for making sure the program is effective; therefore, you will also need the authority to allocate material and human resources to achieve that end. The key to this balance is monitoring the interplay of the team members; from your broader perspective you can see how group dynamics impact work flow and interactions with the school community. Team building enables resources to be used more efficiently because the team can share expertise. The potential price you pay for exercising this supervisory role is being less candid and conforming more. The team might also form internal coalitions. This strengthens team spirit, which can reinforce your need for some separation from the team at the same time that it can gain internal power.

In the managerial role you have referent power because of your position. You probably also have power because of your expertise, and you may also enjoy charismatic power. You must exercise your power to run the library program and manage people. You also have the authority to share that power with the rest of the library staff (both paid and volunteer). When adherence to strict routine is required, you will have to exercise tighter power; however, when staff members become more skilled, you can loosen the reins. Likewise, when the library program entails a number of creative initiatives, you will want to delegate power so that the library team can operate more autonomously and exercise more responsibility. On the other hand, if you have hostile staff, you will need to exert more power. Furthermore, if you "give away" all of your power, staff might not comply with your orders or directions, even though you are ultimately responsible for the library program. In short, recognize and use your power thoughtfully in order to attain the best possible results of the library staff and program.

What Do You Bring to the Role?

School librarians should have these managerial attributes even if they might not be called managers. On the other hand, each person has different levels of each aspect. What strengths do you bring to the position? Fortunately, you can improve in each area through a self-designed plan of action. Besides the usual avenues of reading, conferences, and workshops, you can also seek a mentor who can provide individual coaching.

A simple exercise is to create a line continuum (see below) for each managerial skill, and write down some concrete indicators that exemplify that skill. For instance, good communication skills include active listening, communicating clearly, speaking articulately, being persuasive, using effective body language, and so on. Mark where you think you stand relative to each indicator. Jot down the basis for your stance, such as anecdotal evidence or formal evaluations. Think of your spot on the line as a "slider" that you can move forward as you improve. What would you have to do to move that slider up the line? You might start by taking one concrete action to improve one specific skill, for example, consciously practicing active listening for a month to improve interpersonal skills. Write down your action under that line, and put that sheet where it will serve as a daily reminder. If you can slide up one increment each month, you will soon see visible improvement.

Isolated ———————▶——————— Always in the Know

Additionally, you can look for a team to complement your strengths. For instance, some school librarians have excellent communication skills and ideas, but some tasks may be difficult because they aren't detail-oriented. A well-trained paraprofessional might be able to provide the necessary skills. If your decision-making skills are weak, then you will have a tough time garnering managerial respect from the rest of the library staff—and you probably won't enjoy managing.

How Do You Decide?

School library management requires constant decision making: which materials to buy and withdraw, how to catalog, how to prioritize tasks, which person to help first, how to teach, how to allocate money, how to handle conflicts, when to say no, and so on. Your decisions may be reactive, if they are made in response to external circumstances, or proactive, if you try to make changes deliberately and anticipate future occurrences. Some decisions are dictated by existing policy, but many more are not prestructured but rather novel or unique.

People have different approaches to making decisions, which demonstrate different decision categories or models. Although a gut reaction can sometimes result in a good decision, it is hard to justify to administrators. As much as possible, managers should make their decisions systematically, that is, by using an organized and analytic process. This approach requires identifying and defining the problem, establishing criteria for making a decision, gathering and analyzing information, considering alternatives, making a decision, acting upon it, and assessing implementation. Within this framework, different decision models exist (Dumler and Skinner 2005):

- A rational decision model is prescriptive, based on logical analysis. It works best in unambiguous situations where adequate information is available.
- An administrative decision model is descriptive and is based on human nature. It seeks to find a satisfactory, "good enough" solution rather than a perfect one. This model is appropriate when alternatives are unclear and group preferences should be considered.
- A political decision model seeks group acceptance in cases where conflicting goals may exist and information is ambiguous.

On a personal level, several factors influence decision-making: values, personality, attitude towards risk taking, and aversion to conflict. Marakas (2002) identified four personal decision-making styles based on individual tolerances for ambiguity and ways of thinking (e.g., rational versus intuitive):

- Analytical: tolerates ambiguity, and decides rationally.
- Directive: has a low tolerance for ambiguity, and decides rationally.
- Conceptual: tolerates ambiguity, and decides intuitively.
- Behavioral: has a low tolerance for ambiguity, and decides intuitively.

No one decision model is perfect, and different situations may call for different types of decision processes. However, it is useful to determine your preferred decision style, and to remember that other people may make decisions in completely different ways. Being able to reconcile those differences helps you manage, particularly in the complex environment of schools.

What Is Your Management Style?

There is no single way to manage any organization, including a school library program. Certain tasks are required to meet program standards (e.g., managing resources), and there are standardized procedures (e.g., cataloging). However, the means by which these functions are implemented may vary depending on available resources, staffing, time, school demands, and the specific situation. In addition to different circumstances, different organizational structures and cultures impact management style choices.

The classic differentiation of management styles falls into a few broad categories.

- Autocratic managers make all important decisions and monitor workers closely. This style can be effective in times of crisis or when dealing with many low-skilled workers.
- Paternalistic managers pay attention to workers' social needs and listen to their opinions. However, the manager makes the final decisions and directs the workers.
- Persuasive managers spend time convincing workers to comply with existing decisions. Workers understand the tasks and the rationale for them, but might not agree with the decision itself.
- Democratic managers empower workers to make decisions based on discussion. This style is effective for complex decisions that require specialist skills.
- Laissez-faire managers mentor and stimulate workers, but the workers manage themselves. This style works best in entrepreneurial organizations with strong workers who share a common vision.

Blake and Mouton's 1964 management grid provides a good illustration of different management styles. Management decisions are based on two dimensions: concern for production or results and concern for people.

- When there is little concern for people, management exerts minimum effort to sustain the organization.
- When concern for both people and production is high, all staff should be committed and interdependent via a common stake in the organiza-

tion's purpose, which leads to mutual trust and respect. Managers tend to delegate.
- When concern for people overshadows other concerns, management focuses on satisfying social relationships and a friendly organization. Workers participate actively, and the manager avoids conflict.
- When production concerns overshadow people, management must minimize human elements that might interfere with efficient operations. Managers tend to tell people what to do, and may need to "sell" the task.
- In the middle zone, managers balance performance requirements and morale.

Blake and Mouton assert that interdependent management is the ideal style, but stress that it requires several steps to attain that degree of organizational development, which must progress from the individual to the organizational level. First, people have to identify their own behaviors and problem-solving approaches. Then they should establish performance objectives. At that point, intergroup development can occur. Only then can top management determine the most effective structure and mechanisms to achieve organizational and personnel goals.

Albrecht (1983) developed a leadership matrix that helps identify management style. It presents four management functions: sharing goals, emphasizing teamwork, permitting autonomy, and giving rewards. Each function is then weighted in terms of the manager's emphasis: low, medium, or high.

- Sharing goals can range from dictating work to depending on workers to define tasks.
- Teamwork can range from no group meetings to constant group meetings.
- Autonomy can range from no freedom to no direction.
- Giving rewards can range from constant criticism to feedback to giving rewards to gain acceptance rather than in response to good performance.

By observing a manager's actions and analyzing your own behaviors, you can determine which management style is being practiced. When your style differs significantly from your predecessor's or supervisor's, you will need to take extra measures to work with staff to transition to your style.

Fiedler's contingency model (1981) focuses on matching management styles to situations. He categorizes management style along a continuum of task-oriented or relationship-oriented. He then identifies three factors for determining the most effective management style: leader-worker relations, task structure, and the leader's position power. Task orientation is effective when leader-member relations are good, the task is well structured, or the manager has strong power. Otherwise, the manager should focus more on relationships.

According to Furnham (2008), management styles may employ several kinds of techniques, which depend on the needs of the organization and its workers.

- Management by objectives involves managers and workers jointly defining goals and defining each worker's responsibilities. The objectives thus serve as the criteria for evaluating worker performance.
- Bureaucratic management goes by the book and focuses on following procedures precisely. It is used in routine jobs or where safety is very important (e.g., working in dangerous situations).
- Management by work simplification aims for jobs that require just one method.
- Management by walking around involves active observation and listening, and can facilitate just-in-time interventions.
- Management by exception delegates authority, and intervenes only when problems occur.
- Management by competitive edge promotes healthy competition, and uses rewards and recognition to foster worker competing against worker.
- Management by pacesetting sets high standards for performance, but the stress that ensues can lower morale.
- Active management leads by example, and sets high standards for everyone.
- Management by coaching and development resembles mentoring in that managers nurture workers through a long learning curve process.

Management style choices depend not only on a manager's personality and habits, but also the environment and specific situations. In addition, under stress, managers, just like teachers, tend to revert to their most personally comfortable or habitual style, even if it is not the most effective choice. For that reason, you should avoid making decisions under pressure, and instead give yourself a little breathing room to think about the most appropriate management style for the circumstance.

Think about your own management style. Talk with a colleague or friend to get some outside feedback.

- Which approach do your normally take?
- To what degree does your management style change in response to your setting?
- To what extent does your management style change in response to your library staff?

- To what degree does your management style change in response to specific situations?
- How effective is your usual management style, and how might you want to expand your repertoire of styles?

Issues in Personal Management

Managing a school library is demanding. You need to take care of yourself in order to perform in top form. Here are some issues to consider.

Hypothetically, you could spend 24/7 in the school library developing and maintaining collections, designing instruction, planning programs, and optimizing the technology. There are always demands on the library program for resources, services, meetings, collaboration, reports, outreach, and so on. (In some cases, school librarians have to manage more than one site, which adds to the management burden.) At the same time, you have other aspects of your life: your family, your community, your own personal needs. Finding a happy balance can be a difficult goal.

As much as possible, follow union or other contractual agreements about work hours and workload. Although you should take opportunities to go the extra mile and contribute significantly to the school's mission, you should acknowledge that you are working more than your contract specifies. Avoid working extra hours in the library. If you find yourself doing so, several red flags may indicate that (1) you are not managing your time effectively, or (2) you are setting unrealistic expectations for successors to your job. You may resent the extra time spent at work—which is unacknowledged because that time was off the clock, and you should realize that you are volunteering the hours beyond what the contract specifies. Working extra time can also cut into your personal and social life, impacting relationships with your family and friends. These other demands eventually impair your effectiveness at work, so you should discipline yourself to perform optimally during work hours, but also balance your life socially, physically, and psychologically.

It is important to address gender issues. As mentioned above, family demands can add pressure to your work, particularly when children need special attention because of illness, special needs, or academic or social problems. Even in today's climate, women tend to bear the major burden of family care. In addition, librarianship itself is a service profession, which reinforces your image as a giving person. At the same time, women who challenge the service paradigm may encounter accusations that they are uncaring. To combat these characterizations and cope with women's reality, female school librarians can do several things (Carr-Ruffino 2004).

- Anticipate and prevent possible stressors.
- Develop a support network of peers, friends, and family.
- Maintain a healthy lifestyle.
- Control the immediate daily living environment as much as possible.
- Draw upon personal resources to relax, visualize positive outcomes, live in the now, and realistically deal with control issues.
- Deal constructively with emotions by identifying feelings without necessarily acting on them, responding objectively to criticism, and postponing possibly dysfunctional immediate responses.

In addition, different cultures maintain different attitudes towards management styles, on the personal level as well as interpersonal level. Hofstede (1980) identified several culturally defined factors that can affect personal management behaviors and attitudes:

- Power distance. What is the degree of equality between people? How hierarchical is the organization? Power distance impacts librarians' relationship with the rest of the school community.
- Individualism versus collectivism. People in individualistic societies tend to belong to several groups, each of which is loosely-knit, whereas collectivist societies tend to have a few well-defined groups who are highly loyal. School community members have preconceived attitudes about individual versus cooperative efforts.
- Uncertainty avoidance. How tolerant is the school community of uncertainty and ambiguity? Are different options acceptable or are strict rules the norm? When the librarian's perspective differs from the rest of the school community, conflict can occur.
- Role differentiation. In some cultures, personal and professional roles are highly differentiated by sex, while others draw a more amorphous line between gendered roles. Additionally, different cultures assign different genders to the librarian (e.g., in the United States, a librarian is more likely to be a female), which can impact attitude towards the person in that position.

In most settings, some cultural differences are likely to occur because the term applies to groups with sustained common beliefs and behaviors, be they jocks or conservatives, constructivists or soccer moms. The key is to identify which of your own values and beliefs are culturally defined, and to figure out how to negotiate cultural differences. Usually this entails finding inclusive goals and values, such as student success, which can then provide a basis for constructive working relationships.

When someone acts outside the cultural norm, he or she may encounter resistance from the rest of the community, be it a member of that person's own culture or a different one. People who work in cultures that are not their own have even greater challenges when negotiating between cultures, especially when values clash. School librarianship has its own set of values and beliefs that may challenge some cultural norms, including freedom of information and expression, intellectual property rights, and privacy. The best way to deal with cultural conflicts is to follow existing school policies and professional library association position statements, for example, the American Library Association's Library Bill of Rights (www.ala.org/advocacy/intfreedom/librarybill).

Bringing It Down to You

Are you a manager human pretzel? You don't have to radically change your personality to become an SLP manager. For instance, if you like to work behind the scenes rather than lead the parade, it might make sense to build a strong library team that includes some members who complement your skill in organization. Perhaps you prefer working alone rather than with a group; your management style might consist of clearly defining roles and delegating authority, and regularly checking in with the group to ensure that all the necessary functions are being taken care of. Perhaps you're a big vision type of person who doesn't want to be bothered with mundane daily operations; if so, you should include s detail-oriented person on your team. Recognize and praise team contributions to make the vision a reality. In other words, the most important factor in management is knowing yourself and deciding how to optimize and complement your own personality.

References

Albrecht, K. 1983. *Organizational Development.* Englewood Cliffs, NJ: Prentice Hall.

Blake, R., and J. Mouton. 1964. *The Managerial Grid.* Houston, TX: Gulf Publishing.

Burgoyne, J., and R. Stuart. 1976. "Managerial Skills." *Personnel Review* 5 (4): 19–29.

Carr-Ruffino, N. 2004. *The Promotable Woman,* 4th ed. Pompton Plains, NJ: Career Press.

Collins, R. 1993. *Effective Management.* Chicago, IL: Commerce Clearing House.

Dall'Alba, G., and J. Sandberg. 2006. "Unveiling Professional Development: A Critical Review of Stage Models." *Review of Educational Research* 76 (3): 383–412.

Dumler, M., and S. Skinner. 2005. *A Primer for Management.* Mason, OH: South-Western.

Fiedler, F. 1981. *Leader Attitudes and Group Effectiveness.* Westport, CT: Greenwood.

Furnham, A. 2008. *Management Intelligence.* New York, NY: Palgrave Macmillan.

Hofstede, G. 1980. *Culture's Consequences: International Differences in Work-Related Values.* Newbury Park, CA: SAGE.

Marakas, G. 2002. *Decision Support Systems in the 21st Century,* 2nd ed. Upper Saddle River, NJ: Prentice Hall.

5

Planning

AFTER YOU FORM SOME IDEAS ABOUT IDEAL SCHOOL LIBRARY programs (SLP) and check available resources and responsibilities, you, the school librarian (SL), can start developing an effective management strategy to bridge the gap between the current and ideal situation. Both short- and long-term goals must be considered, and objectives and strategies determined. Data must be collected purposefully and analyzed carefully in order to make informed and effective decisions. This kind of proactive thinking may feel daunting to an SLP manager who is constantly busy putting out brush fires. However, this broader perspective demonstrates what is required from a reflective practitioner, and actually provides a sense of stability and direction for library management. This chapter provides step-by-step guidelines for connecting process and product to provide a top-quality, effective school library program.

Why Plan?

Sometimes it feels futile to plan. So many things lie outside the control of the school library program and its staff. Things change constantly—and others resist change. Brush fire crises, from paper jams to unscheduled classes, from computer crashes to floods, can consume the energies of the school library staff. Because an SLP manager should be responsive to the school community's needs, you should also try to plan ahead and address the school library program on a more systematic basis. Otherwise, the program will have no clear identity or direction.

At the practical level, planning ensures that the school library functions effectively. There should be guidelines for coordinating efforts, identifying priorities, minimizing the time needed to accomplish tasks., optimizing performance, and creating the conditions that enable the SLP to react effectively to change.

Types of Plans

The terms "plans" and "planning" can refer to many things: blueprints, standing orders (e.g., the yearly updates of a reference title), single-use projects (e.g., assembling a task force for creating a special event), as well long-term strategic plans. Some plans represent the status quo, such as a standing plan for handling overdue materials. Other plans are more visionary. Furthermore, plans can vary in scope, time frame, and level of detail. Dumler and Skinner (2005) described three types of planning processes:

- Strategic plans usually take a comprehensive, long-term, broad perspective. They build on the program's mission statement, and identify goals that set the direction for the library program's future.
- Tactical plans identify specific objectives and activities that implement the strategic plan. To that end, they are short-term actionable options.
- Operational plans are the usual type of library planning, which focuses on effective uses of available resources to meet measurable objectives and solve immediate problems.

As an SLP manager, you should conduct both short- and long-term planning. To help make long-term planning more manageable, you should develop benchmarks (concrete indicators of progress) so that the library staff and the rest of the school community can acknowledge efforts that have shorter-term results.

In any case, you should plan for continuous improvement. This type of planning requires continually monitoring the impact of the library program's resources and services.

- How can services be provided more quickly, efficiently, and qualitatively better?
- How can the collection best meet the needs of the school community?
- How can the physical facility be arranged for optimum use?
- How can the library's virtual presence best serve the school community?

In sum, how can the library program optimally meet its mission—and surpass it?

The data collected can be analyzed in order to identify more effective practices that will bring the school library program closer to its vision.

Steps in Planning

Planning resembles problem solving in that

1. An issue is identified and defined.
2. A desired outcome is determined.
3. Data are collected.
4. Significant factors are identified.
5. Alternative actions are considered.
6. A set of actions or strategies is chosen.
7. Resources are identified.
8. The decision is implemented.
9. The impact of the actions is assessed.
10. Necessary modifications are determined.

The main difference between the two processes is that planning is more proactive, and problem solving is more reactive. Details of the comprehensive planning process follow.

STEP 1: ESTABLISH A PLANNING TEAM

Depending on your personality, you may prefer to plan by yourself, or you may want to surround yourself with many supporters. The rest of the library staff, both paid and volunteer, should be involved because they have firsthand experience and insights about the program's implementation as well as interaction with the rest of the school community. Indeed, because the school library program exists within the framework of the school, the SL needs to work with key stakeholders from the start in order ensure that the plan will be supported and implemented properly. In addition, these influential people can convey important information to and from their constituents.

Choosing these individuals is itself a significant planning task. Most likely, a couple of people already support the library program, for example, a classroom teacher who uses the library regularly or brings in classes frequently. Perhaps you have a good collegial friend in the school community. Some students and parents may be strong library users and advocates. Hopefully, at least one administrator also appreciates the library program and your efforts. In all of these cases, these potential teammates should have good reputations and have influence, which will help them to spread the word about the library program effectively. All members should be dependable and competent, and each person should bring specific skills to the team: writing, public speaking, budget acumen, political savvy, community networking, familiarity with the school's history and culture, organization, or attention to detail. It is also important that team members do not use the library for their own agendas, unless they happen to mesh well with the library's; if agendas veer away from the library's mission, you are likely to lose that person's support. Because the number of team members should remain small, ideally five to eight individuals, you should try to ensure that a variety of demographics and perspectives are represented: age, gender, culture, subject matter, role, seniority. At the same time, you want to make sure that everyone can work well together and can trust one another. You should feel comfortable confiding in the planning team and asking for their honest opinions. It might be a good idea to start with three or four individuals whom you trust, and then build the team formally from that point.

Regardless of the composition of the planning team, remember to keep a site administrator in the communication loop. The SLP plan exists within the framework of the school, and therefore may impact the rest of the school community. Theoretically, systematic planning should be regarded as a positive activity from the standpoint of administrators, especially if it aligns with and supports the school's mission. Furthermore, most administrators appreciate the efforts of problem solvers; they would rather praise positive results than have to deal with problems themselves. In any case, it is best to get the administrator's approval so that you have the political support (if in words only) to develop and implement the plan. One of the worst mistakes is to surprise administrators after the fact, or to find out about library plans from an outside source. Remember that as a manager, your role is to make both the SLP program and the school as a whole look good; this requires keeping the administration informed so that they, as the school leaders, look good too.

STEP 2: DESCRIBE THE CURRENT CONDITIONS

Before you know what direction to take, you have to know where you are beginning. To some degree, steps one and two operate simultaneously because you must have a solid understanding of the SLP before you ask individuals to join the planning team, and you will need to look outward to the school community before you can gather some of the necessary data that describes it.

Gathering information is a core SLP management function, and certainly plays a major role in planning. On the practical side, here are several questions to consider when determining effective ways to assess the current situation.

- Why assess? To gather baseline information, to diagnose strengths and weaknesses, to evaluate, to facilitate planning, to redirect efforts, to change content or instruction, to allocate resources, to motivate, to reward or punish (e.g., promote, fail), or to maintain accreditation or licensure (Mowl 1996)?
- What is being assessed? The needs of learners, instructors, or the community; the learning environment; or support, content, instruction, or outcomes?
- Who is being assessed? Students, classroom teachers, library staff, administrators, other school staff members, district personnel, pre-service teachers, families, or the community-at-large? Will you assess the entire population or a sample (representative or targeted)?
- Who is assessing and analyzing data results? Students, classroom teachers, library staff, administrators, other school staff members, district personnel, other librarians, or outside consultants?
- When does assessment occur? Before, during, or after planning; upon starting a position; during schoolwide accreditation; at the end of a semester or year; or on a specific day or week?
- Where does assessment occur? In libraries or classrooms, in meetings, at institutions of higher education, at home, or online?
- How is assessment conducted? By survey, observation, work analysis, test, rubric, interview, focus group, self-assessment, circulation statistics, usage analysis, or systems analysis?

Assessments may reflect inputs (e.g., resources and services) and outputs (e.g., circulation figures and sample student work). Librarians are familiar with metrics that relate to the collection, circulation, budgets, and visit numbers. Less obvious measurements include database usage, library portal hits, wear and tear on materials, student reading scores, student status post-graduation, or teacher evaluations. Just as one person cannot represent all perspectives, no single measurement can tell the whole story. The planning team can compare, or triangulate, multiple measures to gain a multifaceted picture, and to determine if there are any discrepancies that will be necessary to explain.

Another piece of the current environmental puzzle can be addressed using a SWOT (Strengths, Weaknesses, Obstacles, Threats) analysis. In school libraries, internal strengths and weaknesses may arise from personnel, boards, support groups, facilities, money, collections, services, technology, user database, open hours, and so forth. External issues might include local demographics, competition, technology, politics, governments at different levels, public and private agencies, economic environment, legal environment, and so forth.

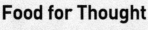

Food for Thought

A good way to approach an environmental scan is from a marketing perspective. Basically, marketing tries to match and promote an entity's products and services with the potential market or population. Remember that the library's purpose is to support the school community, so you should begin from that standpoint; what does the school want to accomplish, and what can the SLP uniquely or most effectively contribute? (Huber and Potter 2015). Guidelines for questions that you should consider when gathering data about the school library environment follow. This is not a definitive list, but rather a course of action for areas you can examine and describe. You do not have to answer every question listed, and you may choose to add some that are not listed.

1. **Environment.** What kind of organization is it? Start with the school library. With what entities/organizations does the school library have relationships? Is the school library affected by technology, political influences, economic influences, societal influences, or other influences? Are conditions surrounding your school library stable or changing? Next, ask these same questions about the school site and the district in which the school library resides.

2. **Users.** Describe the current and potential users of your school library. The library staff may serve several sub-populations or market segments, such as AP biology students, graphic novel fans, or recent immigrant parents. Describe these and try to understand their relationship to the whole or a proportion of the whole. The primary public, which is internal, is the school community, which may be subdivided into students, teachers, support specialists, support staff, administrators, and parents. These subdivisions can be further segmented: kindergartners, science teachers, club advisors, and so on. Secondary publics can include schools in the same or neighboring districts, local libraries and librarians, and the local community at large (including day-care centers, postsecondary institutions, recreation centers, local agencies, bookstores, media outlets, and other businesses). What is each entity's demographics? What is their perception and use of the library? How might they influence and support the library? (Guth and Marsh 2012).

3. **Products and Services**. What products and services does the school library provide? Which products and services are primary, or core, and which are secondary? Are these traditional or innovative products and services? Are they tailored to the users served? Are they branded? How does the school library publicize its products and services?

4. **Place.** Place refers to a geographic location less than it does a distribution channel. How and where does the school library deliver its products and services? Do users come to the school library, or does

the school library go to the users? Does it go to them physically or virtually? Does it go to them in their homes or their classrooms? Is there an intermediary? These questions may have more than one answer, as there is often a mix of distribution channels.

5. **Price and Cost.** Are products and services free to users or are they offered for a fee, as for photocopying or overdue fines? Are there different price levels depending on a user's status? If there is no monetary cost, consider choices that the user has to make in order to benefit from the school library's products and services. Choices can be in terms of ways to spend time, or psychological choices (i.e., asking for help).

6. **Promotion.** What kinds of promotion does the SLP do? This can be direct advertising and/or publicity. Are some products or services more heavily promoted than others? Is promotion sometimes more focused on a particular market segment?

7. **People.** This refers to those delivering the product and service, in other words, the library's paid and volunteer staff. Describe the school library setup and the interactions between library staff and users. Are there intermediaries? If so, describe them.

8. **Service Scope.** Describe the physical surroundings where products and services are delivered. Describe the appearance and atmosphere of the facility, the website, signs, marketing materials, the immediately surrounding environments, and so on.

9. **Competition.** Consider who or what might be a competitor to your school library. Think outside of the box and beyond the obvious if appropriate.

A SWOT analysis can be based on the total school library program, or it can focus on one aspect of the program. Because one of the library's functions is instruction, a focused SWOT analysis might identify:

- current library-related curriculum that is provided in the school library and offered by competitors such as classroom teachers, public libraries, and online information providers
- existing and potential instructors and instructional designers in the school library and elsewhere
- existing and potential resources, including learning aids, in the school library, and elsewhere
- existing and potential learners *and* learning needs in the school library and elsewhere

You should align SLP efforts with schoolwide priorities. In that respect, SWOT analysis can help clarify a compelling situation in terms of what the SLP can contribute. For instance, students might be performing poorly on standardized tests (which is a significant concern for administrators). Alternatively, a growing incidence of cyberbullying might be negatively impacting the school. A SWOT analysis might uncover the following factors for the second situation:

- Strengths: a rich digital collection that supports the curriculum, class set of Internet-connected computers, access to the computers throughout the day, flexible scheduling, a tech-savvy library staff, filtering software, an acceptable use policy (AUP) in place
- Weaknesses: no library lessons on cyberbullying, no discussion of cyberbullying or digital safety beyond AUP on library website
- Opportunities: e-rate compliance requires instruction on digital safety; administrators and teachers don't know how to deal with cyberbullying (the school librarian can serve as an expert)
- Threats: no digital safety instruction in the curriculum, administrators and parents who want to cut off access to all social media, and technicians who don't want to deal with intranets or social media

At this point, you can gather more specific data that can inform SLP planning decisions. A needs assessment is an effective way to find out about the current knowledge, capabilities, interests, and values of each school community segment. For example, through a schoolwide survey, you may find out that no one understands cyberbullying or how to deal with it. On the other hand, you may discover that 97 percent of students use social media, and 36 percent have been involved in cyberbullying. You should also assess the learning context; how might lessons on cyberbullying fit into the curriculum? How might the school schedule fit in cyberbullying instruction?

STEP 3: SET GOALS AND OBJECTIVES
As a framework for this step, you and your planning team should carefully review the existing school and SLP vision and mission statements.

- What values and assumptions do they express?
- How and why were they developed?
- How are they used in planning and implementation?
- How well do they align?

Sometimes these statements have "image" value, but little programmatic substance. However, in theory they can serve as benchmarks to measure how well

Food for Thought

As you gather data about the school community, the library, and how they align, you may notice a gap between the school's goals and its current situation. Huber and Potter (2015) adapted Maslow's 1954 hierarchy of needs to describe the health of communities. They further posited that each level must be satisfied before addressing the next, higher level. The hierarchy follows, noting the school's situation and library's contribution.

1. **Physiological needs.** Do students come to school clothed and fed? Do they have a home? Schools often provide meals for free or at discounted prices, and parent groups might gather clothing for students. Can the library provide a resource list for food banks and other social services for the school community?

2. **Safety and security.** Do students feel safe at school? Schools might partner with correctional officers or security staff, and could establish anti-bullying and peer support programs. Is the library a safe place where students feel secure? Can the library ensure data privacy and confidentiality? Does the library provide resources or programs that help students defend themselves against cyberbullying?

3. **Belonging.** Does every student have opportunities to belong to a group where they feel accepted and appreciated? Are academic courses or cocurricular activities such as clubs or sports offered? Does the library have aides and book club groups? Do library staff advise interest clubs or services groups?

4. **Self-esteem.** How do schools help students gain self-confidence, and empower them to assume more responsibility for themselves? How do schools recognize student accomplishments? Does the library provide opportunities for students to shine by displaying their work, providing certificates for reading progress, creating "techie of the week" posters?

5. **Self-actualization.** How do schools facilitate lifelong learning and success? Do students have leadership opportunities and ways to contribute to the school and community? Does the library provide resources and services that help students find opportunities for volunteering, interning, and otherwise contributing to society? Does the library help students generate new knowledge or creative expressions, and ways to share those original ideas?

Where does your school fit in this hierarchy? Where does the library fit in this hierarchy? Where is the alignment between school and the library? What can you do to provide a closer fit?

the organization is accomplishing its mission. The planning team has to determine these statements' roles, and identify possible gaps between the statements and the actual practices of the school and the SLP. Only then can the planning team determine how to address those gaps either by bridging them, or redefining the statements (at least for the SLP). In either case, the vision and mission statements—as well as the environmental scan and SWOT analysis—inform the planning team's determination of goals for the SLP.

Goals define future conditions that enable the SLP to fulfill its mission. Goals reflect effective and impactful practice. Objectives provide short-term, specific, and measurable targets to accomplish goals. For instance, a goal might be expressed as "developing a culture of reading" with supporting objectives of "providing a rich collection of current, attractive, and appropriate reading materials," "collaborating with classroom teachers," and "expanding storytelling activities." Although the planning team may identify several worthwhile objectives, they should also research existing best practices in the field. As an information professional, the SL is best positioned to spearhead such investigations.

Effective plans usually focus on just a couple of goals in order to marshal resources efficiently. Likewise, only a handful of objectives should support each goal, and the planning team should prioritize those objectives based on a number of possible factors: importance, time-sensitivity, degree of difficulty, target audience, greatest return on effort, and even motivation. Note that the planning team is likely to agree on goals, but may differ on the prioritization of objectives. Ultimately, it is usually the SL and the site administrator who have the final say in the implementation strategy of those goals and objectives.

When determining objectives, the planning team should also develop indicators that operationalize (make concrete) the objectives. For example, what does collaboration look like? Indicators of collaboration might include: communicating frequently, meeting regularly, planning together, identifying roles and tasks, sharing resources, coaching one other, co-teaching students, and co-assessing student work. Assessments can then measure the quality of those indicators. Good practice is evidence-based, so determining upfront how those objectives will be measured and assessed are key tasks, and will help the planning team implement and effectively adjust their action plans.

STEP 4: CREATE ACTION PLANS

At this point, the planning team has enough data to decide on a specific course of actions, or strategies, necessary to meet the objectives and overarching goals. Just as several roads may lead to the same destination, so too can several actions enable the SLP to meet identified objectives. Thus, the planning team must determine which actions will be the most effective, that is, give the best return for the amount of time, effort, and resources needed to carry out the action. Of

Table 5.1
Action Plan

	Resources	Library Staff	Skill	Other Personnel	Time	Space	Cost	Total
Face-to-face story hour read-aloud	Books, document stand (option)	Student aide, parent, library clerk, school librarian	Effective oral reading, class management	Classroom teacher cooperation (option)	10–60 minutes	Library, class, other room, outdoors	0 (possible cost of document stand)	
Real-time online story hour read-aloud	Books, Internet-connected computers, webcam, conferencing application	Library clerk, school librarian, others with training	Effective oral reading, web conferencing skill	Classroom teacher cooperation (option), tech specialist if needed	10–30 minutes	Library, class, other room	Net cost, equipment, software cost	
Face-to-face storytelling	Books (as basis)	School librarian, outside storyteller	Storytelling	Classroom teacher cooperation (option)	10–60 minutes	Library, classroom, other room, outdoors	Storyteller	
Videotaped storytelling	Optical storage, player, and monitor	Student aide, parent, library clerk, school librarian	Use of video equipment (player or recording), optional video production and editing	Classroom teacher cooperation (option), tech specialist if needed, video expert	10–60 minutes	Library, class, other room	Video supplies, video product	
Digital storytelling	Computer, digital storytelling application	Student aide, school librarian	Use of digital player, digital production and editing	Classroom teacher cooperation (option), tech specialist if needed	10–60 minutes	Library, class, other room	Computer, digital resource product	

course, several actions may be implemented, the assumption being that each one produces a desired effect, and that together the total will optimize results. A grid (see table 5.1 on the previous page) can facilitate decision making, as shown in this example. For example, if one of the objectives is to expand storytelling activities to support the goal of creating a culture of reading, several possible actions may be considered. Each criterion, listed across the top of the grid, can be weighted to reflect relative importance. Some criteria can even be considered nonnegotiable, for example, the speaker must be a volunteer.

Strategy choices also depend on predictability, determined by the likelihood of previous success of similar actions at the site or in other settings, and the stability of internal and external environments. Usually, predictability is more likely when the SL can control the factors and does not need to depend on others. On the other hand, impactful actions usually require collaboration and pooling of resources, along with shared control.

Regardless of the action plan, the above criteria usually have to be delineated so that everyone knows what tasks are required, who is responsible for each task, and the time line for the activities. Although the grid shown above does not include benchmarks and assessments, these two elements should be part of the action plan in order to ascertain the action's progress. Table 5.2 shows a sample action table heading.

Table 5.2
Action Plan Table Headings

Tasks	Target Groups	Person Responsible	Progress Notes/ Benchmarks	Date Completed	Evidence and Assessment

STEP 5: ALLOCATE RESOURCES

Allocation of resources goes hand in hand with the action plan because material, human, fiscal, time, and other resources are needed in order to act. Because staff time is usually required to implement the plan, as the manager, you will need to determine how to reallocate the workload. In some cases, the proposed task will replace an existing practice, but in other cases the new action means that another, unrelated task will have to be left undone or accomplished by another person. In general, most functions should be performed by the lowest-level staffer who can accomplish it; for example, displays might be handled by volunteer aides. Thus, when a new task is assigned, you can take the opportunity to review staff workloads and redistribute them as applicable.

Although it is easiest to use existing resources, sometimes requesting—and getting—additional resources can make a significant difference, such as hiring a staff person or procuring a cart of laptop computers. SLP managers can acquire materials using existing library budgets if the resource is a line item on the budget, or if budget lines can be redistributed. Sometimes the site or district budget can accommodate existing need. You will need to justify the expenditure to the decision maker, whether an administrator or school board. This process will be detailed in the budget chapter, but it is safe to say that you should use a one-page request stating: (1) what is needed, (2) why, (3) the impact of the acquisition, and (4) a budget with comparative source figures.

STEP 6: IMPLEMENT THE PLAN

As a manager, you are responsible for making sure that the plan is implemented. Normally, you will not accomplish this on your own. Rather, you make sure that resources are available for the action team to carry out the plan. Most importantly, you must motivate the action team (be it the library staff, students, teachers, or other community members) to carry out the task, training them as needed; monitoring and redirecting their performance as necessary; and rewarding them for their successful efforts. Dumler and Skinner (2005) suggest three tactics for working with others:

1. Authority: Use your position as the SLP manager to ensure compliance; for complex tasks, authority alone usually does not suffice.
2. Persuasion: Convince others about the merits and feasibility of the plan. Persuasion requires clear and compelling communication, which often involves leveraging the target person's own interests.
3. Policies: Draw upon existing policies or create them as guidelines to implement the plan and achieve its objectives. Policies tend to be used for permanent actions, and should be flexible enough to enable staff to modify specific procedures as needed. Policies usually must be approved by the school board, so they should be carefully crafted by the library staff and planning team.

STEP 7: CONTROL THE PLAN

Action by itself does not suffice; each action must be done competently, and must contribute to meeting the plan's objective. Typically, the manager explains the tasks, and trains the workers as needed, then monitors and provides specific feedback until they can work competently without supervision. This process will be detailed in the chapter focusing on managing people. It should be noted

The following planning guide (table 5.3), based on the library program planning guides of the American Association of School Librarians (1999, 2012), can help you make sure that you align the school library program with the school's efforts, and consider the implementation details needed to ensure success.

Table 5.3

Planning Guide

	Target	Acceptable	Emerging
Planning process preparation	Includes logical key persons, clear and useful criteria, appropriate resources, thorough and feasible time frame, valid and reliable assessment methods	Includes key persons, appropriate criteria, appropriate resources, feasible time frame, valid assessment method	Lists few key persons, few and unclear criteria, inadequate resource, unrealistic time frame, inadequate assessment method
Mission statement	Memorable and appropriate, involves key stakeholders, aligns with and supports school mission	Clear and appropriate, involves other people, aligns with school mission	Unclear, done without input, ignores school mission
Goals and objectives	Goals linked to assessment and *Information Power* (IP), effective objectives and strategies, triangulated evaluation plan	Goals linked to assessment, reasonable objectives and strategies, valid evaluation plan	Goals not linked to assessment or IP, vague or unrealistic objectives and strategies, inadequate evaluation plan
Action plan	Specific and clear plan of action, good alignment with prior work, reflects good use of time, has good potential of impacting the library program and student success significantly	Clear plan of action, aligns with prior work, reflects good use of time, has some potential of impacting the library program and student success	Unclear or sparse plan of action, reflects ineffective use of time, has little potential of impacting the library program or student success
Supporting evidence and assessment	*Includes strong evidence of the plan's implementation and assessment*	*Includes some evidence of the plan's implementation and assessment*	*Includes little evidence of the plan's implementation or assessment*

that many action plans involve interdependent tasks performed by several people, so juggling overall performance can challenge the SL. In his book *Good to Great* (2001), Jim Collins asserted:

> There is no single defining action, no grand program, no one killer innovation, no solitary lucky break, no miracle moment. Rather, the process resembles relentlessly pushing a giant heavy flywheel in one direction, turn upon turn, building momentum until a point of breakthrough, and beyond. (Collins 2001, 5)

A simple approach is to employ a plan, do, check, act (PDCA) quality planning cycle (Dumler and Skinner 2005): plan the action, have staff perform the task as a pilot project, check the process and results of the process in terms of the desired outcome, modify the action as needed, and redo the action until it is performed consistently at the necessary quality level.

Both the process and the product, or result, need to be assessed. For example, an author visit might be well planned, but might have resulted in a disappointing turnout, or the author might have been late because of a traffic accident. In some cases, the specific circumstances might not be predictable or controllable; but in others, the underlying reasons for a disappointing result can be identified, and taken into consideration the next time that a similar activity is performed. Following the above example, perhaps few people attended the author visit because of upcoming exams, a big game scheduled at the same time, or because the author is not well-known. The first two reasons can guide future scheduling, and the latter reason points to the need for better communication and more careful author selection.

The goal of controlling the plan is sustainable implementation. If the plan is worthwhile and impactful, it should become the new status quo, the new normal. Nevertheless, the SLP will never be perfect, so planning should strive for continuous improvement, should be considered as an ongoing cyclical activity.

A Few Words about Change

Planning involves change. Although most people like novelty, permanent change is less appealing. Thus, a vacation from work is attractive, but unemployment is not usually embraced. One of the reasons that people prefer the status quo is that it is a known quality. Even when change is expected to be positive, the unknown can be unnerving. As a manager, you need to provide the conditions for effective and sustainable change from the SLP and its stakeholders. For that reason, planning and managing for change require careful consideration and communication. Generally, when change is communicated rationally and supported through incentives, people are more likely to view it favorably. Agreement on SLP goals and objectives is critical because it signals an acceptance of change, a desire for improvement, and a sense of ownership and responsibility for implementing it.

Ely (1999) focused on the conditions that should exist or be created in the environment in order to facilitate change. Those catalysts include:

1. Dissatisfaction with the status quo
2. Sufficient knowledge and skills to accomplish the change
3. Availability of resources
4. Availability of time
5. Rewards or incentives to engage people to change
6. Participation in decision making
7. Commitment to change
8. Leadership of expectations, commitment, and support

Resistance to change is also a reality. As the SLP manager, you need to identify possible negative reactions so you can know how to deal with them. Furthermore, resistance to change may be an indicator that the plan is off course. When resistance is encountered, it can be a learning opportunity to reconsider the reasons for change and the strategies being used to affect it, and to root out the reasons for resistance. Zaltman and Duncan (1977) provide the most thorough examination of the factors that contribute to resistance.

- Social barriers: group solidarity, rejection of outsiders, conformity to norms, and group introspection
- Organizational barriers: threats to power and influence, organizational structure, behavior of top-level administrators, climate for change in the organization, and technological barriers
- Individual psychological barriers: perception, conformity, and commitment, and personality factors

At the very least, you should involve stakeholder representatives in the planning process in order to identify and address possible resistance. Stakeholders have to see that a plan will improve the existing SLP and ideally the school community as a whole, that the proposed practices are preferable to the existing ones, that the actions are feasible, that the resources are available, that the changes are socially acceptable, and that the plan can be changed if need be.

To convince library staff and other stakeholders about the value of a plan for improvement (and change), it helps to show concrete examples of successful action-plan implementation. Visiting model school libraries and talking with their employees can lower your library staff's stress (of course, you should visit the library ahead of time to make sure that the picture is realistic and that their staff are happy with the situation). If visits aren't feasible, you can locate and share articles and personal accounts about the desired outcome so that stakeholders can see how the outcome can impact the school community positively. Indeed, finding such examples should constitute part of the early planning process. You can also contact SLs at those sites to gather tips on optimizing planning and implementation.

It should also be noted that the scope and degree of a particular change impact the ease with which it is accepted. For instance, internal change that barely impacts the rest of the school community, such as rescheduling shelving responsibilities, can be easy to implement. However, change that impacts the entire school, for example, shifting from a fixed to a flexible class-use schedule, will usually require effort to convince others that the change will improve educational practices and student outcomes. Documenting and reporting the results are critical to show stakeholders how the change has improved the overall school community. Once they are won over, stakeholders can become effective supporters for the plan and the positive change it facilitates.

In terms of deploying a plan that involves many people, here are some tips:

- Start with volunteers.
- Do a pilot test or small-scale version of the intended change.
- Aim for a critical mass, and then push for inclusion.
- Base the first steps on existing structures and services.
- Employ available, easy-to-use resources.
- Focus on relationships.
- Do personal coaching, and then have participants buddy up.
- Be responsive.
- Empower people to shape change.
- Have people share their successes.
- Give incentives and recognize performance.

Bringing It Down to You

Most of the discussion in this chapter has focused on strategic planning, which provides a long-term, big-picture approach to school library program development and improvement. Even in the midst of day-to-day management, you should take time to review and reflect on the SLP's mission and goals. This can be as simple as posting your mission or goals by your computer, then reflecting on them at the beginning and end of each day. By doing so, you are practicing the role of the reflective practitioner.

As noted above, planning comes in all sizes and at different levels and time frames. Planning can start when you open the library door in the morning and prioritize the day's tasks. It can happen after a dismal first period class, when you realize that you have to remind the kindergarten teachers about how their classes are expected to behave, and that you will have to plan an engaging, age-appropriate learning activity about library manners. As you run out of printer ink yet again, you may decide that you need to plan how to handle library supplies more systematically. As you see students having troubles locating relevant articles, you may realize that it is necessary to plan ways to integrate the use of database aggregators into the curriculum. When you receive a notice that books are misshelved, you understand that you should monitor and maybe retrain the library shelvers. In short, you must be a reflective practitioner. By constantly scanning the environment, identifying needs and problems, examining the reasons behind the contributing circumstances, and thinking of alternative solutions and ways to address the issues, you are practicing a fundamental management activity. Be the change you wish to see in the world.

Take a few minutes to do a planning reality check.

- What is working well in the library? How can you tell? Why does it work?
- What is not working well in the library? How can you tell? Why is it failing?
- What is one process or product that you would like to improve? Why?
- How might you address the needed improvement?
- Who will you include in the planning?
- What is one activity your staff can do to improve the library program?
- What is one way you can measure the staff's efforts and the success of their results?
- How will you manage your staff's efforts and reward results?

Each time you systematically plan, you will find the process becomes more manageable.

References

American Association of School Librarians. 1999. *A Planning Guide to Information Power.* Chicago, IL: American Library Association.

———. 2012. *A 21st-Century Approach to School Library Evaluation.* Chicago, IL: American Library Association.

Collins, J. 2001. *Good to Great.* New York, NY: Harper Business.

Dumler, M., and S. Skinner. 2005. *A Primer for Management.* Mason, OH: South-Western.

Ely, D. 1999. *New Perspectives on the Implementation of Educational Technology Innovation.* (ED 427775). Syracuse, NY: ERIC Document Reproduction Services.

Guth, D., and C. Marsh. 2012. *Public Relations: A Values-Driven Approach,* 5th ed. Boston, MA: Allyn and Bacon.

Huber, J., and S. Potter. 2015. *The Purpose-Based Library.* Chicago, IL: American Library Association.

Maslow, A. 1954. *Motivation and Personality.* New York, NY: Harper.

Mowl, G. 1996. *Innovative Assessment.* Newcastle upon Tyne, England: University of Northumbria.

Zaltman, G., and R. Duncan. 1977. *Strategies for Planned Change.* New York, NY: Wiley InterScience Publications.

6

Managing Resources

SCHOOL COMMUNITIES CONTINUE TO THINK OF THE LIBRARY IN terms of its books and other material resources. Therefore, school library program (SLP) managers must manage those resources well in order to meet these expectations. In our digital world, the scope of resources has grown exponentially to include a variety of print items (including graphic novels), multimedia products (including videos and audiobooks), digital resources, and the associated equipment. Furthermore, SLP managers need to manage resources they *access* as well as those they own. How are those resources selected, acquired, organized, stored, and maintained for effective retrieval and use? What is the life cycle of collection management? These core management issues are detailed in this chapter.

The Role of Resources and Resource Management

School librarians straddle two professions: information professionals and educators. They seek to provide their stakeholders with both physical and intellectual access to information and ideas. Because textbooks continue to play a role in K–12 education, the school community must learn how to gain knowledge via a wide range of informational resources. The United States Common Core State Standards for English language arts (2010) asserted: "Through wide and deep reading of literature and literary nonfiction of steadily increasing sophistication, students gain a reservoir of literary and cultural knowledge, references, and images; the ability to evaluate intricate arguments; and the capacity to surmount the challenges posed by complex texts" (35). Furthermore, the Common Core State Standards for mathematics (2010) noted: "Because the mathematics concepts in [US] textbooks are often weak, the presentation becomes more mechanical than is ideal. We looked at both traditional and nontraditional textbooks used in the US and found this conceptual weakness in both" (3). As the SLP manager, you are uniquely positioned to evaluate, select, acquire, organize, store, and facilitate the access and use of a wide variety of recorded resources across the curriculum.

School libraries provide the most cost-effective way for the school community to access and use relevant, developmentally appropriate informational resources. One book on ecology, for instance, might address the needs of an advanced student in a ninth grade social issues course or a struggling senior in a biology course. A podcast of a Martin Luther King Jr. speech could be useful in an eighth grade U.S. history course, a high school rhetoric unit, or a Black History Month event. A simple video clip about the reason for seasons might be appropriate for second graders, and a more sophisticated video clip might be more appropriate in a high school earth sciences class. Different resources about the same topic can provide unique points of view, complement each other in content and presentation, and address the varied learning needs and preferences of a diverse student population. Because SLPs serve the entire school community, library workers can develop and maintain collections that address all content standards at every grade, and optimize the use of those collections in collaboration with classroom teachers and support specialists.

The concept of a collection, both physical and digital, cannot be overemphasized. The library is not a bookstore with ever-changing stock. Although you do need to keep library collections dynamic and responsive to the moving target of curriculum, you also must maintain core materials in several formats that can be dependably accessed upon curricular need. As classroom teachers plan their lessons and learning activities, they must be assured that the resources they are required to teach—and for students to use—are available according to plan. SLP managers usually try to acquire materials at the last moment upon request, but such practice should be kept to a minimum because it undermines systematic instructional planning and implementation; furthermore, immediate funding and easy access to a copy might prove challenging. Neither the classroom teacher nor you are then well prepared to integrate that resource thoughtfully into the curriculum. In addition, that last minute resource might not be high quality or well reviewed. Especially when budgets are often tight, you will need to acquire materials selectively and systematically to ensure equity across grades and subjects. In the case of a last-minute request, you might look for available copies at another local library, and suggest that the requester (or library worker) borrow it for the short term. Such access points out the advantage of ownership: sometimes a resource is not accessible because other people are using it, be it physically or virtually. Older physical resources can go out of print within a year, and digital resources can disappear overnight.

Each resource goes through a library life cycle that must be managed: from its publication and selection to maintenance and withdrawal. The entire collection (or set of collections) of resources exist within the framework of the school community, which also calls upon your management skills. Thus, the management aspect of collections requires careful and systematic attention throughout the life cycle of recorded information in order to optimize the learning environment for the entire school community.

Analyzing the School Community

The library's collection supports the school community—not only the curriculum but also the personal needs of that community. Determining what resources are needed requires you to assess the community's demographics, information needs, and available resources.

Most public school students attend the school closest to their home, and the elementary level is most likely to reflect neighborhood demographics. Community information can be found in

- census figures (www.census.gov/epcd/www/zipstats.html)
- housing information (www.zillow.com)
- socioeconomic factors (www.claritas.com/MyBestSegments/Default.jsp)
- maps (http://maps.yahoo.com and http://maps.google.com)
- city websites

Such data will help you determine the information role that the school library program provides. For example,

- Is the school situated in a residential area, a commercial area, an industrial area, or near a park? Students' after-school habits, such as shopping or playing sports, are typically determined by the locale. Where few activities exist outside of school, after-hour clubs and library activities might fill an important gap—or students might simply go straight home.
- How do students usually come to campus: walking, bicycling, public transportation, private vehicle? Students might stay at the library longer if they can easily get to and from school. If public transportation is the

main way to get to school, then school hours might well be controlled by the transit system's schedule, impacting after-school library use. In areas where parents routinely transport their children, it may well be the case that they would prefer that the library stay open until 5:00 pm or later so children can stay at school after class hours.

- What ethnic groups are represented in the area? School libraries usually try to honor family cultural traditions. The collection might also include non-English materials if the need arises. Depending on the culture, methods for transmitting and sharing information may differ; some may honor the oral tradition, and others may prefer images or text.
- What is the economic background of the school's families and the community? Poverty impacts access to, and ownership of, reading materials. Parents who have to work long hours, especially to make ends meet, may have less opportunity to supervise and read to their children, and older children might have to take care of younger siblings. If the population is highly transient, perhaps the collection should focus on paperbacks.
- What competing entities provide reading material: libraries, bookstores, and some chain stores? Children especially need to experience print environments, and in some cases, the school library may be the only local example.

Within this context, you can then focus on the school community itself, particularly the regular staff and students. Here are several questions to guide the assessment, based on Loertscher, Woolls, and Felker (1998).

1. Who are the potential target populations of the school library collection? Most of these data are available from school reports compiled for their communities.

   - Students: grade range, age range, ethnicities represented, languages spoken, academic records, socioeconomic needs (e.g., free and reduced lunches), special needs, dropouts, and graduates
   - Staff: specialists, and administrative employees, grade range, age range, seniority, ethnicities represented, subject matter, and technological expertise
   - Families: socioeconomic status, family configurations, ethnicities represented, languages represented, and home access to resources

2. Who currently uses the library resources?

   - Who uses the collection regularly? What parts of the collection are used most frequently? How is the collection used? When do they use it? Where do they use it? Why do they use the collection?

- Who are occasional users—and why do they attend only infrequently?
- Who does not use the library resources and services—and why?

3. Who will be the potential users of the library's resources?

- Who will be the target audience?
- What will motivate them to use the library's resources?
- What feasible changes to the library program should be changed?

Analyzing information about the school and larger community is just the first step. You should also look at these populations' information needs, particularly in light of the library's mission. In school libraries that mission is to support the school, so you will need to examine the curriculum. You should look at texts, course guides, state content standards and frameworks, as well as assignments and other student work that rely on library resources. Make sure you think about cocurricular activities and personal needs, including the needs of the staff and families. Here are some guiding questions.

1. Subject matter

- What subject matter is required—and for which grades?
- What courses are elective—and for which grades are they offered?
- Is curriculum tracked, that is, do different student subgroups take different curricular pathways?
- What textbooks and other resources are routinely used?
- How are technology resources, including hardware and software, integrated into the curriculum?
- What school initiatives, such as writing across the curriculum or instilling mutual respect, could be supported by library resources?

2. Teaching and learning

- To what extent can students choose materials that support the curriculum?
- What kinds of assignments integrate library resources? What assignments could potentially integrate library resources?
- What instructional approaches are typically used: lecture, memorization or rote learning, problem solving, inquiry, Socratic method, debates, collaborative work, competitive work, and so forth?

3. Cocurriculum and personal content

- What cocurricular activities are offered? How high is the demand for such activities?
- What cocurricular activities already do—or could potentially—integrate library resources?
- What are the personal interests of the school community that could be supported by library resources (e.g., career information, hobbies, and recreation, lifestyle choices, personal health and well-being, human relationships)?

4. Adult education

- What role does professional development play in the school?
- What library resources support professional development?
- What role does instruction for families play in the school?
- What library resources support instruction for families?

The answers to these questions can help shape collection development decisions. For instance, if textbooks are used heavily, then the library should collect at least one copy of each textbook for convenient referral. If the school focuses on career exploration, then materials in those areas should be provided. If peer counseling is available, then library resources can help train student counselors. If the community is known for its sports, then the collection should feature those activities. If professional development is highly valued, perhaps a separate collection for teachers should be developed. If the school has strong ties with its alumni and community, then the library might keep school publications and information about community events.

Analyzing the Library's Resources

With this information, you can then more accurately assess the library's current collection and map it. What is used most often? What resources are missing? What is the school's and library's niche? This analysis will help you identify gaps, which will inform your collection development plan.

Although print materials remain a core aspect of most school libraries, information is represented in many formats, and SLs have a responsibility to introduce students to these formats. OCLC (2003) provides a two-pronged approach to library collections that transcends formats (table 6.1).

Table 6.1
Library Collections

		Stewardship/Scarcity	
		High	Low
Uniqueness	Low	Books and journals (e.g., periodicals, government documents, maps)	Freely accessible web resources (e.g., open source, newsgroups)
	High	Special collections	Research and learning materials

Johnson (2009) offers a two-dimensional approach to collection analysis based on use versus collection that employs both qualitative and quantitative assessment instruments.

- Circulation figures (total, by collection subgroups, by user subgroups identified by demographics and curriculum). The library's integrated library management system provides the most data on library resources. If it is linked with the library portal, these tools can offer many insights on inventory and use.
- In-library use. When the library is primarily used for student study and research, materials may well be consulted without being checked out. A good practice is to keep a book cart close to the research area for students to fill rather than trying to reshelve the books themselves. Not only does that make materials handier for the next set of users (and less likely to be misshelved), but a book count can be done regularly to track in-house use. Materials that are left on the tables can be carted and counted.
- Interlibrary loan (ILL) requests and delivery. Schools tend to use ILL infrequently for a couple of reasons: most assignments do not require extensive resources, and students' work habits usually preclude waiting for the material to arrive. On the other hand, if ILL services are well publicized, they may attract attention by teachers and administrators. Requests for items may be a good indication of a need, although the basis for the request should be determined; for instance, is the item being previewed for possible course use, or is the item being used for professional development? As another option, the library might feature suggested books or use e-mail to determine interests.
- Tracking hits of online resources (e.g., websites, ebooks, articles, etc.). Most computers can track hits, and database aggregators can compile access statistics.
- Observation of users. Do students grab newspapers when they come to the library? Are students surfing the net or skimming text? Are they deep

into a magazine article? Are they sharing what they read? Do they participate in literature circles or book clubs (physical or virtual)?

- Content analysis. Analyzing citations used in student research products can point to resources owned by the library—or in other collections. Students might indicate favorite reads in book reports, book talks, social media sites, and online reading discussion websites. Some library catalogs enable users to post their favorites on that site.
- Surveys. Library surveys can solicit information about users' reading habits and library use, as well as use of other centers of information, such as other libraries and bookstores.
- Focus groups and interviews. Probably the richest source of information about the library's resources is the school community itself. Both users and nonusers should provide input. It is a good idea to hold these sessions in a neutral place, such as a conference room, instead of the library itself. Focus groups are particularly good for identifying issues, and interviews are especially useful as a follow-up to surveys designed to ferret out the reasons for response trends.

Johnson suggested several ways that the collection itself may be measured.

- Quantity (total, by format, subject matter, curriculum focus). As with circulation figures, the library's integrated management system (ILMS) provides the quickest and most detailed statistics.
- Material-to-student ratio. Schools' annual reports list student populations by grade and demographics so that some collections can be more finely analyzed, such as non-English or DVD holdings.
- Budget (total, and disaggregated by type of expenditure). It is important to also include other funding sources such as categorical funding, donations, grants, and gifts in kind. In addition, some library materials might be provided by state plans (e.g., database aggregators), or hidden under the school's budget for resources (e.g., equipment and Internet connectivity).
- Number of items added and withdrawn over time. These data indicate patterns of acquisition and deselection. The basis for deselection (e.g., physical condition versus outdatedness) reveals collection maintenance practices. Patterns may also indicate changes in funding allocations or possible changes to the library, such as moving a collection (which is a good opportunity to weed thoroughly). Table 6.2 is an example that illustrates which parts of the collection have shrunken because of withdrawing older materials, shown by the newer copyright dates.

Table 6.2
Collection Statistics

	2007	2012	2007	2012
	Number of books	Number of books	Average copyright date	Average copyright date
Fiction	3,133	4,593	1994	2001
Nonfiction	5,537	4,845	1989	1999
Reference	996	854	1988	1996

Visuals can be compelling, too. Figure 6.1 shows additions only, and Figure 6.2 shows net collection gains (i.e., additions minus withdrawals).

Figure 6.1
Collection Additions

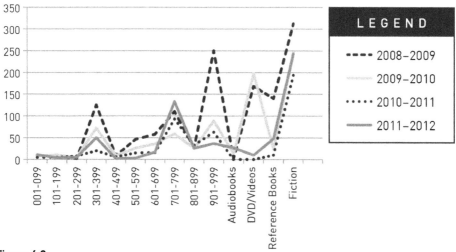

Figure 6.2
Net Collection Gains

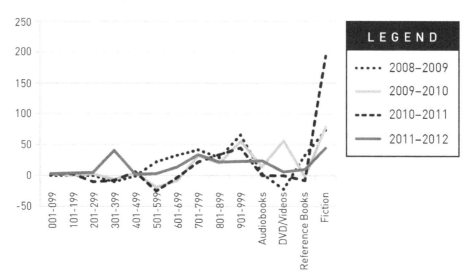

- Age. As with quantity, many library ILMS can quantify the copyright date of resources. Spot checks in trendy collection areas such as astronomy (is Pluto still a planet?), health, travel, and technology can give clues about the collection's relative currency. Who are the two most recent presidents whose biographies are in the library, for instance? In one sad school library, it was Lincoln! Curriculum-based age offers a more insightful picture than a strict call number approach, as seen in figure 6.3.
- Physical condition. Wear and tear of the collection indicates use, but may also indicate a lack of weeding (deselection). Pristine collections may be new—or just unused. Even the amount of dust on materials can be an indication of use and currency. As with age, physical condition should be examined by curricular area in order to make more precise collection management decisions.
- Comparisons to collections of similar schools and to collection standards. Statistics drawn from a school district library union catalog can reveal possible inequities in local school library collections. It is also a good idea to compare school libraries in other districts that serve a similar population; as library catalogs are increasingly accessible remotely, gathering such data has become easier. The Institute of Education Statistics maintains data about public school libraries, which can be compared. *School Library Journal* and the American Association of School Librarians sponsor budget and resource surveys that provide national and regional figures about school library collections. Many states maintain statistics and offer guidelines about school library collections.
- Checklists of published core collection. Wilson's core catalog publications and Follett's Titlewave service provide two useful ways to measure a collection for peer-reviewed choices and popular titles.

Figure 6.3
Average Age of Collection by Subject Area

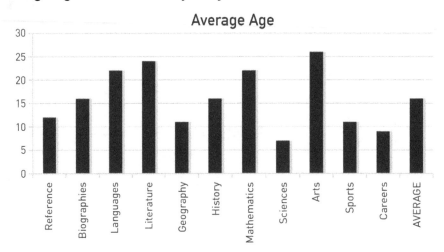

Infographics can help represent and clarify the data. For instance, an annotated time line of collection addition and deselection data over time can facilitate resource management decisions and communication. Likewise, a visual collection map can show the relative size of resources for reference, major curricular areas, and specialty areas (e.g., non-English language, professional reading, and magnet schools) beyond Dewey Decimal Classification, which might not reflect curriculum needs as clearly. OCLC's quadrant approach to collections offers another way to visualize the library's resources.

Technology deserves special mention, not only because it constitutes a growing percentage of many school libraries' resources but also because the criteria for digital resources should consider both the content and the equipment and connectivity needed to access them. In analyzing the school library's electronic resources, the following factors should be addressed:

- Hardware and peripherals: quantity and specifications, platforms, age, physical condition, repair records, etc.
- Software: titles; productivity and curricular-specific quantities; regularity of upgrades; local installation and access practices; cloud access and storage
- Online subscription services: quantity and scope of text-based and video-based database aggregators; tutoring and other online services; ebooks; audiobooks; ereader and other player quantity, quality, and platform; license agreement specifics (e.g., number of simultaneous users versus total school population, access basis, fee basis, and file transfer options); and the quality of vendor services
- Network issues (connectivity—T1, 56K modem, etc.): server quality; network connectivity to the rest of the institution and the community; information transfer and storage options; conferencing capabilities; technical support and management quality
- Access issues: circulation of equipment; in-library use of resources; websites and portals; remote access: to what extent and for whom? (to offices/classes, other sites, other libraries, home)
- Video technologies (quantity and quality): video titles (curriculum coverage); storage format; related equipment; video production software and hardware; droplines; remote connectivity
- Other equipment (quantity and quality): projectors (overhead, data, document); cameras; mobile devices; response systems; circulation policies and procedures

A full analysis links user data with collection data to reveal collection needs. For instance, a library may have a vast and current collection of philosophy materials, but if related courses are no longer offered, then other areas might need more attention. Similarly, if school demographics have changed, the collection should also respond to those changes; for example, if new Americans now constitute a significant percentage of the school community, then culturally relevant materials and information about local social services should be strengthened. As the OCLC collection grid indicated, technology has become a cornerstone of the library's collection (or at least access gateway); do families have access to these resources at home—and the equipment to access them? In some Internet-rich communities, the library may ramp up its web portal and digital resources; in other less-connected communities, the library might require more equipment and longer hours to provide students with the access necessary to become technologically competent—this need also depends on the degree to which teachers integrate technology into instruction and learning. These factors underscore that you must have information about the school community, the curriculum, and library resources in order to provide top-quality resource management.

Selection

Selection is complex. It should be based on user needs, involves selection criteria, requires careful review that involves the school community, and should be supported by policies to systemize decision making.

SELECTION CRITERIA

Selection of library resources should start with a selection policy, which lists the criteria for evaluating resources. A written selection policy that covers different formats provides a consistent, objective basis for collection development. Typical factors include:

- Interest: alignment with the curriculum, personal interest
- Language(s)
- Writing style: clear, engaging, age and developmentally appropriate
- Organization: logical sequence of information, design and visual aids such as headings and summaries, easy access to information (including cross-references), presence and organization of indices
- Coverage: depth and breadth of subject matter, scope, specificity
- Treatment: perspective or approach, balanced view, presentation of different views
- Esthetics: layout, images, typography quality, paper quality, attractive cover
- Accuracy: information should be correct and not misleading or stereotypical (pictures should represent all populations)
- Currency: timeliness (for certain subjects, of it is essential that information be up-to-date), reprinted information that has a current date but contains information that may be very old

- Authority: creator's reputation and expertise, publisher's reputation
- Unique features: images, charts and tables, accompanying resources, website connection
- Added value to the collection: unique treatment and/or complementary content
- Physical quality: paper sturdiness, readability of type, binding quality, ease of handling, durability
- Cost relative to the resource's quality: discounts for buying a series, multiple copies, and/or joint purchasing with other sites

Electronic resources require additional criteria:

- Interface: ease of navigation, site map, search features, networking options, ease of use, user control, interactivity, help options
- Readability: ease of viewing, need for plug-ins. accessibility features for individuals with special needs
- Technical quality: working links, image and sound quality, reliable performance
- Administrative features: documentation, customization, access levels, monitoring options, authentication and authorization procedures, statistics generated
- Equipment and other technical requirements needed to use the resource: specifications, platform, input/output needs, peripherals, Internet connectivity
- File features: transferability of files, printing options, save options
- Licensing details: scope, duration, location of content, digital assets and rights management, access, sharing, service, upgrade/version options, customization

Each format has its unique features:

- Ebooks: platform interoperability, layout, sound features, ease of customization, viewing and downloading options
- Software: installation requirements, file corruptibility, network options, storage options, interoperability with other software
- Optical storage products (e.g., CDs, DVDs): stability of the format (including file corruption), capacity, platform and interoperability, resolution quality, interactivity, format proportion (e.g., wide screen), unique features, presence of advertisements
- Database (aggregators): thoroughness of content, search options, simultaneous use, location of content, choice of collection titles, trans-database lining software (i.e., ability to access content from a different database aggregator)

- Graphic resources: dimensions, ease of storage, preservation considerations (e.g., lamination)
- Games: ease of handling game pieces, risk of a child swallowing them, nontoxic?
- Kits: interaction of parts, dimensions of parts, ease of finding replacement parts, labeling, storage needs
- Hardware: functionality, capacity, interoperability, safety, reliability, ease of repair, upgradability, documentation, service

REVIEWING

Nothing beats looking at a resource before deciding whether to acquire it for the library. It's a good idea to browse public libraries and bookstores to get an idea of what's out there, although many resources supporting the curriculum might not be available in these public venues. Electronic resources can sometimes be harder to test out, although many publishers provide demo downloads.

Reviewing groups can supplement firsthand examination of resources. Although librarians focus on reviewing in their areas of interest, they can also complement each other's expertise. Face-to-face sessions provide rich insights, but online chat and written reviews can serve as a good basis for most selection purposes. Sharing professional insider information about resources saves time and money, and offers a reality check about possible acquisitions. In some cases, joint reviewing can lead to resource sharing of seldom-used but still worthwhile items. You might also consider developing a review group that includes both teachers and students in order to broaden the selection criteria.

SLP managers often rely on professional selection tools, which will require more effort than using a vendor's catalog or database or clicking on www .amazon.com. Professional library selection tools are written by librarian professionals like yourself. They usually don't get paid to write the review, but they generally get to keep the item. Professional library periodicals often include reviews; some periodicals are devoted entirely to reviews. Note that some periodicals publish only positive reviews (omission of a resource is a sign that the item is inferior); others publish both positive and negative reviews. Several review products are available both in print and digital formats:

- The American Library Association and its divisions have several periodicals and websites devoted to reviews.
- Several K–12 professional associations (e.g., the International Literacy Association and the American Association for the Advancement of Science) publish magazines that include reviews.
- Organizations such as the Center for Children's Books and the New York Public Library also publish reviews.

- Good commercial review journals include *VOYA* (Voice of Youth Advocates), *Teacher Librarian, The ALAN Review,* and *Horn Book*, as do a number of Reed-Elsevier publications (e.g., *Publishers Weekly, School Library Journal*).

Books on selection are also good sources of information because they are usually edited by a small committee who agree upon the selection criteria and review components. Selection books may list a core collection, focus on a genre, or cover a specific format. Leading publishers in this area include the American Library Association, H. W. Wilson (now owned by EBSCO), Bowker, Brodart, and Libraries Unlimited (acquired by ABC-CLIO).

Note that it is harder to find nonprint reviews. Here are a few good sources of review information:

- Children's Software Revue (http://childrenssoftware.com)
- CNET (www.cnet.com)
- Computer Information Center (www.compinfo-center.com)
- *PC World* (www.pcworld.com)
- Information Today (www.infotoday.com)

Here are sources that list professional selection tools:
- Arizona State Library, Archives and Public Records Selection of Library Resources (www.azlibrary.gov/cdt/selection.aspx)
- University of Houston Collection Development and Acquisition Selection Tools and Manuals (http://library.uhd.edu/collection development)
- Resources for School Librarians Selection Tools for Books, Videos, and Computer Software (www.sldirectory.com/libsf/resf/selection.html)

Collection Development Policies and Procedures

As noted above, selection policies help SLP managers make collection development decisions. Relevant policies may exist at the site, district, state, or even national level. Usually, local policies are more specific than those at the state level, but they still must comply with their states' legal documents. Johnson (2009) suggested the following topics that the overall collection development policy should include:

- purpose statement
- library's mission, goals, and objectives, and its alignment with the school's mission and community

- collection development responsibilities
- financial information
- collection scope and formats
- selection criteria and selection aids
- resource sharing
- acquisition policies, including gifts and exchanges
- intellectual freedom and intellectual property
- maintenance, including preservation and digitalization
- deselection

Collection development procedures complement these policies by providing guidelines on how to implement the policies. In some cases, school districts may have collection development manuals of procedures, which usually include cataloging procedures as well. However, every site has unique practices, which should be documented to facilitate training and ensure quality control. Every school library policy should be developed with input from the school community, and needs to be approved by the local school board. Here is a beginning list of collection development policies:

- Arizona State Library, Archives and Public Records Collection Development Policies (www.azlibrary.gov/cdt/colldev.aspx)
- California State Department of Education Library Services (www.cde.ca.gov/ci/cr/lb/policies.asp)
- Resources for School Librarians Collection Development Policies (www.sldirectory.com/libsf/resf/coldev2.html#policy)

Acquisitions

Once materials are selected, then you, as the SLP manager, have to make decisions about acquisitions. Should the item be acquired for the collection or just accessed? From whom should the item be procured? What is the process of acquiring a resource? Even if the library has no acquisitions budget, you should keep a wish list of desired items in case money becomes available. Furthermore, all SLP managers need to know how materials are ordered and acquired, both in terms of the processes as well as the personnel involved.

Increasingly, the argument is put forth that access to information trumps ownership to information, largely because of digital resources. In today's school libraries, both aspects of resource management are required. Especially with cloud storage, libraries can save valuable shelf space, increase access, decrease processing cost and labor, minimize maintenance, decrease material damage and losses, keep material more current. However, such benefits come at a cost.

Depending on license agreements, access may still be limited to one user at a time, require equipment, and usually Internet connectivity. Furthermore, some digital resources are platform-specific, and may require that the library staff download the file manually. Library catalogs must be able to handle digital resources and ensure secure authentication and authorization procedures. The cost per digital item might not be less than a print resource, and some publishers make the site pay for another copy after a certain number of uses. Although people can browse digital resources online, physical browsing opportunities may decrease. Few vendors allow the library to actually download and own a permanent copy of the digital resource, so if budgets are cut and subscriptions to these digital products have to be cancelled, the library will be left with nothing if downloads are not permissible. Therefore, while SLP managers are encouraged to incorporate digital resources into the library's program, they should continue to acquire physical items for a physical library collection.

Choosing a good vendor is vital. One of the best ways to choose vendors is to ask advice from local librarian peers. In some districts, school librarians must order only from preapproved vendors. Vendors should be stable and reputable, and they should provide timely, cost-effective service that fulfills the purchase order's demands. Some vendors provide value-added services such as materials processing and cataloging, which can be cost-effective if the site or district does not process materials, and if site library staff do not have the training and expertise to perform these tasks effectively. Cataloging services typically require a profile guide, which stipulates processing preferences such as the location of bar codes, the preferred designation of call numbers, and book covering options. Sometimes publishers or jobbers (wholesale dealers) package titles together to offer a better deal to the buyer. However, if several of the titles are not relevant or interesting, then the per-title cost might not be as attractive as it seems at first glance. Sometimes discounts are given if several titles are purchased from the same publisher; you should investigate possible deals.

Online subscriptions are especially complex endeavors because of intellectual rights issues, technical requirements, and leasing agreements. In most cases, online database vendors license their products, which can seriously limit the resources' use, especially in comparison with fair use laws under copyright regulations. In addition, the site or district's technology center should be consulted about connectivity with the vendor, interface issues (particularly between databases), networking protocols, authentication and authorization procedures, security assurances, technical issues impacted by the number of simultaneous users, and service agreements.

As with print resources, database aggregator vendors often package together various resources—some high-demand and others less well-known but costly—in a mutual fund model. You will have to examine possible overlap of coverage as well as the specific features and services within each vendor's product line. Many libraries choose one vendor as their base product, melding the searching engine and full-text access; additional subscriptions with other vendors might pay for only the search function rather than the full text, depending instead on trans-database linking software such as SFX to provide access to the requested article. It should be noted that most states underwrite database subscriptions that all public and school libraries can access. This approach benefits site and district library budgets at the same time that it increases equitable access to digital resources.

The actual process of acquiring a resource for the library can vary widely, even within a site. For instance, the SLP manager might have a small slush fund or school credit card for just-in-time purchases. More typically, the SLP manager creates a purchase order with a jobber, and submits the order form to the school site's business office, which then requires site administrative and district controller approval. The order is usually fulfilled by the jobber and sent to the district, and ultimately makes it to the school library. No matter how many people have worked on the order, you should check the order to make sure that the invoice matches the received items, and that all the items are free from defect. Jobbers often cannot fulfill the complete order, so it is a good idea for you to list about 20 percent more items than the capped order amount total because it can take months for refunds to be processed.

Theoretically, technology can help with the ordering process. For instance, digital wish lists can be repurposed into purchase orders. Increasingly, as digital orders progress through institution and vendor checkpoints, electronic reviews and signatures can make for seamless tracking *if* all the stakeholders have compatible programs and can agree on the logistics and legalities of such transactions. MARC records can also be incorporated into this process, which can be downloaded into the integrated library management system upon arrival of the document. At this point, technology is less of an issue than business agreements. This convenience comes with a price. Some professionals have a hard time trusting vendors to select, deselect, and manage on behalf of their institutions. Catalogers may assert that outsourcing results in declining cataloging standards.

Processing

Even when items arrive shelf-ready, they require some processing. At the very least, make sure that the resource has no defects, is properly labeled or tagged, and inventoried. Cataloging records and other processing should be reviewed for thoroughness and accuracy. Purchase orders, license agreements, and service warranties must be carefully filed. Understand that other library workers can perform these tasks; you just need to make sure that they are done.

Some school districts provide centralized processing services. If the school library has this responsibility, the SLP manager still prefers to outsource processing in order to decrease workload and improve cataloging quality; vendor processing costs may prove to be less than the cumulative cost of supplies, training, and staff labor time. On the other hand, you may choose to process materials on-site because of unique needs, limited budgets, cataloging expertise, or a surfeit of trained library volunteers.

Generally, books undergo the most processing: cataloging and classification, labeling, covering and other physical protective efforts such as reinforcing bindings, adding security strips or other detectors, barcoding, and marking other information such as reading level and genre. Other formats may omit some processes. For instance, some SLP managers might not choose to fully process some leisure reading paperbacks, such as graphic novels. Magazines may just be stamped and checked in, although some high-interest issues may need security detectors.

Cataloging Issues

With integrated library management systems (ILMS), users can access resources using keywords and call numbers along with author, title, and subject. Bare-bones original and copy cataloging practices may tempt school librarians, especially if they rely on easy-entry input templates. Nevertheless, controlled vocabulary headings, such as Sears, are still needed to ensure consistency and optimize retrieval. Furthermore, when library staff use CIP (cataloging in print), they may forget to cross-check the cited Library of Congress subject headings with Sears, and thus mix up the two sets of headings. School library managers should develop cataloging profile sheets to guide cataloging efforts, be they in-house or outsourced. Prime areas to consider include added entries, notes, leveled reading, awards, curricular links, and holdings information.

Call numbers, the "address" for an item, pose special challenges because they usually reflect local practice. For example, in most school libraries, Cutter numbers are not used to indicate the main entry author; instead, a shortened version of the name or title is used. Here's a nice simple explanation:

> 973.7
>
> COMMAGER or COM or C
>
> (the bigger the collection, the more likely to use more letters)

If a Cutter # were used for Commager, the call number would look like this:

> 973.7
>
> C734

Likewise, school libraries also often use letters for Fiction (F or FIC) and Biography (B or BIO). As the manager, you have to decide how to handle these call number issues by creating a processing profile to ensure consistent assignment of call numbers (e.g., Baker and Taylor's form; see www.btol.com/pdfs/marc _school_quick_form.pdf). If jobbers process material, they follow the profile to process each item.

SLP managers must also address RDA (Resource Description and Access), a new content standard that impacts cataloging. MARC fields are changed to some degree, and more options are available for describing resources (e.g., use of abbreviations, title transcription). SLs should ask ILMS vendors how they are incorporating RDA practices. You also need to decide what options to choose in creating RDA-compliant records. Veering away from standards will result in confusing procedures and less efficient retrieval by users.

SLP managers also must determine how much of the collection to catalog. For instance, increasingly, nonprint items are frequently cataloged, but posters and software are seldom cataloged. A few libraries even catalog websites. Unlike most other processes, which can be done by trained volunteers, cataloging requires specialized training and monitoring.

Access

If the digital resource is held locally, then the main process is installation; otherwise, the resources need to be accessed remotely. In any case, authentication and authorization constitute the main issues to resolve. Ideally, school networks take care of authentication issues. Many database aggregators have their own authentication processes, based on the IP (Internet Protocol) address. If access is based on a static address, that means only predetermined equipment and connections at one site can be used; the advantage is that log-ins and passwords are not required. Dynamic addresses enable remote access, but require log-in and password authentication and authorization. Elastic IP addresses are static IP addresses designed for dynamic cloud computing. This decision largely lies with site principals and network administrators, who are likely to prefer static or elastic addresses; however, such a decision severely limits use of important resources by members of the school community who want to access them from home or public places.

On the user end, most people prefer a one-stop access point, similar to the Google model. Instead, most libraries have a list of access tools: a public access catalog to access information containers (e.g., books, videos, journal titles), a directory of subscription databases, perhaps a metasite for relevant websites, a local repository of in-house learning objects, and so forth. Increasingly, though, libraries are incorporating frontloaded shells to library catalogs or web portals that serve as a single point of entrance to access the desired source, be it physical or virtual.

Circulation

The SLP provides a cost-effective, efficient way for the school community to access needed resources. As the library program manager, you must develop and oversee circulation policies and procedures that optimize convenient use. Issues that should be considered include:

- What materials should stay in the library? Reference? Periodicals? Software?
- Is the library in charge of circulating technology, such as equipment?
- Who can borrow materials? Can kindergarteners? Can parents?
- Can the borrowing time period vary? For example, should DVDs be borrowed for a shorter period of time than a book? Can reference books be borrowed overnight? Should materials being used for class assignments be borrowed only overnight? Can teachers borrow materials for an extended period of time?
- Can teachers borrow materials for their classes, and check those materials to their students?
- Should there be any limit on the number of items borrowed?
- Can materials be reserved?
- What fines, if any, will be accessed for late, lost, or damaged materials? What district or state policies impact options for fines? Should teachers be fined?

Most libraries use the ILMS to catalog and circulate resources. Some sites include a date due slip, which can be used as a bookmark. If that feature is not available, library staff (or students) can pre-stamp date due slips for borrowers to use upon request. In some elementary schools, the library staff provides teachers with bins to collect their classes' borrowed books. Although this may be more convenient for students, this practice can lead to students informally borrowing their classmates' books and not returning them properly, which can impact the real borrower. Furthermore, teachers may feel put upon with this extra responsibility.

The school community usually likes to borrow magazines, but those resources can be easy to lose—and may be hard to replace. Here is a workable procedure to facilitate magazine circulation and help preserve the magazine's physical condition at the same time.

Sample Magazine Checkout Procedure

1. Large envelopes with barcodes are located below the drawers at the circulation desk. Take an envelope.

2. Ask patron to complete the magazine checkout form as below:

   Name
   Homeroom Teacher
   Magazine Title
   Issue's month/day/year

3. Pull up patron record on computer.

4. Scan the barcode on the large envelope (see step 1) so that it records "periodicals" on the patron's record. Hit "Checkout."

5. Write the last three digits of the barcode on the upper right-hand corner of the magazine form, and on the upper right-hand corner of the inside first page of each magazine.

6. Place the magazines inside the envelope.

7. Stamp the envelope and the magazine form with the three-day stamp.

8. Ask patron to please return all magazines at the same time in the same envelope.

9. File the magazine form with the other magazine forms, by barcode number.

Sample Magazine Check-in Procedure

1. Find the magazine form that matches the last three digits of the barcode on the envelope.

2. Verify that all magazines have been returned.

   a. If some magazines are missing, cross off the returned magazines.
   Refile the magazine form.
   Place envelope in "Unreturned magazines" Princeton file until the remaining magazines are returned.

   b. If all magazines have been returned, throw away the form.
   Scan the barcode and hit "Check in."
   Place envelope in the pile of envelopes leady to check out.

3. If magazines are returned without the envelope, then check the magazine form. Follow step 2.

   [Note that you will need to manually type in the barcode number. All barcodes for periodicals begin with "3003," followed by the three digits on the form or magazine.]

Textbooks can be another source of circulation concern. In most schools, textbooks are handled separately from library sources, although some sites use the same integrated library management system. A case can be made that handling textbooks reinforces the library as Resource Central, and provides another opportunity for library staff to interact with the rest of the school community. On the other hand, textbooks constitute a labor-intensive service that takes away precious time from other library management functions. Regardless of the situation, SLP managers are required to work with the rest of the school community to determine responsibilities and policies. If the library program includes textbook management, scheduling becomes a major issue; in some

---

Textbook Loan Policies

The textbooks checked out to you with your high school ID card are the property of the school district and it is your privilege to use the books while you are a student at this high school.

Only students with a current, valid high school ID card will be issued books. Students will be issued textbooks only for those classes in which they are enrolled. Students are required to return all textbooks at the conclusion of the class, at the direction or request of the teacher and/or the library staff, or if the student leaves the high school.

Please read the following rules and responsibilities carefully.

1. If you receive a book that is torn or damaged, please bring it to our attention, and we can let you know when it can be repaired or replaced. If you do not take care of this issue at that time, it will be concluded that any damages found when you return the book are your responsibility.

2. All texts are to be covered with a paper, nonadhesive book cover—do not use tape on the book or the cover.

3. Protect all textbooks from damage. If lost or damaged in any way, student will pay all costs before a new textbook is issued.

4. Do not write, underline or highlight in textbooks, including textbook novels checked out for English classes (use sticky notes!).

5. All texts checked out to the student must be returned in good condition, with the barcode still attached to the book at the end of the class. A book returned without a barcode will be considered a lost book and the full cost of the book will be billed to the student.

Students will not be allowed to complete registration for the new school year or have records transferred until all textbooks and library books are returned and outstanding fines are paid.

cases, students can check out textbooks as part of schoolwide opening registration and end-of-the-year shut-down procedures. See page 103 for a sample set of rules about textbook use.

Overdues can also pose problems. In some school libraries, the way that this issue has been solved is to eliminate due dates—hopefully the borrower simply returns the material at some point. Such an approach requires training the school community about this new expectation—and to manage their resources with others in mind. The main reason for due dates is to ensure that resources can be accessed by as many people as needed; the due date is a way to nudge people into managing their time to facilitate resource sharing. In any case, people should be able to request an item in circulation, with a notice going to the borrower to return that item as soon as possible. So even with no due dates, some kind of notification and possible repercussions for non-returned materials seems appropriate. Whatever the system, timely notification is key. Usually a notice is sent to the person's homeroom, although nowadays an e-mail or text message might be more appropriate—and faster. In addition, sending the notice directly without teacher intervention lightens that intermediary's workload. Some public libraries have an automated system to phone the patron about overdue materials, which might be a (costly) solution for SLP managers. You also should ensure that the library is part of a student's transfer process: when students enter or leave the school throughout the year, they will have to see the library staff about borrowed materials.

Maintenance and Repair

The best resource maintenance is preventive maintenance. When items are prepared optimally for eventual use, they are more likely to stay in good condition. For example, resources should be kept in clean areas with good air circulation. A yearly inventory can also ensure that resources are in good condition. Library staff should also teach users how to handle materials responsibly. Some simple measures for print resources include:

- reinforcing liner pages
- reinforcing front cover corners
- reinforcing magazine staples
- adding an extra security tag to high-risk books in case the first tag is removed
- covering those trade paperbacks that are intended for long-term use with laminated clear covers

Here are some good sources of information on the proper care of print materials:

- www.tcpl.lib.in.us/find-a-good-book/book-care-and-repair
- www.dartmouth.edu/~library/preservation/repair/?mswitch-redir
  =classic
- https://www.nedcc.org/resources/introduction.php
- Printed materials may be subjected to heavy and harsh treatment by library users, if for no other reason than backpack-based transport. A minor distraction while turning a page can result in tears. Spilled food and weather can damage items. Because students may be embarrassed to admit these accidents, librarians should convey an attitude of acceptance when students report these incidents. Usually library workers do not have time to examine each item thoroughly when it is returned, so students need encouragement to report any damage. They should be reminded that timely repairs can ameliorate damage and lengthen shelf life—and that money can be spent on new titles rather than in replacing old ones. Any repairs, even if as insignificant as a tiny rip, must be done with professional grade supplies (e.g., those available from Brodart, Demco, Gaylord, and Kapco). Several vendor websites include repair manuals and tutorials, and these companies also welcome the opportunity to provide live training. Sometimes public libraries have volunteers with excellent skills who can teach school library staff. Such training is a good investment because it results in print materials that stay in better shape longer. Here are a few websites that address book repairs:

  - www.dartmouth.edu/~library/preservation/repair/
  - www.library.state.ak.us/hist/conman.html
  - www.lib.rochester.edu/index.cfm?page=3242

Technology maintenance requires more attention because of moving parts and other complexities. In addition, all library staff should know how to use and maintain the library's equipment well enough to operate it and teach others how to use it responsibly.

- Keep an inventory diagram sheet and set-up instructions with equipment.
- Protect equipment with padded containers.
- Strap monitors to stands, especially if the stands are on rollers.
- Label cords and cables, and color-code ends with corresponding colored dots on the appropriate equipment ports to facilitate correct connections.

- Maintain a binder or database of each piece of equipment, noting specifications (date of purchase, vendor, and cost should be included in the catalog record).
- Try to keep technology physically secure through visual monitoring, securing parts, and installing motion detection equipment.
- Cover equipment when not in use.
- Keep electronic resources in darkness, or at least away from sunlight.
- Use virus detection software.
- Back up digital files regularly. Back up circulation records nightly.
- Set up a regular maintenance schedule that includes weekly computer scanning, monthly defragmenting, and a thorough yearly cleaning.
- Check cables and cords regularly, and toss out any with frayed and exposed wires.

Here are some beginning websites about computer maintenance:

- www.microsoft.com/athome/setup/maintenance.aspx#fbid = dzQ DqNaWagC
- www.infohq.com/Computer/computer_maintenance_tip.htm
- www.sensible-computer-help.com/computer-maintenance-tips.html
- http://tips4pc.com/articles/computer%20maintenance/computer _maintenance.htm
- www.5starsupport.com/tutorial/basic_maint.htm
- www.pcworld.com/article/2010982/28-pieces-of-computing-advice -that-stand-the-test-of-time.html

As the SLP manager, you will be working with the rest of the school community to plan ahead for possible disasters, natural or intentional. Electronic assets are vulnerable to security breaches, electrical problems, demagnetization, water, heat, and even solar flares. The school's emergency checklist should be posted in the library. All library staff should be trained in responding to disasters as well as in first aid and CPR. After a disaster, the first steps are to stabilize the disaster's effects, assess the damage, and start recovery efforts. The Association of Research Library's SPEC Kit *Institutional Repositories* (Bailey et al., 2006) provides valuable advice about disaster planning. Here are some factors to consider:

- What backup provisions exist? Can the vendor ensure uninterrupted service? Can the institution legitimately back up content?
- What institutional disaster planning policies and procedures exist?
- Are all assets inventoried?

- What insurance coverage does the institution or vendor carry relative to disaster damage?
- What plans are in place to replace damaged equipment?
- What collaborative plans among school systems exist to help replace, or at least provide access, to damaged resources?
- What recovery companies are readily available?

Deselection

Part of a resource's life cycles include its deselection or withdrawal. There comes a point when repairing an item is not worth the time and trouble. When materials are outdated and falling apart, they lower the credibility of the other resources. SLP managers typically use MUSTY criteria for deselecting materials: **m**isleading information, **u**gly (worn or unattractive) physical appearance, **s**uperseded information, and **t**rivial content. Because the school curriculum changes, the library's collection must reflect that dynamic. Of course, the acceptable age for information differs by area. As long as the item is attractive and in good physical condition, a classic fiction title can be retained as long as it is being borrowed regularly. On the other hand, scientific resources need frequent reexamination. Some school librarians may be reluctant to weed out resources because it would leave holes in the collection; however, such gaps can provide strong justification for acquiring new items.

Similar weeding criteria apply to digital resources, including poor physical appearance and irregular operational condition. Not only do older systems retrieve information less efficiently, but those systems are less energy efficient; especially as equipment tends to cost less over time, school librarians should refresh equipment every three or four years.

Whatever resources are deselected, they should be disposed of properly. First of all, their records should be taken out of the library catalog, and inventory lists updated. If the resource was purchased with federal funds, its withdrawal should be recorded in that fund's account. In addition, items should be visibly marked "withdrawn." In most cases, the withdrawn item should be recycled rather than passed on to someone else. Books, in particular, should not be given to others; if they are not good enough for the library, they will not be good enough for anyone else. In some cases, withdrawn magazines can be reused for collages; if so, they should be placed in a separate area far away from current holdings (perhaps in the art department) to avoid possible mix-ups with newer issues. Many recycling centers accept technology hardware. Sometimes schools partner with centers to raise money while providing a valuable service by sponsoring recycling days when the local community can get rid of old and possibly dangerous technology. In addition, some computer user groups collect and repurpose technology, which advances green technology.

The library's physical collection constitutes a sizeable financial investment, and as the SLP manager, you are responsible for its security and inventory. Preventative measures have already been suggested: security gates, security strips within books and high-demand periodicals, secured computers and peripherals. You should also keep accurate records about the status of each item, noting all additions, deselections, and losses. A yearly inventory enables every item to be checked, which can reveal misplaced books or additional lost items. This process can also help you identify collection gaps and discover materials that should be withdrawn from the collection. The task is worth the time and effort.

Green Resource Management

As responsible global citizens, the school library program should practice green technology and try to lessen its carbon footprint. The phrase "reuse, recycle, reduce" can be a library mantra. Libraries are built on the premise of reusing and sharing resources, which reduces the acquisition of materials. As libraries transition to digital resources, fewer print resources are required. On the other hand, digital resources require equipment in order to physically access the information, and that hardware may well increase, rather than decrease, the carbon footprint.

As an SLP manager, you can model green technology, and encourage library users to go green. (Remember that in some cases, actions that sound like good practice may not help, so carefully weigh the possible consequences of your decisions.) Here are some suggestions:

- Libraries can serve as recycling centers for print cartridges, batteries, and pens.
- Libraries should provide recycling bins that separate different kinds of garbage.
- Library guides and research handbooks should be digitized rather than printed out. As a physical reminder, the library can keep a binder with one laminated copy for easy user referral, and also post reference posters or signs as a reminder (e.g., how to use the catalog, cite resources, use databases).
- Leftover printed pages can be cut up for scratch paper. It should be noted that turning printed paper over and reinserting it into printers can harm the printer, so that practice should be avoided.

- Users should be encouraged to e-mail information to their accounts rather than printing it. Although downloaded information could be stored on personal flash drives, school librarians need to be careful because these devices might have viruses. Virus detection programs should scan all input devices.
- Technology has the potential to cut down on paperwork for processing orders and other business communication. Nowadays, most schools conduct transactions largely through telecommunication channels.
- Libraries can serve as a green professional development center by providing a venue for web-based conferencing, which saves time and reduces transportation costs and pollution.
- Libraries can facilitate green thinking by acquiring and promoting information about ecological practices.

Such initiatives usually require that the school librarian work with site administrators to ensure a schoolwide, systematic approach to ecological measures. Librarians can leverage their expertise by researching promising practices and sharing viable solutions with decision-makers.

Bringing It Down to You

What does the collection say about the school library program—and you? Even though the school community's needs and wants constitute the focus and context of the library's collection, it also reflects your selection philosophy and perspective. In most cases, you inherit the library collection, so you will need to get to know it first before you start to make your mark on it. As you browse the stacks, what images of the curriculum and the school community come to mind? As you get to know that community and its agenda better, does the library reflect it well? What do you bring to the collection? How can your contributions be represented in the collection decisions you make? Making your mark on the collection is important because the library staff impact service, and the quality of service depends on the collection. It is a great opportunity to let your personality shine.

References

Bailey, C., Jr., et al., ed. 2006. *Institutional Repositories.* SPEC Kit 292. Washington, DC: Association of Research Library.

Common Core State Standards for English Language Arts and Literacy in History/ Social Studies, Science, and Technical Subjects. 2010. Washington, DC: Council of Chief State School Officers.

Common Core State Standards for Mathematics. 2010. Washington, DC: Council of Chief State School Officers.

Johnson, P. 2009. *Fundamentals of Collection Development and Management,* 2nd ed. Chicago, IL: American Library Association.

Loertscher, D., B. Woolls, B., and J. Felker. 1998. *Building a School Library Collection Plan.* San Jose, CA: Hi Willow.

OCLC. 2003. *Environmental Scan: Pattern Recognition.* Dublin, OH: OCLC.

7

Managing Facilities

SCHOOL LIBRARY RESOURCES AND SERVICES COMPRISE A POTEN-
tially rich learning environment, be it physical or virtual. A digital library requires, at the very least, housing for a server and an
office for managing these digital assets. In that respect, the technical infrastructure for supporting this environment has become
increasingly significant. As soon as people open the physical or virtual door of
the library, they form an impression of the library, which may instantly determine whether they will enter or not. The facility can drive the quality of the
library program in terms of collection use as well as instruction and other interactions. For instance, if the room is tiny, few classes can work in the space; if
no differentiation in space exists, it is hard to provide different types of learning
experiences. This chapter examines the spatial elements of resources and services, taking into account their physical relationship and use for the intellectual,
social, and emotional development of the school community.

The Impact of Space on Learning

Space impacts teaching and learning, whether or not it has been designed for
those purposes. In 1933 educator John Dewey stated that "whether we per-
mit chance environments to do the work, or whether we design environments
for the purpose makes a great difference" (22), asserting that educational settings are better served by explicit planning rather than serendipity. In his meta-

analysis of environmental impact on human behavior, Moos (1986) determined that "the arrangement of environments is perhaps the most powerful technique we have for influencing human behavior" (4). Moos also contrasted the terms "formal learning" (curriculum-based, which generally refers to classroom-based intentional opportunities for learning) and "informal learning" (serendipitous human interaction that involves learning).

Cannon's 1988 synthesis of research on the impact of the environment on learning provides a starting point for learning space discussion. Basically, contemporary design of learning spaces builds upon an educational philosophy of active and social learning. This approach starts with the learner, examines desired outcomes, and plans the physical conditions for an optimum learning environment. To serve a range of instructional and learning styles, learning spaces are designed to provide different types of areas and grouping arrangements. In addition, items within these environments should support modification and customization that reflects users' interests and needs. The school library is uniquely positioned to provide a range of learning experiences: group learning, individual learning spaces, social learning, immersive environment, and virtual exploration.

The introduction of digital technology changed the definition of learning spaces. Increasingly, the space in which learning occurs has broadened to include cyberspace as well as physical space. With the advent of the Internet and social media, the world of the school library has changed dramatically. Increasingly, the school community wants remote access to library resources and services, sometimes via course management systems. Paradoxically, online environments can inhibit social learning, particularly for individuals who have little or no experience developing academic social networks.

It is therefore important to examine and plan library facilities purposefully in order to optimize learning experiences.

Learning Theories and Space

Research on learning spaces addresses the physical attributes of space, psychological factors, and cognition. Social constructivist philosophy posits that environments, especially those in close proximity, can stimulate the senses (e.g., attractive visuals and unexpected structural features), encourage interaction (e.g., furniture groupings and open spaces), and provide opportunities for practice (e.g., labs and studios) to improve learning (Oblinger 2006). MIT researchers Turkle and Papert (1990) found that the medium of the campus inspired learning, with ready availability of people and resources fostering creative reassembly of complex thought, a situation that affirms the library facility as Idea Central. Similarly, situated learning theory asserts that learning occurs in a community of practice, and that learning space can refer to both physical places and learners' mental constructs of their experiences within the social environment (Lombardi 2005). Vygotsky's activity theory of social cognition (1978) conceives learning as a transaction between an individual and the social environment. In elearning environments, that transaction occurs in the physical experience of user interface with the elearning space as well as the interactions of individuals in cyberspace.

Oblinger (2006) synthesized many of the key features of effective learning spaces:

- *Flexibility* that can provide quick reconfiguration to meet changing educational tasks, needs, and is amenable for student customization
- *Decentralization* that allows learning to flow from classroom to corridors and eating spaces, so that students can co-construct knowledge, so that learning and living commingle
- *Ergonomic comfort* (both young and older bodies are becoming more "substantial"; at least some furniture should be adjustable)
- *Stimulating to the senses* using engaging visuals, varied levels, unexpected areas or pathways, a sense of nature (e.g., organic shapes, texture, greenery, reflective surfaces)
- *Ubiquitous technology* to support access to active, social learning, for example, Wi-Fi, plug-and-play; frequent outlets, "smart" classrooms with presentation and online conferencing capabilities, and 24/7 presence

Learning Spaces and School Libraries

To improve learning, school librarians should examine the library's physical and virtual learning spaces in order to optimize learners' interactions with those spaces to meet the affective, perceptual, cognitive and behavioral aspects of learning. Specific recommendations include providing spaces for:

- conversational learning (e.g., circular seating or virtual chat/classrooms with whiteboard space)
- customizable group areas to facilitate privacy while inviting interaction
- developing expertise (e.g., labs or simulations)
- action and reflection (e.g., display areas or discussion boards for threaded discussion)

- thinking and feeling (e.g., carrels or blog space)
- play, exploration, and projects (e.g., areas that can be messy)
- large-group events (e.g., spaces that can be easily modified for different purposes)
- services (e.g., reference, technology, writing, thesis/research assistance, instructional design, and faculty development)

School library facilities should connect different types or configurations of learning spaces in order to facilitate the flow of learning (e.g., learning commons or course management systems). In addition, a space should provide students with opportunities to take charge of their own learning (e.g., tackable walls or wikis).

Research centers, particularly for technology enterprises, have developed sophisticated and playful environments that stimulate symbiotic innovation, balance "I" space and "we" space, and provide fixed infrastructure while supporting adaptive areas and fluid options (Hempel 2006). If these philosophies guide school library facilities design, learners will not only be more engaged with the subject matter and interact more with other people, they can also blend formal and informal learning, and maximize interactive learning.

Functional Areas of the School Library

As mentioned above, the school library should offer a variety of learning spaces to match different functions and different needs of its users. School libraries should balance predictable, orderly areas with elements of novelty that can delight and surprise users, such as reading nooks and playful decorations. The following list reviews functional areas.

Study areas. The school community needs space to engage in intellectual study, both individually and in groups. Typically, study areas are located by the reference collection. Both quiet spaces and group study areas are needed. Quiet spaces tend to be located further away from entrances and service areas, such as at the end of shelving or in far corners. Ideally, the library should provide glassed-in group study rooms. An interesting option is a fabric sound "cone" to dampen sound reverberations within a specific function area, as shown in the photograph (figure 7.1).

Story area. Typically, elementary libraries have a separate area where children can sit on the floor or on risers for story activities. Ideally, this area should be located near tables for follow-up hands-on activities. One interesting layout is a corner that can be blocked off by shelving or display wall, or even a curtained-off "wall" (see figure 7.2). An open area between back stacks can serve as a puppet show stage. Usually, story hour supplies are located near the story area for easy retrieval. The same area can be used for instruction and presentations.

Figure 7.1 **Mölnlycke Bibliotek (Sweden) Children's Room**

Figure 7.2 **Addams Elementary School Library (Long Beach, CA)**

Production area. Students are not just consumers of information; they are also producers of information. As such, they need production or "maker" space such as drafting or other large tables, supplies bin, creative materials (e.g., recycled magazines), storyboarding surfaces, and recording and editing space. This area should adapt easily to situational needs, so multiple outlets and flexible lighting are vital. The production area is likely to be a conundrum in terms of noise, because recording needs surrounding silence, whereas videotaping involves talking. In some cases, the library oversees a separate production studio, which requires adult supervision and regular maintenance. On the other hand, a production studio can serve as an effective room for online conferencing, which is increasingly used for professional development and virtual class trips. If a school has the room for such a production space, the benefits can outweigh possible managerial issues.

Meeting and presentation areas. Public libraries offer events or programs more frequently than do school libraries. However, a school library can gain name recognition and prestige by collaborating with the rest of the school community to host guest speakers and hold events such as student media festivals. Small facilities might consider using movable shelving, along with portable seating and tables, in order to make space for the occasional event. However, it is preferable to have a designated area for instruction and presentations. In some cases, the production studio can serve that purpose. The librarian's office can also be used as an occasional meeting room if a small conference table can be placed there. Set-off study rooms work well as meeting rooms, and may be scheduled in the same way that other class visits are scheduled. It should be noted that meetings and other events often involve food and drink, so the library should have a sink and food storage/preparation space, which would normally be provided in the workroom.

Workroom and storage areas. Every library should have a separate work area for processing materials and securing supplies. This area can also be used to store little-used materials. In some cases, the workroom can also be used by teachers, with professional reading within easy reach. There should be adequate storage for supplies, seasonal or seldom-used books, class sets, software circulated only to teachers, periodicals, books to be repaired or discarded, and so forth. Some school libraries that have very little extra space use compact shelving or remote storage for low-use items. Some storage areas need to be temperature-controlled to preserve materials such as servers. The work area should also include a sink; a microwave and refrigerator can also be a welcome addition for library staff and visiting teachers.

Office. If possible, the school library manager should have a separate office to keep important files, administrative computer and program archives, a telephone, and a work surface. Even though the librarian is likely to conduct most business in other parts of the library, and have another desk, having an office provides the privacy needed for quiet communication or sensitive work.

Restrooms. A restroom should be located near the library, especially if the library is heavily used. Larger or remote library facilities often include a restroom, either for staff or for the community.

Lighting. If possible, lighting should fit the function as well as comply with building standards. For instance, study lamps are better for reading spaces than are general ceiling light panels. Direct light should not fall on computer screens. Indirect lighting is also more effective than direct lighting because it spreads light more evenly. Ambient light through windows softens the harshness of artificial lights, although it can be uneven in quality at different times of the day and year. At the least, full-spectrum lights should be used rather than traditional fluorescent bulbs. Because some projection systems need almost total darkness, which is hard to achieve in a windowed facility, windows should have blinds and other window treatments such as drapes or screens.

Access Issues

One of the core characteristics of a library is that it is organized for optimum physical access. School library program (SLP) managers will need to make several decisions to achieve this goal. The details below show how user behaviors form the basis of many decisions. On the other hand, school librarians (SLs) can sometimes change user behaviors by the way that the collection is arranged and accessed.

Shelving. Usually the collection runs left to right, left-justified, top-to-bottom, per each set of shelves. To maximize shelf space, SLs may choose to put oversized books on the bottom shelf nearest to the corresponding call number area; alternatively, oversized books might be gathered together in a separate wide-shelving area, with dummy books or signs indicating the physical location of the oversize collection area. Freestanding racks and displays, especially for paperbacks, encourage browsing. For marketing impact, some books might be shelved in bookstore fashion with the covers turned outward or placed on a zigzag shelf insert to show their front covers; alternatively, one book per shelf might be featured at the end of the shelf. Ideally, each shelf should only be two-thirds full to accommodate additional titles without the need to readjust several rows of items. Shelving should also be age-appropriate—picture and beginning books should be placed on lower shelves; in addition, stable upright dividers should be placed about every foot to keep thin books from sliding. Some elementary schools put picture books in bins for easy browsing.

Subcollections. Traditionally, reference materials are placed in a separate area for quick research use; today, separate reference areas usually consist only of ready reference such as general encyclopedias, dictionaries, almanacs, and atlases; specialized references are integrated into the regular collection. On the other hand, school (and public) libraries tend to maintain a separate section for fiction, individual biographies, and children's picture books. To save space, some libraries rotate holiday collections, keeping out-of-season items in storage or rolling cabinets. Most libraries also continue to separate resources by format, mainly because users are looking for an item by its format, such as an audiobook; however, many media can be easily integrated into the print collection, which will then reinforce the idea that information comes in many kinds of packages. A few school libraries arrange books by reading level, but that is usually not considered a good practice, especially if only part of the collection is "leveled." In other cases, libraries may separate non-English books, or maintain genre-specific subcollections such as mysteries and science fiction and fantasy. Subcollections like these usually reflect users' habits of focusing on one genre. Because school libraries have the educational function of introducing students to different genres to broaden their reading interests, alternative methods can address the needs of genre-lovers: placing genre stickers on book spines, creating temporary displays by genre, producing genre-specific bookmarks, and adding genre subject headings when cataloging. Once in a while, a donor may want to underwrite a special collection, and will stipulate a separate shelving arrangement. SLs must think carefully about accepting such demands, and determine the impact that such donations would have on the rest of the collection (i.e., the degree of physical variation or disruption, the value of the donation, the amount of publicity and goodwill generated, and so on).

Displays. Literacy promotion constitutes a core function of library programs, and displays are a way to attract and engage users. Indeed, the library as a whole can be considered to be a display that conveys a message about its purpose through the style of the furniture, the drapery and flooring, plants and other decorations; even the sense of order—or clutter—indicates the state of the library. Reading promotion is the most common use of displays, via posters and other signs, as well as books and accompanying artifacts. One or two bulletin boards, preferably with cork or fabric surfaces, can provide an easy way to post timely materials. Some libraries have murals, which provide permanent art that helps shape the atmosphere of the library (but can limit otherwise available display space); they are ideally placed near the ceiling, which is generally underused. Almost any space can be used for displays: shelves, table tops, cabinets, freestanding racks, walls and windows, bookcarts, even hanging banners and mobiles. Library resources can also be displayed at the entrance (figure 7.3) and throughout the school; circulating library posters in classrooms is another easy way to spread the library message. A quick tour through a bookstore can inspire ideas, including point-of-sale mini-stands by the circulation or checkout desks, staff-favorite bookmarks, face-out book covers, and tie-ins with movies or current events. Libraries can also display student work based on library resources, which can go beyond the typical book report or research paper to include art projects. Cultural artifacts from the school community can also be

Figure 7.3 **Entrance to Rio Branco School library (Brazil)**

displayed and linked to library resources. Photos of students and staff reading or otherwise using the library can be mocked-up as "READ" posters. Such displays can attract new users if students' works are shown; they are likely to come in and show off their "stuff" to their friends, and thereby enlarge the library audience. In any case, involving the school community in displays offers them a way to help shape the library program. Technology-based displays should also be considered: from desktop screens promoting genres to in-library monitors streaming video. As the library manager, you don't have to create these displays, just find a willing person to do the job. Be sure, though, that displays are esthetically appealing, and changed frequently enough to keep users' attention engaged. (Some appealing display ideas are posted at http://schoollibrary displays.blogspot.com.)

Signage. Libraries can seem intimidating and hard to navigate, so signage is imperative. It is a good idea to mark each area of the library with appropriate signage, be it on the wall or hanging from the ceiling as a banner. Signs should also indicate library hours. They should be of uniform design, large, and easy to read. Each book range should be marked, and even each shelf can have a small indicator of its subject matter. Signs can also double as displays, for example, as images to complement classification designations; they can be even be repurposed from old calendars.

Security. In order to ensure that the collection, including equipment, is available for optimum access and use, security measures must be taken. Because high schools have more resources—and more users— they typically require more security. The increasing value of resources, and the savviness of users, can also lead to more theft or other inappropriate use. Security measures can be as simple as using a single portal for entrance and exit or as elaborate as locking down equipment or installing electronically sensitive gates and room security systems. It should be noted that because even the most guarded facility should be barrier-free to those with disabilities; security "gates" should not include physical bars per se, but rather employ signal-sensitive archways. As noted elsewhere, security systems often should be located some distance from circulation equipment, so placement can be tricky. Windows should not open in ways that allow books to "escape"; and safety screens can take care of that problem easily.

Safety. Access must be safe. To that end, make sure that furniture is stable and safe (i.e., no sharp corners or poking elements) and can be repaired quickly if needed. The facility, its furniture, and even its air ducts, need regular cleaning to reduce allergic reactions. Bean bags and stuffed toys should be avoided because they can carry allergens. Tall shelving units must be bolted securely, and high book shelves may need to be stabilized with bungee cords or straps in case of tremors. Shelf pins should be secure and tight. Likewise, large glass panels and windows should not be adjacent to student seating. Flooring should be free of rips or holes. Outlets should not be located on the floor. Cords and cables should not run across walking areas; if people must cross them, they should be covered, ideally with rubber inner-tracked runners. In addition, equipment and cords should be checked regularly to make sure they function properly and are not frayed. On a more general level, power standards must meet OSHA standards, and backup power systems should include surge protection. Regular preventative measures and ongoing maintenance optimize safe and healthy access. More profoundly, though, safety is a mindset. The library is a safe haven for many students, sometimes the only place where they feel comfortable.

Furniture Issues

Furniture constitutes a central feature of the facility because it physically holds the resources, and facilitates the users' interaction with those resources and each other. Managing furniture involves careful selection and oversight. Whether local or national, a vendor should have a good reputation. Nonlibrary furniture suppliers may serve if their furniture addresses library needs. It makes sense to ask other librarians for advice, and to talk with vendors at library and other trade shows.

Overall, furniture should be sturdy, functional, and comfortable; appropriate for the intended age group; low-maintenance; and safe. Wood is the usual choice of material because of its lasting quality; it can often be resurfaced and repaired instead of having to be completely replaced. Ideally, items should have a similar, timeless design and appearance that conveys a sense of unity and order. Erickson and Maruson (2007) provided a great deal of useful advice.

Seating. Unpadded chairs are usually best for studying. Seating for recreational reading may be stuffed, but any covering should be of darker patterned fabric rather than plastic or leather. Couches should usually be avoided in order to minimize sleeping, although story hour corners with platform seating can work nicely. Seating should be at the right height for the student's body. Vendors often let libraries test potential chairs with their users before purchasing items.

Tables. Small rectangular tables with rounded corners work well because they can be regrouped for different function and provide more surface area than round tables. Long "bar-style" tables with tall chairs appeal to teens, especially if they face a window. "Genius bar" arrangements are also popular, arranged to seat two to five people around a semicircular or rectangular table with a monitor at the end and electrical outlets for multiple computers. The most efficient table support design is four legs at the corners. Table tops should have laminate or linoleum surface. Some students like slightly sloped tables for reading. Counter-height tables work well for OPAC use, and one station must be at the right height to accommodate wheelchairs. users.

Computer work station surfaces. The surface for the computer should include space for other materials such as books or writing, at least thirty-six inches in width. For elementary libraries, a sixty-inch table for two students to work on one computer is effective. Ideally, the furniture should have a "trench" or other half-hidden space to hold cables and cords; otherwise, cords that stick out can be easily disconnected. If a tower is used, it should not rest directly on the floor but have air circulating all around it; avoid placing the tower in a space that can be kicked.

Separating areas. Some students like carrels, which can be placed at the end of shelving ranges that provide optimum isolation but are easy to monitor. When students need to have private space, one alternative is to provide temporary barriers by placing interlocking panels on table tops to divide the space. A sense of separation between tables or grouped areas can be achieved by providing portable panels on which to write.

Library-specific furniture. Usually the circulation desk is counter height (thirty-nine inches) to facilitate stand-up checkout functions, but should also include a section that is desk height (thirty inches) for younger students and people using wheelchairs. The furniture should include spaces for sitting (including knee clearance), drawers, and storage, and be suitable for telecommunications functions. Modular furniture is a good alternative. Depending on what functions occur at the desk (e.g., book drop, "behind-the-desk" reserves, or cash transactions), and what other desk centers exist (e.g., instruction or reference), the circulation area could be relatively small. A secure (and cushioned) book drop should be located outside the library so people can return materials anytime.

Technology Facilities Issues

Technology plays a central role in design and specification requirements. Regardless of the learning space, technical requirements must be addressed: terminal and workstation requirements, system platform configurations, network hardware, Internet connectivity issues, and administrative software. The introduction of social networking requires cross-device sharing, parallel awareness, group archiving, as well as general groupware functions. Additional security and privacy measures (including issues of remote access) should also be taken into account when social media is incorporated. Online 24/7 technology support must be calculated as part of planning and implementation endeavors. Some factors have already been mentioned: workstation furniture, ventilation and temperature control, and cable management. It should be noted that equipment needs to be cleaned and kept dust-free.

Computer arrangement. Ideally, computers should be placed against walls to impede possible cable disturbance and optimize visual supervision and access. Other acceptable arrangements include: (1) an "island" grouping, which gathers cables and maximizes work space but impedes supervision; (2) rows of computers with the monitor facing a library staff desk, which can make power connections difficult if the bank is freestanding; (3) a U-shaped set of computer desks coming out from the wall (as in *_UUUUU_),* which can facilitate group work, supervision, and cable control; and (4) "genius bar" semicircular setups where several computers can be switch-linked to a display monitor for joint viewing. Normally, groups of computers should be located near service centers rather than off in a far corner. If computer furniture is in a carpeted area, static control mats should be used to control static electricity. Viewing areas are also required for technologies such as televisions and DVD players; their arrangement can mirror what is used for computers.

Power. Because users now routinely bring their own technology to the library, the demand for power outlets continues to increase. Power strips are useful, but not always safe, and they can hide electrical power drainage. Long commercial stabilized power strips allow for safer distribution of equipment.

The library should also invest in a commercial-grade power surge protection system, especially because computer crashes can seriously impede circulation processes.

Storage. Ideally, the computer server and physical copies of programs should be stored in a separate, secure, temperature-controlled room. The librarian's office is often allocated to such a function.

Security. Besides securing computer content through firewalls and system-specific security programs, the librarian should also make sure that hardware itself is physically secure. A simple solution is physically linking systems together using security cables with end locks. Having the room wired for security can protect the library from all kinds of theft, assuming that the security alarm is set consistently.

A Word about Maintenance

Ongoing care and preventative measures can prolong the life of facilities and their interiors. Here are some good practices:

- Dusting should not be the measure of a library's well-being, but basic housekeeping tasks such as keeping the library neat and clean fosters an atmosphere of care.
- Although it is good practice to prohibit food, librarians might want to relax that regulation a bit—but they should make sure that no food or beverage is left at the end of the day.
- Facilities should be checked for evidence of pests and their entry points located to minimize their presence. Graffiti should be removed at once, ideally by the individuals who created the writing.
- Some school libraries take the effort to cover machines at night, but all should at the very least clean equipment yearly.

In other words, the library should be clean enough to be "healthy" for resources and happy for people.

Making Adjustments

Most school librarians inherit the library's collection and facility, and try to make the best of the situation. However, even if shelves are built in, you can make some adjustments by such measures as moving furniture to optimize traffic flow as well as applying interior design esthetics to make the place more functional, comfortable, and welcoming.

The starting point should be existing school library standards, in terms of the library's mission and possible physical facilities standards. The American Association of School Librarians' 2009 standards provide a solid foundation for guidance. For instance, for students to collaborate, the facility should include tables and areas for group work. Because students also need to work independently, both quiet and conversation spaces should be planned. For students to become effective producers of information, they need a physical production area, supplied with the equipment, table space, and other tools in order to create physical products. States have education facilities standards and building codes, which should be consulted.

Food for Thought

To make sure that changes have a positive effect, school librarians should do a reality check by observing users—and consulting nonusers. Taking photos can help to analyze use patterns, and can serve as baseline data for photo editing explorations of color schemes and enhancements.

- How do people use the facility?
- What areas do they use—and how?
- What obstacles impede movement? For instance, computer stations might block useful print resources located behind them.
- How are users grouped: individually, in pairs, in groups of four or five, or in large groups? How does the space facilitate or impede groupings?
- How are work areas used? Can users spread out their work, or do they have to pile up their materials? Computer areas tend to lack surface working space. Different heights of working spaces impact how they are used; for instance, OPACs are often placed on counter-high surfaces to facilitate quick access and short-time use, although lower surfaces are needed to accommodate users with motor limitations. Increasingly, "bar-style" tables and stools are favored by teens.
- What kind of seating is preferred? How do users sit: feet planted on the ground or tucked under the seat? In some cases, seating is deliberately designed to discourage relaxation.
- Do users bring their own equipment, such as laptops, that require power outlets? If so, do sufficient outlets exist, and are they easily and appropriately accessed?
- Where do pockets of noise exist? Do they impede the learning experiences of other users?

- How does lighting impact use? Do users seek or avoid specific kinds of lighting?
- Do heat pockets exist? Is air well-ventilated?
- How does the library facility connect with the rest of the school? Is it physically central—or isolated? Even if the library facility cannot move, it might be possible to ease the transition from one part of the site to the library through "gateway" murals, displays, or glassed-in walls.
- What is the sound level? Can you differentiate between constructive sound (e.g., group work) and just chatter? Is the sound level spread out throughout the facility, or are there specific areas that are quieter—or need to be? Occasionally, noise may be concentrated due to furniture configuration, such as a circle of higher stacks that funnel up sound. Acoustic ceiling tiles and carpeting can cut down noise levels. Some librarians use background music to provide white noise.
- Does the library physically connect to the outdoors? What ways can the two spaces relate? Can users go between the two areas easily, or do security issues impede such flow? Are outdoor elements incorporated into the library, such as vegetation, open windows, or sky lights? How do users interact with these natural elements?
- How well does the facility support usage by individuals with disabilities? Are working surfaces at appropriate heights? Are pathways accessible? Is signage accessible? Have accommodations been made to facilitate retrieval of materials and information?

Doshisha Secondary Girls School Library Interior Atruim

By observing what works—and doesn't—in your facility, you can identify problems and then seek ways to resolve them. Of course, the library staff has additional insight, similar to that of the kitchen in a restaurant, so they understand how well a facility supports library services such as materials processing, circulation, and security. Some other issues include ease of access to equipment, storage characteristics, ease of visual supervision, options for displays, climate control, and telecommunications availability. This usage analysis, therefore, should be done with the input of key stakeholders. Ideas can range from informal (suggestion box, graffiti wall, "slam" book, and/or tweets) to formal town hall meetings and advisory committees. Soliciting nonuser input is also important because it can reveal why people do not use the facility. The goal is broad-based consensus and sense of ownership, which can optimize the library's effectiveness.

Some of these conversations should include references to other facilities and sources of ideas, such as architectural magazines and Pinterest. Every year *American Libraries* has an architectural issue that can provide inspiration. It should be noted, though, that form does not always follow function in "eye candy" facilities, so library staff and other stakeholders should visit other libraries and interview staff and users to check out how facilities work. In any case, collecting fun ideas and feedback on what to avoid can help when modifying or remodeling library facilities.

When thinking about shifting furniture, including shelving, first locate or make an accurate scale floor map, noting significant elevations such as steps or lowered ceilings and immovable lighting. Each piece of furniture should be carefully measured. Simple CAD (computer-aided design) programs or graph paper can be used to virtually shift items around. It is also a good idea to scan or otherwise record all feasible plans in order to compare them later. These scenarios should also take into account existing power and telecommunications outlets, air and heating ducts, sprinklers, and lighting fixtures. For instance, rearranging shelving can result in light or dark spots if light panels run perpendicular to those ranges. The linear footage of shelving and material in general also must be measured accurately.

Moving

Library collections sometimes have to be moved because the facility is being refloored, repainted, or rewired. Consider the following:

- What is the time frame? Is school in session? How long will the changes take?

- Is the library expected to be open? What services, and to what extent, must it provide? For major renovations that will take weeks, it may be necessary to establish a core library collection, which should include reference materials and items for upcoming assignments; school librarians should work closely with classroom teachers to ensure that needed materials are available.
- Who is in charge of the changes and library moving?
- Who is available and able to help? In some cases, student or adult volunteers can contribute. Insurance coverage might need to be reviewed. All personnel should be trained on how to shift the collection.
- What safety considerations must be addressed?
- What resources are available to transport the collection: boxes, book carts, dollies? If items should be boxed, they should be clearly marked on the top and side according to classification number. If the timing is right (e.g., the summer), other local libraries may be able to loan book carts—and even personnel.
- Where will the collection be stored, even temporarily, during the change? The distance between the library and the storage area can be a significant time factor. If a library facility includes two rooms or differentiated spaces, materials in one area can be stored in the other area while the first area is being worked on; then those two areas can be shifted. Given enough book carts and tables or other work surfaces, moving the collection can be done fairly painlessly with a small, well-organized group of people.
- What signage needs to be made ahead of time, such as end cards indicating where materials should be shelved?

As the SLP manager, you should develop the moving plan (perhaps mapping it as well), and then test-run part of it to make sure the process works smoothly. It also helps to ask veteran library movers for their advice. Share the plan with the person in charge of the facilities activity to ensure that it does not conflict with his or her plans, including the impact on staffing. Make sure that the move is documented visually before, during, and afterwards. Explain the overall library plan, including service accommodations during the move, to key stakeholders well in advance in order to minimize disruptions and stress.

Thinking Green

When thinking about improving the library's facilities, the school librarian should also consider how to make the space more ecological, or green. The motto "reduce, reuse, recycle" can serve as a guideline. Space can be reused and repurposed for different activities, and some furniture and other resources can be reused from other places or given to other groups when no longer appropriate for the library. As noted before, wooden furniture can be resurfaced instead of being replaced. Libraries should use energy-efficient LED and full-spectrum light bulbs, and should optimize natural lighting. Automated heating systems can be more fuel efficient. Low-flush toilets save water. Certainly, outdated technology can be recycled. The library can also serve as a recycling center for ink cartridges, pens, and batteries. The chapter on resource management suggests a few other actions that apply to facilities management, including recycling bins and virtual conferencing. The website Green Libraries (http://greenlibraries. org) maintains a list of ways to maintain an ecologically sustainable library.

Renovations and New Facilities

Occasionally, SLP managers have the opportunity to renovate their library, or to develop the facilitate from the ground up. This is an ideal situation to reconceptualize the library in terms of its potential functions, and to also construct a greener facility.

As when making adjustments to existing facilities, you should start by consulting existing library and educational standards and building codes. Visit recent library facilities, and brainstorm needs with key stakeholders. Sometimes schools have student competitions to draw the ideal library, and those ideas can transfer to real-life elements. One way to approach overall functional design is to use the metaphors of "clouds" or "zones," terms used in the retail industry. The concept is to identify different areas for different functions, and see how they relate to one another (consider IKEA and bookstores as sources of inspiration). Some other factors to consider when determining layout (*Gale* 2006) include future expansion or change; flow of movement; orderly materials handling; production and output needs (for both library staff and users); space utilization including storage, ease of communication, and support; impact on staff morale and job satisfaction; promotional value; safety; and ADA compliance.

A team approach is used to plan new or significantly renovated facilities, and as the SLP manager you should participate early and throughout the process. From the beginning conceptualization through the blueprint stage onto construction, you will need to review ideas and provide input. At any point, details may change that can negatively impact the final configuration—and ensuing library program. You can also help sell the plan to stakeholders. Surprisingly, sometimes the school librarian is overlooked in this process until the very end, when it is difficult and expensive to make changes, so it is important to assert your role. Sometimes architects are hired who do not have significant experience designing library facilities, and they might not consider important factors such as the standard length of library shelving, the dimensions of specialized library furniture, electrical and telecommunications requirements (e.g., placement near both the circulation desk and the office), security requirements (e.g., a security gate should be placed several feet away from the check-out system), or the need for clear sightlines for group monitoring (which can be very challenging for split-level or two-story spaces). Sometimes the architect is more interested in form than function, which can result in a long-term dysfunction.

Of course, participation requires background knowledge. Can you answer the following questions? If not, you will have to track down the answers. If the questions have not been asked, you will need to pose and answer them.

- How will the library be used? Think about both the school community and the library staff. Also consider linked activities such as researching and organizing.
- How should students be monitored?
- How much shelving is required?
- What are the shelving dimensions: width, height, depth? Take into consideration the size differences among paperbacks, children's books, and reference books.
- What resources need special handling, such as oversized books, posters, DVDs, equipment, and realia (e.g., puppets)?
- What other library specific furniture and functions should be considered, such as atlas stands or storytelling corners?
- What facilities are needed to process and circulate materials?
- What other workspace is needed? Consider needs for water and food.
- What storage space is needed? Consider how to deal with periodicals.
- What instructional space is needed? Consider lighting for projected images. Consider group study rooms.
- How much flexibility is needed? Consider how furniture or areas might need to be reconfigured in response to different functional needs.
- What kind of atmosphere is desired? Desirable behavior impacts several decisions. For instance, wood tends to convey a warmer feeling than metal. Dark colors lend themselves to a more studious mood whereas light colors convey more activity.

You should also review the accessibility guidelines for buildings and facilities (www.access-board.gov/adaag/html/adaag.htm), and determine which apply to the library (e.g., doors, entrances, storage, windows, aisles). For instance, the aisle width between stacks should be forty-two inches, and at least 5 percent (or one instance of each type of furniture) should be ADA compliant. As well, signage is often overlooked.

It should be noted that funding obstacles can impact facilities development and maintenance for rural schools. Sometimes governmental funding is tied to student enrollment, both in terms of a baseline number as well as anticipated growth patterns. Rural schools often do not meet those minimal numbers, and their student populations are likely to decrease due to migration trends. Furthermore, some funding caps renovation costs as a percentage of normative formulas, which may disadvantage rural districts that will incur additional transportation costs for materials and labor (Lawrence 2001).

Virtual Spaces

These days, the school library's virtual presence is just as important as its physical presence. Just as with physical spaces, school library virtual spaces need to be functional, content-rich, flexible, accessible, and interactive. The Young Adult Library Services Association (YALSA) (2012) developed guidelines for virtual spaces for teen service that apply well to K–12 school libraries.

- Access must include options for user input and interactivity. The website must be accessible on multiple browser platforms, and be ADA compliant.
- Technology properties should organize and display content to enhance understanding and use.
- The library's web presence should include social media, and include links to other online communication.
- The site should include areas for users to share ideas, including reviews of information sources.
- Features such as RSS feeds should facilitate the creation of personalized learning.
- Web content and design itself should be reviewed and updated regularly.

Rural schools can run into more obstacles relative to virtual spaces because of their locale. For instance, the "last mile" syndrome still impacts them as the cost for Internet, and cable connectivity is tied to the distance required to make the connections. Satellite transmissions have helped in this regard, but reception can still be problematic because of hilly terrain.

Disaster Planning

As the SLP manager, you must also plan ahead in case of possible disasters. Because it is considered to be a learning space throughout the day, the school library must participate in the federal government's mandate for a continuity of operations plan (Halsted, Clifton, and Wilson 2013). At the very least, as a manager, the school librarian should take first aid and CPR training. Take advantage of existing school district disaster planning documents and training. Ideally, a library worker should serve on the school's disaster team.

The first part of disaster planning is preparation. The library should store a library map and an inventory list (both in print and digital formats) of the library's resources off-site, and keep disaster and insurance contact information handy. Emergency and disaster procedures should be posted prominently, and library staff should review them each term. The library facility should house the following provisions: first aid kit; vacuum; boxes; flashlights and batteries; writing materials; emergency radio; camera; plastic sheeting and trash bags; and salvage supplies (e.g., gloves, safety glasses, cutting tools, tape, string, bins, blotting materials, sponges, and water). In collaboration with the site disaster team, you should also develop a disaster plan, noting the following elements:

- lines of authority
- actions to take if advance warning is given
- first response procedures and communication
- procedures for specific types of emergencies (e.g., flood, earthquake)
- rehabilitation plans
- lists of maps, resources, contact people

When as disaster strikes, the school library staff must respond immediately. The Northeast Document Conservation Center (2008) provides valuable guidance. First, the librarian must assess the damage, and decide how to salvage materials. The collection must be stabilized to make sure no further damage, such as mold, occurs. Usually the most important items to salvage include records (e.g., the library catalog, finances, legal documents), equipment, and other resources needed to provide library service. Ideally, the library's disaster plan should rank the importance of resources and actions, so the librarian does not have to ponder priorities in the midst of typical chaos. During this time, you should communicate with site administrators and disaster team members.

Next, rehabilitation can begin. The collection must be cleaned and dried (moisture is usually the most damaging factor). Several procedures are effective: air drying, sun drying, and freeze drying. Some materials should be discarded, especially if they are mildewed or moldy because these bacteria spread quickly.

Other items may need repair or conservation treatment. Sometimes materials will need to be rehoused, as least during the time the facility itself is treated. When items are reshelved, it is a good idea to inventory the remaining collection and update the catalog accordingly.

Electronic assets are surprisingly vulnerable to security breaches, electrical problems, demagnetization, water, heat, and even solar flares that can knock out services. The first steps are to stabilize the disaster's effects, assess the damage, and start recovery efforts. The Association of Research Library's SPEC Kit *Institutional Repositories* (Bailey et al., 2006) is an excellent source of sound advice. Here are some factors to consider:

- What back-up provisions exist? Can the vendor ensure uninterrupted service? Can the library legitimately back up content?
- What library and institutional disaster planning policies and procedures exist?
- Are all assets inventoried?
- What insurance coverage does the library, institution, or vendor carry relative to disaster damage?
- What plans are in place to replace damaged equipment?
- What collaborative plans among library systems exist to help replace or at least provide access to damaged resources?
- What recovery companies are readily available?

Because the library contains so many important and irreplaceable documents, preventative care is vital. Particularly for digital data, such as the collection catalog and inventory, systems should be backed up daily, and a copy kept off-site in case of disasters. Most libraries use special software to back up files automatically (vendors include Iomega and Mozy). In the worst-case scenario, data may become unreadable, and costly recovery service will be required. Having an archive copy, or mirroring data, is a much more cost-effective strategy.

Several organizations have assembled useful disaster planning and recovery resources. These include:

- The International Association of School Librarianship's disaster planning and response resources (http://iaslidsig.wikispaces.com/Disaster+recovery)
- The American Association of School Librarians' disaster preparedness resources (ala.org/aasl/aaslawards/beyondwords/disasterprep)
- The Northeast Document Conservation Center's emergency management leaflets (www.nedcc.org/resources/leaflets/3Emergency_Management)

- Lyrasis's disaster prevention and protection checklist (www.lyrasis .org/LYRASIS%20Digital/Pages/Preservation%20Services/Disaster %20Resources/Prevention-and-Planning.aspx)
- The Ohio State University's disaster manual (http://ati.osu.edu/library/ files/disastermanual.pdf)

Bringing It Down to You

Imagine the ideal library facility. What elements make it perfect? What changes can you see done to the current library facility that help it approach perfection? At the very least, to work effectively in an environment, you must feel comfortable. What makes the school library comfortable for you? What additions or rearrangements would make your work more productive and pleasant? Does the rest of the staff agree? What personal touches can they contribute to the overall atmosphere of the library? Are there areas that users can personalize? Your job is to manage the facility by including others in the design and maintenance of the facility. In that way, you can broaden the sense of ownership and responsibility, which will make the library program itself more effective and supported.

References

American Association of School Librarians. 2009. *Empowering Learners: Guidelines for School Library Programs.* Chicago, IL: American Library Association.

Bailey, C., Jr., et al. 2006. *Institutional Repositories.* SPEC Kit 292. Washington, DC: Association of Research Libraries.

Cannon, R. 1988. "Learning Environment." In *Encyclopedia of Educational Media Communications and Technology,* edited by D. Unwin and R. McAlees, 342–58. New York, NY: Greenwood Press.

Dewey, J. 1933. *How We Think.* New York, NY: D. C. Heath.

Erickson, R., and C. Maruson. 2007. *Designing a School Library Media Center for the Future.* Chicago, IL: American Library Association.

Gale Encyclopedia of Small Business, 3rd ed. 2006. Farmington Hills, MI: Gale.

Halsted, D., S. Clifton, and D. Wilson. 2013. *Library as Safe Haven.* New York, NY: Neal-Schuman.

Hempel, J. 2006. "Space Matters." *Business Week*, July. www.businessweek .com/innovate/NussbaumOnDesign/archives/2006/07/jumps_new_space .html.

Lawrence, B. 2001. *Effects of State Policies on Facilities Planning and Construction.* (ED 459970). Charleston, WV: ERIC.

Lombardi, M. 2005. *Standing on the Plateau Looking Forward: The Croquet Project.* Durham, NC: The Croquet Consortium.

Moos, R. 1986. *The Human Context: Environmental Determinants of Behavior.* Malabar, FL: Krieger.

Northeast Document Conservation Center. 2008. *Preservation Education Curriculum.* Andover, MA: Northeast Document Conservation Center.

Oblinger, D. 2006. *Learning Spaces.* Washington, DC: EDUCAUSE.

Turkle, S., and S. Papert. 1990. "Epistemological Pluralism: Styles and Voices within the Computer Culture." *Signs: Journal of Women in Culture and Society* 16 (1): 128–65.

Vygotsky, L. 1978. *Mind in Society.* Cambridge, MA: Harvard University Press.

Young Adult Library Services Association. 2012. *National Teen Space Guidelines.* Chicago, IL: American Library Association.

8

Managing Funding

IT'S HARD TO MANAGE A LIBRARY WITHOUT FUNDING. EVEN HANDLING a small budget can be challenging. Nevertheless, the school library budget can constitute a sizeable amount compared to other school departments, and the teacher librarian must demonstrate sound money management skills. This chapter explains how to develop and work with budgets, how to obtain additional funding (e.g., grants, donations, other soft money), and how to work with other entities to support the school library program. Financial management highlights the need for strategic planning, and can help you weather stormy budget times.

The Hidden Cost and Funding of School Library Programs

The school library program (SLP) reflects a significant financial investment by a school and its district. Even a small room with a range of books probably has more physical inventory than most other classrooms. As Information Central, responsible for a rich collection of resources to support the entire school curriculum and the staff to manage the optimize the access and use of those resources, the SLP should be allocated a significant budget to address the diverse needs of the school community.

Much of the allocation of resources remains outside the control of the SLP manager. In fact, most school librarians do not know the total amount of funding that supports the school library program, largely because school finances involve many accounts. The largest expense in education is salaries. Even that amount's total is not evident, and certainly not reflected by the pay stub, because benefits and insurance are not easily calculated by program; nor do those costs reflect the cost of recruitment and hiring, professional development, sick and maternity pay and substitute costs, and separation costs. Facilities expenses can be difficult to calculate as well.

School districts often employ program cost accounting, which includes both direct-charged and allocated costs. Categories of costs may include:

- Instructional costs: salaries and benefits for teachers and aides, textbooks and instructional supplies, reproduction costs, professional development, instructional equipment and its maintenance
- Instruction-related services costs: instruction supervision; salaries of librarians, technicians, and administrators; library expenses; technology
- Pupil services costs: salaries of support personnel such as counselors, social workers, health workers; supplies; testing service costs; food services; student transportation
- Community services
- Central administration costs: accounting, data processing, legal services, school boards, superintendent
- Plant services: facilities operations, maintenance, rentals, and leases; facilities acquisition and construction; costs can include salaries, supplies, equipment, repairs. In other cases, costs may be spread across programs depending on the function, such as telephone lines for instruction versus for data processing.

In addition, there are also indirect costs that are not easily identified with a specific program, such as utilities, custodial services, budgeting, personnel management, and warehousing. School site budgets usually separate out capital outlay for land acquisition and improvement, major facilities expansions and equipment deferred maintenance, and debt services. Different revenue streams exist for adult education, child development, and foundations. In addition, categorical funding and expenditures occur for special education, disadvantaged student population services, and so on. In sum, even if you have no direct control of any money, several other offices are allocating funds to support the library through plant and administrative services.

Nevertheless, you will need to examine school and district finances in order to determine what funds are available, from whom, and for what purposes. For instance, who manages telecommunications funding, including discounted e-rates? How can the library get money allocated for new carpeting? Which source can pay for a paperback rack? Does the school or district have a computer "refresh" program that can apply to the library? Most schools have a general school-supply fund, which should fund the materials for materials processing. Not only should librarians follow the money trail, but also the decision process used for allocating resources in order to determine at what decision points they should participate. In most cases, financial decisions are made at site councils; even if library staff are not officially represented on the council, they can—and should—attend in order to learn how resource allocations are made. Grade- and department-level meetings may include funding on their agendas, and parent organizations may also consider financial support for school initiatives. School librarians should also volunteer for task forces that involve finances; one-time opportunities may arise that can benefit the library program.

Budget Basics

Financial planning and implementation requires knowledge about some basic budget practices. A budget may be considered a policy statement because it reflects an organization's goals and values. It gives an idea of the status of the library program: what resources are required to accomplish the program's goals? As the year progresses, the budget is reviewed to measure how well the revenue and expenses enable goals to be achieved.

FINANCIAL REPORTS
Several financial reports exist, each with a unique lens for evaluating the effectiveness of fiscal management (McPheat 2010).

- An operating budget estimates revenue and expenses, usually for one year. It is often presented in terms of the actual budget for the prior year, the approved budget, a project actual budget, and the "yield to date."
- A chart of accounts lists assets (cash, accounts receivable, equipment) and liabilities (salaries, benefits, public relations, accounts payable); school districts group accounts by category and then number them according to a standard format.
- A general journal, or book of entry, records daily transactions, as shown in table 8.1.

Table 8.1
General Journal

FY 20xx		Description	Account	Debit	Credit
Oct.	2	Webcam	440	50.00	
		Donation	140		20.00
		Accounts payable (store credit)	320		30.00

- A general ledger keeps entries in chronological order, as with a general journal, but separates activities by account and keeps a running total (usually by month).
- A balance sheet, also called a statement of financial condition, summarizes the library's assets (items of value), liabilities (obligations to pay), and equity or net assets; normally it consists of the monthly totals from the general ledger.
- A revenue or income statement, also called a profit-and-loss statement or a statement of operations, is described in terms of revenues (incoming assets), expenses (outgoing assets or liabilities), and net income; a monthly income statement is probably the most commonly seen report.
- A cash flow statement charts how money is gathered and spent on operations, financing, and investment; school libraries usually do not generate this report.

Typically, each state has a standardized accounting code system, which designates certain numbers and placement to indicate specific kinds of information. For example, in California, the number 01–6296–4-0000–2420–4210–624 can be translated as follows:

- FUND: 01 (01 is General Funds; Food Services is 13)
- RESOURCE: 6296—AB 862 funds
- YEAR: 4—year four of AB 862
- GOAL: Whom are we serving? (0000 for libraries, 1110 for classrooms)
- FUNCTION: 2420 (means library; nursing, food services, maintenance are different)
- OBJECT: 4210—books
- 624—the site: in this case, DeMille Middle School

This code becomes especially important when transferring money.

In any case, you will need to make sure that all transactions are recorded in a timely manner in the general journal in order to be transferred to a monthly revenue statement. This task can be delegated to another library worker, but you should monitor it and review monthly reports in order to make adjustments as needed.

APPROACHES TO BUDGETING

It takes money to run a library, so part of library program planning involves thoughtful budgeting. Several approaches exist in budget development (Rounds 1994).

Incremental budgeting. The prior budget and committed expenditure forms the basis for negotiation, and then adjustments are made. How well did the prior budget support the library program? What changes in library plans or revenue streams are projected? This is an easy approach, but it is not very strategic or analytical.

Priority budgeting. This approach starts with a known revenue amount, and prioritizes resource allocations according to their alignment with site priorities rather than by department. In this case, the library might be vying for books or technology in competition with academic departments. Within the library, the allocation is usually calculated in terms of time dedicated to the activity.

Function budgeting. Each library carries out several functions (i.e., activities and services such as technical services, circulation, instruction, administration). A line-item budget is calculated for each function: labor (calculated by multiplying time by hourly wage) and resources. The functions can then be analyzed to determine relative cost-effectiveness, and alternatives can then be explored (e.g., eliminating fines, sending overdue notices by e-mail rather than print, etc.). The functions are then prioritized. This process works well for new or changing functions.

Program-based budgeting. Objectives are listed, noting intended activities and resources needed to meet the objective. A cost is then attached to activity and resource; labor and time should be included in this calculation. Costs for additional labor and resources should be listed. A program approach differs from function budgeting in that it is usually more goal-based and may include a mixture of operations or functions. For instance, a reading outreach program might include collection development, public-relations activities, and instruction.

Performance-based budgeting. Library inputs, such as labor and resources, are measured in terms of cost. Outputs, be they products or services, are likewise calculated in terms of costs. Cost per activity determines the efficiency or productivity. The level of goal achievement then determines the performance's effectiveness.

Zero-base budgeting. This approach resembles function budgeting. It is often done at the beginning the budget process, and encourages creative ways to deliver services. The costs and benefits of the library's operations are detailed: materials processing, circulations processes, and instruction. Benefits can be difficult to quantify; some measures include circulation records, class visit numbers, turnaround processing time. Each operation or function is translated into a decision package that includes the purpose, process, alternatives, and impact of doing—or not doing—an operation. The operations are then analyzed in terms of their cost-benefit ratios. For instance, if students rather than library staff shelve books, the cost savings might be substantial, but if the shelving is done inaccurately and users cannot find the materials, then the circulation benefit also decreases significantly so that the analysis will find that the use of student shelvers is not cost-efficient. Zero-base budgeting can be used to calculate new or different operations, and justify their cost.

As noted above, you will need to figure out the cost of labor and materials. It also helps to compare budgets with similar school libraries. Being able to state that comparable middle school libraries had budgets of $7,500 or spent an average of $9 per student can help school librarians justify added fiscal support (Farmer 2012). *School Library Journal* publishes articles based on data drawn from national surveys, which discuss the costs of resources as well as relative school library revenues and expenses. Such information can simplify cost calculations, such as the average cost of printed books; for instance, the 2012 average cost of hardcover children's titles was almost $20, and $21 was the average for teen titles (*School Library Journal* 2016). Other good sources of information are state school library statistics and data garnered by professional library associations.

Whatever budget process is used, it is wise to prepare three versions of a budget: a minimum budget that lists the bare essentials needed to meet the lowest acceptable level of the library's program goals; a target budget that shows the minimum funding needed to fully support the library program's stated objectives for the year; and a "stretch" budget that states what additional level of objectives could be met if allocated that level of funding (McPheat 2012). It should be noted that the minimum budget should specify the negative consequences of funding at that level, such as fewer class visits or longer turnaround time for materials processing and circulation. Even if no budget is allotted, the process of budgeting helps to concretize the SLP's vision. Furthermore, if money does become available, you will be immediately ready to take advantage of the opportunity it presents.

Presenting a budget in itself requires specific skills and techniques.

- Time the presentation to optimize the budget's reception.
- Know the audience, and use terms that resonate with them. Why is the library important to them?
- Anticipate tough questions and obstacles ahead of time, and prepare

well-justified answers.

- Provide a professional-looking one-page summary, ideally with some clear infographics.
- Identify clear specific priorities, and align them with school initiatives. Make student learning foremost.
- Defend the budget by program rather than line item.
- Note those areas for improvement that will not incur additional funding.
- Show all sources of revenue, including donations and gifts in kind.
- Mention external and internal factors that drive the budget.
- Tell your story: provide a mix of factual, anecdotal, and emotional, inspiring stories.
- Give a clear call to action.
- Be prepared to negotiate—which is another reason to draw up different levels of budgets.
- Thank the audience, regardless of the outcome.

TYPICAL FUNDING SOURCES

Ideally, school sites and districts would allocate all the fiscal resources needed for the library program to achieve its goals. However, such is not necessarily the case, but it is good to know that the school librarian can access funding from a variety of sources. The important thing is to be aware of these different funding sources, and to leverage them efficiently.

Schools are typically funded on three levels: local, state, and federal. Property taxes are the main source of local contributions; parent-teacher organizations may contribute "soft" money but are not usually dependable sources. State contributions usually come from state income taxes and sales taxes. Each state has a different formula for distributing funds; in some states, schools are largely funded at the state level in order to compensate for geographical areas that have low property values. In addition, both state and federal levels provide supplemental categorical funding for specific needs such as special education or state-dictated priorities such as reduced class size. In some cases, the federal government gives block grants for the state to determine how to allocate funds. Making the issue more complex, even in these states, most school districts can exercise a local option to level a higher level of taxes, which is not equalized by the state. The resulting disparities usually impact allocations to school library programs.

On the federal level, the 2015 Every Student Succeeds Act (ESSA) singles out libraries for the first time in decades. Funds can support instructional services provided by effective school library programs, and encourage school districts to use part of their Title 1 plans to ensure access to school libraries, for example, by extending service hours. A new literacy program within the act funds planning time and professional development for school librarians. The act further

Food for Thought

What is the Price of a Smile?

In the midst of calculating library program costs, it is important to remember the MasterCard tagline "priceless." The library staff can work very productively, but if they do it with a sour attitude their effectiveness may be undermined. It is hard to put a price on public relations, but one can calculate its worth in terms of library usage and library reputation. Time dedicated to have a good conversation can be a priceless investment that results in greater collaboration and program support. Consider adding public relations to the program "formula," and explicitly budget in time for positive human relationships.

addresses the library program for high-need schools, such as those in low-income communities. The Literacy through School Libraries program was consolidated with five other Department of Education literacy programs, so school libraries have to compete with other entities for that money; fortunately, at least half of the money must to go low-income school libraries under the Innovative Approaches to Literacy program umbrella. Other federal funding that may apply to some extent to school library programs include:

- Innovative Approaches to Literacy
- The Institute of Museum and Library Services
- The Library Services and Technology Act
- Native American and Native Hawaiian Library Services
- The National Library Service for the Blind and Physically Handicapped
- Supporting Effective School Library Programs (SKILLS Act)

Keeping appraised of these different governmental programs takes time and effort, which few SLP managers have. Some states have school library consultants or professional associations that can keep an eye out for funding opportunities. To keep in the loop, you should belong to such associations and subscribe to relevant listservs.

Ways to Optimize Fiscal Management

School librarians have to manage finances resourcefully and flexibly. As the SLP manager, you have the responsibility to confirm that resources are effectively used to fulfill the library's charge and support the school's mission. Having a stewardship role without accompanying financial control can be frustrating. Nevertheless, school librarians who show that they can manage resources responsibly are better positioned to request funding, be it to address specific resource gaps, support special projects such as a union catalog, or provide seed money. Especially in tight economic times, you have to work—and budget—smarter. That includes prioritizing tasks, training others to assume responsibilities, standardizing procedures, cutting out extraneous steps via technology, and finding creative solutions such as keeping bookcarts at the end of book ranges to facilitate reshelving.

You will need to learn about the many little pots of money and informal ways of acquiring resources that exist in schools. In the process, enlist the input of stakeholders who are likely to have their own wish list of resources for the library and may know of funding sources that might otherwise be overlooked by librarians. Include teachers in on-site vendor sessions, or let them choose a couple of books for the library when book fairs are held. At the least, survey classroom teachers about their priorities for library resources, and encourage teachers to suggest materials for the library; in some cases, teachers may be surprised to find that their desired items are already available in the library. Such collaboration is especially important when teachers have classroom or department resources. You might consider including these resources in the library catalog, at least at the administrative level, to help staff keep track of their own inventory as well as keep abreast of resources throughout the site. Here are some other tips:

- Look for alternative support. Seek teacher help if administrators block the way. Get user support if school boards do not see the library's value. Fight selectively and negotiate based on each stakeholder's priorities.
- If the school site allows fines for late returns, check to see if that money can be used at the library's discretion.
- If the library provides photocopying services, parent or student-body organizations might be able to fund it.
- Some schools charge students for ripped-off barcodes and other damages to materials that require supplies to mend.
- Check with vendors, including bookstores, for possible freebies that can be used as rewards for volunteers and students.
- Most schools have parent or community volunteer programs whose services the library can enlist. With administrative approval, the library might also be eligible to participate, with other local volunteer group opportunities. For instance, some colleges have relevant volunteer and intern programs.
- Parents or other local artists may donate time to create displays or paint decorations.

- Book fairs can provide substantial funding and books in kind, particularly in elementary schools. Coordinating book fairs, however, can require a great deal of time and effort, so librarians should get dependable adult volunteers to handle them. Alternatively, book fair companies are usually willing to take care of all the details for a well-deserved commission. Book fairs can also be complemented with birthday and graduation book-donation programs whereby a family donates a book—or preferably money to buy a book from a wish list—to the library. A personalized bookplate is placed in the book, and the family's child can be the first borrower.
- Always keep a wish list of library resources in case someone wants to give a donation, or some fiscal window of opportunity opens.
- Graduating classes often donate something to the school, and the library should be ready to suggest something memorable such as a reading center or cart of laptops.
- Libraries can get into the product sales or penny-drive business. Such efforts should be considered as much public relations efforts as ways to raise funds, because they can be time-consuming and not very profitable. Consider whether that time is well spent in relation to other library functions.
- Keep sales receipts for any library items purchased with personal funds, in case they can be reimbursed. At the least, these items can be considered tax-deductible business expenses.

Fiscally managing technology requires an additional level of expertise. The following suggestions can optimize your work:

- Check if the school district has a vendor or brand list of acceptable hardware and other equipment from which to choose. These lists can result in more standardized equipment and easier servicing. In some cases, brands may be limited, and not be available in the configurations needed for a specific library function, in which case a special bidding process may be required. Therefore, when writing specifications, describe features in a very detailed manner so that only the desired product will be eligible for bidding.
- Know about site and district service contracts. Most equipment is covered under preexisting service agreements, so additional service contracts are usually not needed except for integrated library management systems.
- Check with other librarians before purchasing technology in order to find good pricing and high-quality products.
- Consider district-wide library management systems. Group purchases typically receive discounts, and the option of a union catalog can facilitate cataloging and resource sharing.

- Explore corporate donation programs. Community parents may be employees in the technology sector, and might be able to donate equipment.
- Maintain computers and other equipment in good condition to decrease repairs and replacement. For instance, install virus- and hacker-protection software, keep computer areas clean, and store equipment such as cameras in padded containers. Additional ideas are found in the resource chapter.

When thinking about the fundraising aspect of fiscal management, also consider expanding into the online environment. Probably the most common, and easiest, method is a tie-in with vendors such as Amazon; the librarian posts a wish list, and Amazon account users can choose items to be sent to the library upon purchase. Enterprises such as Network for Good are entering the library world, offering online communication tools and event management for a cost. Online fundraising involves several potential factors:

- an effective home web page with a donation button, which describes the need for funding, and includes testimonials and endorsements
- social media such as Facebook and Twitter with links to and from the library web page
- online one-page interactive donation forms with automatic e-mailed tax receipts, ways to offer gifts and facilitate repeating donations, and the ability to incorporate web analytics
- an effective e-mail list that facilitates personalized online marketing and social networking
- methods of thanking donors, including personalization, gifts, stories, and ways to tie back the donation to the appeal
- online events that educate, interact, and raise money

As with other kinds of fundraising, modest targeted success trumps over-ambitious and uneven results. Additionally, online efforts need tech- and communications-savvy personnel to manage them. As with book fairs, it may be cost-effective for you to delegate this task to a qualified person who has a proven record and a passion for the library.

Finding Alternative Funding Sources

In today's educational environment, getting sufficient funding for SLPs is a challenge. You must know how to locate and "go for the money" in order to help students succeed. Of course, the best scenario is to have an abundance of financial support *and* get grants to do innovative services. In the worst-case scenario, you may have to seek outside funding in order to provide the library program required to address at least some of the needs of the school community. It should be noted that even then, administrators must approve such initiatives, so invest time and energy to build positive relationships with decision makers, especially those who control the purse strings. Any efforts should be seriously considered to make sure that the returns are worth the investment of labor.

Whenever asking for funding, you should have on hand:

- specific goals and objectives
- specific and compelling needs (which drive the objectives)
- strategic plans for meeting the objectives, including detailed costs
- means to show results and impact, especially on student learning aligned with standards
- information on the benefit to the funder
- facts and figures in visual form, such as infographics

Articulating the library program's ends and means facilitates locating appropriate funders and making a better case to such funders. Although it is usually better to start with a specific need and then match the funder, you can also begin by finding likely funders and then shape an SLP initiative accordingly.

As the SLP manager, you are often more likely to get funding if you align efforts with the priorities of other school community members. By working with other groups, you will find fiscal and moral support, and accomplish more. For instance, the science department might be pursuing a STEM (science, technology, engineering, mathematics) grant. Part of that grant could fund library sources about STEM topics, so you should consider participating in the grant application development. You can then work with the science department to select and house those resources as well as co-teach students how to use those resources productively. Potentially, you bring several skills to the grantsmanship table: research, technology, resource evaluation, cross-disciplinary connections, instruction, and communication. By contributing significantly to fundraising efforts, you can often procure resources or funding for SLP projects. Even the act of providing a grants-awareness service for the school can increase your value.

Funding sources can be as close as the local community. For example, you can brainstorm with parent groups about connections to local enterprises and foundations that have discretionary funds for fiscal contributions and donations in kind. You might also collaborate with other libraries, be it schools or other types, on local projects that can garner substantial fiscal support, such as after-school programs or health information for at-risk youth. Local service clubs may also donate to worthy library causes, or have members who can provide leads to funders. It is a good idea for you to join service groups, or at least present to them occasionally in order to build a professional network of supporters. SLP managers usually have better luck getting funded from local funders because of greater community pride, more personal connections, and less competition. You should also feel comfortable asking previous donors to give again, especially if the return on their investment has positive, concrete outcomes and benefits the donor. A good idea is to start small, be successful, and then leverage that success for larger funding opportunities. When applying for grants and other funding, several practices have been found to increase the chances for success:

- Start with a strong paragraph that describes the intent, the need, and the potential impact.
- Establish credibility quickly by mentioning the library's reputation and successful efforts.
- Know the audience. Use terms that they understand. Make sure that your request fits their intent. Explain how funding the library will benefit them.
- Follow directions carefully and completely.
- Explain how the resources will be used, and how their impact will be measured.
- Prepare the budget carefully and realistically.
- Check to see if matching funds are required, and make sure that the school or district is prepared to match those funds. Find out if in-kind contributions can be used in matching funds.
- Check funder and school district requirements and limitations for indirect or overhead costs.
- Provide a realistic, specific time line.
- Be sure that the people involved in the grant are qualified and have enough time and support to do the work.
- If a cover letter is permitted, write a one-page summary that gives a clear compelling message—without begging.
- Ask for advice before applying. Read the proposals of successful grantees. Ask for rubrics or other review guidelines that can help in writing the proposal. If possible, make personal contact with decision makers. Sometimes these people will preview your proposal, and give valuable suggestions.
- If letters of support are permissible, have prominent supporters and participants write on the library's behalf.
- Have successful grantees review your proposal.
- Make sure the proposal looks professional, is well written, and is error-free.

- Meet deadlines. Hand deliver the proposal, if necessary, rather than risk missing a deadline. Check if the deadline refers to the date and time the proposal is submitted, or the time it is received.
- Thank the potential funder even if the proposal is rejected.

The websites of several library groups offer valuable advice on fundraising:

- www.ala.org/tools/libfactsheets/alalibraryfactsheet24
- www.metgroup.com/assets/326_libfundraisingbestpra.pdf
- www.libsuccess.org/index.php?title = Fundraising
- http://libraryfundraising.pbworks.com/w/page/16953264/FrontPage
- www.fundraising-ideas.org/find/library.htm
- www.folusa.org/sharing/fundraising.php

Administering Grants

It can take a great deal of time and effort to write a grant or other funding proposal, but it takes even more work to administer successful awards. Thankfully, SLP managers have the required skills: organization, attention to detail, communication, and collaboration.

Once you receive notice of a grant or award, send copies to notify administrators and other relevant personnel such as development officers and school boards. Also work with the school's public relations personnel to announce the award to the community. Acknowledge the grantors, and check details about funding disbursement. All time-sensitive activities or products should be marked on a master calendar.

Grants tend to focus on materials or personnel. The consequences can be substantial. For instance, SLP managers might procure resources but not be able to pay for storage or training. Sometimes SLP managers hope that local administrators will ante up to fill the resource gap (including both material and human), but such assumptions may prove false. Instead, you should try to anticipate all consequences of requests to make sure that it is probable that the resources can be implemented.

Many grants involve partnering with other school community members or off-site entities, so allocate time for team building and implementation plans. Surprisingly, the more sophisticated the technology the greater the need for human interaction; roles and responsibilities for tasks must be determined, and technologies must be interoperable. Furthermore, make sure that partners are involved in assessment activities. All stakeholders must determine assessment methods, collect data, analyze results, and make adjustments in the initiatives. In any case, grant administration requires full documentation of plans, efforts, products and other deliverables, assessments, finances, and adjustments.

Grant administration requires effort, but it also offers opportunities to partner with stakeholders and offer additional funding for mutually beneficial projects. Most important, such collaboration can result in greater student achievement, which is the main goal of any good library program and school charge.

Bringing It Down to You

So what is the school library program worth to you and to your school community? And where is the money? What is the return for your investment of time and resources? Are you spending your time—and the time of the rest of the library staff and volunteers—wisely? Sometimes a task that takes minimal time has big rewards—and vice versa. Sometimes just pausing to socialize can reap great rewards; how do you calculate the benefit of that activity? The trickiest part of resource allocation is agreeing on priorities, especially if the library's priorities differ from the rest of the school's. The optimum situation exists when stakeholders agree with the use of time and money.

Assess how library workers spend their time in the library, and calculate that value in terms of hourly wage. Might time be better spent? Should tasks be assigned to different people? What resources are missing, or are of inadequate quality, for the library's program goals to be achieved? To what degree would filling those gaps make a difference? Identifying those obstacles and bottlenecks can help you decide what resources should be requested in order to get the biggest bang for the school's buck.

References

Farmer, L. 2012. "Brace Yourself." *School Library Journal* 58 (3): 38–43.

McPheat, S. 2010. *Managing Budgets.* Warwickshire, England: MTD Training and Venus Publishing.

Rounds, R. 1994. *Basic Budgeting Practices for Librarians,* 2nd ed. Chicago, IL: American Library Association.

SLJ's "Average Book Prices for 2016." 2016. *School Library Journal* 62 (3). www.slj.com/2016/03/research/sljs-average-book-prices-for-2016.

9

Managing People

EVEN THOUGH MANAGING RESOURCES CAN BE CHALLENGING, managing people can be even more time-intensive and stressful—yet rewarding—because of each person's complexity as well as the dynamics of every-changing interactions. Because school librarians work with the entire school community, they manage a variety of individuals. The most obvious group is the library staff, both paid and volunteer. The financial differentiation is important when trying to supervise and collaborate fairly. In addition, managers of school library programs (SLPs) must take into account the characteristics, experience, and interests of people of different ages as they manage them. This chapter gives concrete guidelines for hiring, training, supervising, assessing, and recognizing library workers and other library team members (e.g., advisory boards).

Although collaboration and partnering are not management functions, per se, such support and sustenance do depend on management skills. What are the management conditions for beneficial interactions? How can partnerships lead to resource allocation and management? These questions are addressed in this chapter. By managing library staff, committee work, and partnerships, you can enlarge your spheres of influence. Tips for working with diverse populations are also provided in this chapter.

What Needs to Be Done?

In order to fulfill the school library program's mission, the SLP manager must identify all the relevant functions and the human resources needed to carry out those functions. Even when the school librarian is the sole staff person in the library, he or she cannot fully implement the library program alone; it requires working with others.

Consider all the library resources and the functions associated with them. How much time do these functions take in terms of time cost per unit, for instance? How often must these functions be done? What skills are needed to do the job? What is the priority of the function? Table 9.1 can jumpstart decision making.

Table 9.1

School Library Program Functions

Function	Unit Time-Cost	Frequency	Skills	Priority: A (top)–C	Personnel
COLLECTION DEVELOPMENT					
Selection	5 min.	1 hour/week	Locating and reviewing resources, linking to curriculum, prioritizing, comparison shopping	A	School librarian
Ordering					
Processing					
Cataloging					
Circulation					
Overdues					
Shelving/storing					
Equipment management					

Preservation/ repairing					
Weeding					
Document production					
ACCESS					
Scheduling					
Website/portal					
Database management					
Student IDs, log-ons, etc.					
Facilities management					
INSTRUCTION					
Reference service					
Programs/events					
Instructional design					
Learning aid development					
Reading promotion					
Repository/ knowledge management					
Collaboration/ planning					
Teaching					
Assessment					

COMMUNICATION					
Among library staff					
Between staff and users					
External					
Document development					
STAFFING					
Recruitment and hiring					
Training					
Supervision					
FINANCES					
Budgeting					
Fund-raising					
Book fairs					
ADMINISTRATION					
Assessment					
Planning					
Collaboration					

This process usually entails prioritization and negotiation of time. It is useful to complete the chart for existing practices as well as using it to start from scratch to conceptualize an ideal or at least cost-effective situation.

Before assigning personnel to each task, list all existing and potential personnel: not only library staff and volunteers but other workers in the school. For instance, a technician might handle all equipment, and an enrollment clerk might handle student IDs. In addition, more than one person or position might be responsible for the function. Increasingly, enterprises cross-train staff in order to prevent work bottlenecks due to absences, and to facilitate career development. A general rule of thumb, though, is to delegate the job to the least expensive or least experienced person possible. For instance, a middle school student volunteer might be able to shelve, but a school librarian should be the one selecting materials to acquire for the library. In some cases, a lower level person might do the job under the supervision, or checking, of the SLP manager, such as placing orders.

Matching Functions with Personnel

The chart above is just a starting point because each person has unique capabilities and interests. Several individuals may have the same title, but how they perform can differ significantly. Any school librarian who manages student and adult volunteers realizes how important it is to match the function with the person, both in terms of the level of skill and of responsibility.

This situation addresses how job descriptions are written. Each function is composed of procedures. A group of related and coherent functions makes up a job and its position. In general, the higher the job position, the less specificity it encompasses, because it assumes more decision making and discretion on the part of the worker. Ideally, the library program staff covers all its functions. It is important to provide space for volunteers to contribute meaningfully to the library program, but SLPs cannot run a program with volunteers alone; that would be like running a library on soft money. Furthermore, when the SLP is implemented principally through volunteers, or is understaffed, then it sends a message that the library is neither valued nor essential.

Typically, SLP managers have little opportunity to design jobs. However, on a small scale you can at least craft volunteer jobs. Some of the factors that should be considered when designing a volunteer position include responsibility and autonomy, meaningful work, variety, learning, and social support (Emery and Thorsrud 1976).

Even with existing jobs, you can make modifications based on personnel or SLP needs. Some job redesign options follow (Collins 1993):

- Specialization. The worker masters one task or function. This can result in more autonomy or responsibility, but it can also lead to boredom or over-reliance on one person.
- More job control. With increased skills, a worker might be able to make more task-related decisions. With more control generally comes more accountability, which the worker should realize. Enlarging task scope and responsibility. Several related tasks can be clustered into a work unit,

with the person taking charge of that unit. Such job increase can increase satisfaction but it requires more training.

- Rotating tasks. Doing a variety of tasks can make a person's job more interesting, and helps as a backup measure in case someone is absent. However, it requires more training.
- Combining tasks. Generally, related tasks could be combined, such as writing content and publishing, be it in print or on the web. Theoretically, combining tasks increases productivity and efficiency.
- Teaming. A group does the task or general function. This redesign can be an effective way to provide more worker control and interdependence simultaneously. However, forming and optimizing a team can be hard to implement because of group dynamics.
- Taking on supervision duties. A paraprofessional, for instance, might supervise volunteers. This option provides opportunities for leadership training, and requires the supervisor to show interpersonal skills as well as task skills.

Job designing can also be conducted as a group process, as outlined by Collins (1993). For example, a library paraprofessional position might be reclassified because of changing library functions or changing personnel patterns. Recent trends include worker empowerment, "rightsizing," technology advances, and increasing health and safety regulations. Typically, a steering committee would be formed, with representatives from administration, union, human resources, library management and other staff, technology, and job design experts. The committee reviews workflow efficiency to identify ways to simplify or streamline actions. They need to identify sources of problems, such as lack of resources or physical obstacles, and reconceptualize the job. In the process, the committee determines whether the worker will be satisfied with the redesign position, what the effect on supervisors and subordinates might be, and whether changes in training will be required. Typically, the redesigned job is pilot-tested and evaluated in order to identify impact and potential gains. Changes also must be approved by administration, unions, and human resource officers.

The job analysis forms the basis of the job description and relevant qualifications. As the SLP manager, you should examine the school district's existing job descriptions, and compare them to similar jobs within the district and comparable library systems, in order to provide the most accurate and relevant information. Several other sources of school library job descriptions also exist. Resources for School Librarians (www.sldirectory.com/libsf/resf/evaluate.html #jobs) lists several sources of information. The American Association of School Librarians provides a sample job description for a credential school librarian at www.ala.org/aasl/sites/ala.org.aasl/files/content/guidelinesandstandards/

learning41ife/resources/sample_job_description_L4L.pdf. More generally, the United States Department of Labor describes the work of librarians at www.bls .gov/ooh/Education-Training-and-Library/Librarians.htm. As noted already, the more senior the job, the less specific it is likely to be. However, higher level jobs usually include more qualifications, including more "soft" skills such as inter-personal skills and resiliency. Furthermore, specific districts may have unique characteristics that require added local qualifications such as bilingual ability.

Staffing from the Start

Competent, personable, and satisfied employees constitute the heart of the SLP. Library workers reflect a significant investment of time and money. Finding the right people for the job, training them, working with them, and retaining them optimizes the effectiveness of the library. This section provides guidance in the recruitment, selection, training, and supervision of library workers, both paid and unpaid.

RECRUITMENT

The information gathered in the job analysis and job descriptions provides a sound foundation for recruiting and hiring qualified library workers who will fit the worksite. It should be noted that hiring entails matching the person to the position *and* the site's culture. No one person is the perfect fit for every setting.

Several sources of qualified people exist. Many positions are filled from within the organization, either as people want to change their jobs or advance in the district. For entry-level paraprofessional positions, a recent graduate, especially one who has worked successfully in the school library, may be qualified for the position. However, because the Every Student Succeeds Act requires highly qualified staff for direct services to students, the requirements for a library tech-nician are likely to include at least an associate's degree as a library techni-cian. Sometimes the best long-term recruitment strategy is developing a strong library volunteer cadre of students and adults who can be encouraged to pursue postsecondary library training.

School districts advertise library positions in local media outlets such as school and college publications, newspapers, volunteer centers, news centers, employment offices, and Craigslist. Word of mouth can also serve as an effec-tive recruitment strategy because parent group members may know of qualified applicants. Similarly, other local libraries may have volunteers, workers, and friends who may be interested; library and information science programs often broadcast job openings to their students and alumnae. Professional library asso-ciations can be another good source for advertising jobs. In any case, you should build strong local networks so that when job openings arise, you can optimize the applicant pool. Sometimes job announcements are publicized in state and national library job list clearinghouses, but the best options are usually local. In any case, let the human resource office, which usually handles hiring processes, know about these important sources of job candidates. Make yourself available to talk with interested individuals; you might be able prescreen individuals to enhance a good match—and to discourage those persons who are either unqualified or have an unrealistic expectation of the job. ("No, you cannot sit in the corner all day and read.")

Volunteer jobs can also be part of the recruitment process. For instance, in identifying tasks that need to be performed, some functions might be done by volunteers, such as shelving, display work, or running book fairs. Schools often maintain volunteer lists of interested parents and community members. Similarly, school counselors may maintain a list of volunteer opportunities for students. Just because the volunteer is not paid monetarily does not mean that recruitment should be any less professional in nature. The person must still be able to do the job and fit into the school and library environment.

SELECTION AND HIRING

As the SLP manager, you should participate in library worker selection and hiring. For volunteer positions, you can sometimes handle that process independently, but for paid positions, the human resource office usually manages the process. Hiring procedures should be consistent, which validates the seriousness of working in the library. Normally, the selection and hiring process includes formal application review, any legal clearances, background and reference checks, personal interview, and extending the offer. If an interview panel is used, you might suggest including a library volunteer or student aide. The applicant should also visit the library before a hiring decision is made.

In any case, you should discuss the position with the human resource officer, and provide input on the questions to be asked in an interview. Hiring decisions are usually based on the person's prior experience, job accomplishments, skills and knowledge, personal attributes, and prior evaluations or letters of recommendation, so questions should address these issues. However, the SLP manager often knows the peculiarities of the library and how it functions, and may be able to develop specific questions that reflect the library's circumstances, such as whether an applicant must be able to multitask, is comfortable working with students who have special needs, can troubleshoot technology, or lift heavy objects. Human resource officers also know what kinds of questions that are not permissible, such as family status, race, age, home ownership status, arrest background, or non-job related affiliations.

SOCIALIZATION AND ASSIMILATION

The hiring process usually entails orientation. The new library worker is introduced to the site and the school library program: key personnel, facilities, basic policies and procedures, and information about the organization and job. Human resource offices typically provide a packet of information about offices, organizational structure, contact information, communication practices (e.g., telephone and computer use), forms, identification, dress code, hours of operations and holidays, vacations and sick leave, scheduling, breaks and meals, parking, school documents, salary and benefits, union and contract details, and safety issues.

As the SLP manager, you should also provide a library-specific orientation so that the worker becomes comfortable with the workplace. In a way, a library walkthrough may be considered a "cook's tour" because it typically not only deals with the general collection, but also includes nonpublic resources (e.g., archives, equipment, software, file cabinets), relevant technology, the circulation area, library-related offices, storage areas, the workroom and its supplies, and break and personal storage areas. Consider creating a library-specific packet of information: a flyer or brochure about the school library's program of resources and services, sample library documents and handouts, teacher-related information such as scheduling and planning, library-specific policies and procedures, emergency practices, passwords and security codes, and contact information.

Probably the most important orientation, though, is personal: getting to know coworkers as individuals. Because library staff work as a team, they need to trust and feel comfortable with each other. It is important to find a few minutes to share a cup of coffee (or other beverage) to start the professional relationship; this is a good opportunity to learn about the context of the person's life, such as family demands. Sharing preferred methods of communication, and figuring out each other's "personal space" are also necessary to optimize interaction. Discussing the library's "culture" and norms should also be done early on so that the new worker has an idea how to relate to library users. In addition, you should talk about the school's culture so that workers can interact appropriately with their counterparts in other offices.

The process by which an individual learns how to interact with others and becomes a member of the group is called socialization. This process is a necessary part of orientation, but it might also improve performance per se. According to Feldman (1976), several accommodations should be made. The new worker has to be initiated to the task and the group. The new and existing workers have to agree on role definition and management. The new worker also has to resolve non-workplace conflicts that might arise because of the new job. With successful socialization, workers will be satisfied, and can mutually influence each other. They are more likely to remain motivated and keep involved in their jobs.

Nicholson (1984) posited four negotiating mental models when assuming a new work role. If the role requires minimal social skills or personal development, then it is easy to replicate; if it requires personal development then the new worker has to master the new job. If the new role is a significant change socially but not in terms of skill set, then the new worker will need to determine if the role feels good. If personal development of skills and knowledge is required, then the person has the opportunity to take an exploratory attitude. It should be noted that this negotiation process involves the existing workers as well as the new one, because they too have to readjust to each other and the resultant group dynamics.

Training

Because orienting new library workers involves a degree of socialization, the new member's focus is on learning the job and doing it well. His or her motto might well be, "Just give me the facts." In the same way, training entails providing a task's overview and main processes, and then deepening understanding and functionality.

Regardless of the job, the training should convey the importance of each task in implementing the SLP and supporting the school as a whole. This perspective highlights the difference between the tasks of cementing a brick and building a cathedral. Showing the interdependence of library tasks and functions creates a compelling rationale, and helps motivate the worker, to perform any task competently and with pride.

Even before training, you should interview the worker to determine the current level of expertise based on prior training and experience. In some cases, the worker has had formal library or technology preparation, and in other cases the worker may have performed the same task in another setting. Of course, each workplace has its setting-specific practices, so a worker may have to adjust to the different situation and even unlearn ways to do things. On the other hand, the worker may be able to suggest better ways to accomplish a task because of that prior knowledge. With new staff who have prior experience in the field, it is a good idea to review the library's policies and procedures related to the task, and then ask workers to demonstrate how they would perform the task, and have them talk through their process. Such authentic assessment provides a concrete foundation for making necessary adjustments to optimize how the task is performed. In addition, this approach validates a worker's current expertise, and sets a tone of collaborative staff development and teamwork.

In many cases, new workers have not done certain tasks before. However, they may have benefited from that function, such as materials circulation or

Food for Thought

You WILL be Assimilated

One of the big challenges of a new job is assimilating to the workplace environment. Especially when a new hire comes in with very specific expectations that are not evidenced in that setting, that worker may feel uncomfortable, frustrated, or disappointed. He or she can adjust, try to change the environment, or leave. Hopefully, the hiring process frontloads that differential of expectations. Nevertheless, adjusting to a new job and a new workplace environment is challenging even in the best conditions, because change itself requires adjustment.

Think about the library's atmosphere. What words does it inspire: reflection, laboratory, haven, bustle, central station, family? When the members of the school community enter the library, what are they likely to see: a high level of activity, displays of student work, a sense of order, lots of equipment, scads of reading material, cozy corners? How are users arranged: in social groups, by gender, in islands, individually? In short, What tone does the library set? How is that tone reinforced?

Ask your new workers what words come to mind when they think about libraries. What are their prior experiences with libraries? Does this school library remind them of other libraries? How is it different? How are their own expectations about library use confirmed or challenged in this school library? In what ways might they feel more comfortable? Are there ways that they would like the library culture to change? By discussing these possibly different expectations early on, the SLP manager can help new workers assimilate more easily, and include them in the process of improving the library's culture in the long term.

computer usage. In those cases, you can build on that "consumer" perspective, and give the "behind the scenes" perspective. Certainly, prior user experience helps provide the rationale for the task, so it becomes easier to explain how to execute the task in terms of how to best serve the user.

In general, training follows these steps, which are much like class instruction:

1. Demonstrate how to perform the task. Do a "think aloud" explaining each process and why it is done. Alternatively, the demonstration could be done by another worker, or recorded as a video or screencast.
2. Share the relevant policies and procedures. A task "cheat sheet" is very useful. Clarify any issues.
3. Walk through the process with the procedures or guide sheet in hand. As much as possible, the worker should go through the motions. For more complex tasks, the worker might start by shadowing an expert worker.

4. Review the task to clarify or polish any aspects. At this point, some exceptions or nuances can be addressed.

5. Observe the worker performing the task independently. Debrief at the end; intervene only when it is critical. For complex tasks, the worker might do the task in tandem with an expert worker.

6. Monitor the task performance to ensure quality control and consistency. The worker may now be able to provide ways to improve the procedures or guide sheet. Sometimes another worker may do the frontline monitoring, although you should check in occasionally. In some cases, such as interpersonal skills, training might consist of role-playing or discussing case studies. For rote tasks, such as shelving, online tutorials or simulations such as those listed at www.kn.pacbell.com/wired/fil/pages/list thedeweli.html can provide timely and private feedback.

Alternatively, some tasks, such as installing and maintaining the integrated library management system, might be taught by the vendor or a commercial trainer. Relevant training may be held by the district or a professional library association. It should be noted that training also applies to existing workers who are broadening their skill set. If an existing worker is assuming a new function, such as technology specialist, he or she might take formal training or academic preparation.

Sometimes a worker may initiate interest in learning new skills, and sometimes a job reclassification requires the additional expertise. Hopefully, any such training aligns with the SLP so that you can support the worker's efforts. In some cases, it may mean that the person's workload might need to be adjusted to accommodate the new learning curve. Such support is a good investment for worker retention, expertise, and satisfaction.

Using Volunteers

Although they should not supplant paid staff, library volunteers offer valuable service and perspectives for the SLP, and they can be the program's best boosters. When volunteers take the initiative to work for the library out of passion and loyalty to the program, and find activities that match their interests and capabilities, they are truly a valued-added human resource.

Library volunteers comprise several populations: site students, college students, library program students, school community members, neighbors, retirees, businesspeople, and members of service groups. They volunteer for a variety of reasons: love of libraries, professional and personal development, career exploration, social activity, sense of belonging, community service, to learn marketable skills, and for school credit.

PROCESSES

Most of the processes of recruitment, application, hiring, and training mentioned above apply to volunteers. However, because volunteers usually work intermittently, matching individuals' skills and interests to tasks is crucial. You should interview potential volunteers to determine their expectations, interests, skills, and availability. It is usually best to start with the volunteer's perceptions and wants, and then expand his or her knowledge to suggest alternative tasks. Because some volunteers want one steady task, such as repairing books or creating displays while others would rather experience a variety of tasks, preferences should be identified in the initial interview. The SLP might be able to accommodate individuals who prefer short-term or project-based volunteering; some possible projects include book fairs, special events, open houses, and fundraising campaigns. You should also identify possible barriers to volunteering, such as transportation and child care, and help the potential volunteer find solutions to those problems. For instance, volunteer buddies could drive together, or watch each other's children. Indeed, pairing volunteers can not only solve logistical problems but also facilitate socialization.

Volunteers may well be very dependable and loyal, helping in the library long after their children have graduated. Others may last just a month, finding that the fit is not good. Because they are not paid, volunteers usually work out of inner motivation. Therefore, recognizing their efforts is a worthwhile and important practice. Perks such as extended check-out periods, printing rights, kitchen privileges, token gifts, thank-you notes, certificates, and annual parties are appreciated. When good volunteers leave, they should receive a letter of recommendation; even if it is not intended or used for other hiring opportunities, the fact that such a letter was written can mean much to that volunteer.

STUDENT VOLUNTEERS

Hopefully, students consider the school library to be "their" library, and they should be encouraged to participate in its operation. From writing web reviews to planning contests, students bring fresh perspectives and ideas to the library program. Moreover, when students learn how to do a task well and contribute to the school through their service, they become positive ambassadors to the community.

Both in middle school and high school, student volunteering may be configured as an activity, service club, or elective course. Students might also want to help out in their free time just because they love libraries. All of these arrangements should acknowledge group expectations and clarify roles, and should balance academic and social aspects. For courses, a contract approach provides a framework for student learning outcomes and responsibilities, and serves as a model for real-life business practice.

Training is an ongoing activity that parallels the needs and interests of students as they grow in their roles at school. Training should be planned, at least at the macro level, and it should be documented so students have a record of their progress. Training may occur in small groups, or be done on an individual basis to leverage the students' needs. Although individualization helps develop good one-on-one working relationships, it is time-consuming. One model of student training is based on the idea of a coordinated intern program. All students meet regularly, say once a month, when they receive training together. This approach allows the trainer to work with an entire group, thus increasing instructional productivity—with the assurance that everyone is getting the same information. If the program is considered a social gathering as well, then a mix of training and socializing can motivate students to attend regularly and build a sense of camaraderie.

Training should take students' developmental issues into account.

- Students are experienced learners. Trainers should build on such expertise, going from the known to the unknown. Nonetheless, training still relies on repetition.
- Students have limited time. Training must be well-prepared and immediately useful.
- Students learn in response to their own interests and needs.
- Students like to interact.
- Students have strong habits. They must feel safe so they can take learning risks.
- Students should see results. They need to practice new skills, preferably while being coached.
- Students have a life outside school—and like training that helps them there.
- Students may find that they have overestimated their library commitment, or they may have seasonal demands (e.g., a sports team), so consider short-term projects as well.

In sum, training should be useful, meaningful, and interactive, and provide students with opportunities to share experiences and have fun.

Student Library Aide Evaluation Form

(by permission of Jennifer Bello of Providence High School)

Name _____Grade _____

Year(s) in this position _____

Period Covered: From _____ To _____

PERFORMANCE CRITERIA

A. JOB KNOWLEDGE—Individual's knowledge of required duties as outlined in the position description

_____ Fully understands and applies the knowledge in performing all phases of job.

_____ Understands and is capable of performing all phases of job very well.

_____ Has adequate grasp of essential duties of job; can proceed without special instructions on all regular work.

_____ Fair knowledge but lacks knowledge of some important aspects of job content.

_____ Poor job knowledge. Does not understand job duties.

Comments and/or suggestions:

B. SUPERVISION REQUIRED—Degree of supervision required for individual to perform job functions

_____ Always follows instructions; you can be absolutely sure you will get the assignment when you want it.

_____ Regularly follows instructions; requires little follow-up.

_____ Necessary on only a few tasks to check up to be sure of deadlines or following of instructions.

_____ Requires regular checking to be sure work will be done on time and in accordance with instructions.

_____ Requires very close supervision and monitoring of all work.

Comments and/or suggestions:

C. QUANTITY OF WORK—Ability of the individual to perform required tasks

_____ Output of work is high; completes all assigned tasks and will ask for more.

_____ Output of work is good; completes all assigned tasks.

_____ Will complete most of assigned tasks.

_____ Work output is occasionally below established standards.

_____ Seldom gets work done in required time.

Comments and/or suggestions:

D. QUALITY OF WORK—Accuracy and thoroughness of the individual's work

_____ Very thorough; mistakes are very rare.

_____ Very few errors, usually minor in nature. Work seldom has to be done over.

_____ Most work done well, usually acceptable in both accuracy and thoroughness.

_____ Work often unacceptable, frequent errors or rejections.

_____ Work constantly rejected because of inaccuracies and mistakes.

Comments and/or suggestions:

E. ADAPTABILITY—Speed with which the individual learns new techniques or duties and understands explanations

_____ Exceptionally quick to learn and adjust to changed conditions.

_____ Learns easily; adjusts to changes rapidly.

_____ Adjusts to changes in methods or duties on request, with average amount of instructions.

_____ Adjusts to changes in methods or duties, but adjustment is slow and requires detailed instructions.

_____ Unable or unwilling to adjust to new methods or duties.

Comments and/or suggestions:

F. TIME MANAGEMENT—Ability of the individual to effectively use available work time

_____ Energetic; loses no time in starting and works right to last minute.

_____ On the job at all times; very little idle time; industrious.

_____ Spends no more time than necessary in talking with or helping other students.

_____ Gets distracted by other students; sometimes causes delays in work output.

_____ Spends much of time off task, often interrupts work for idle talk.

Comments and/or suggestions:

G. COOPERATION—The way in which the individual handles work relationships

_____ Goes out of the way to cooperate with others and ease conflicts.

_____ Gets along well with others and is approachable.

_____ Shows acceptable behavior.

_____ Shows a reluctance to cooperate with others.

_____ Refuses to cooperate with others.

Comments and/or suggestions:

H. PLANNING AND CONTROLLING—Ability to plan out tasks and follow through to completion

_____ Plans and achieves objectives ahead of schedule.

_____ Effectively plans and achieves all objectives on time.

_____ Achieves objectives and schedules with some difficulty.

_____ Occasionally plans and achieves objectives appropriately.

_____ Has poor planning skills and end results.

Comments and/or suggestions:

Supervision, Performance Evaluation, and Improvement

In the final analysis, the SLP manager is responsible for the implementation of the library program. The overall library program depends on the assessment and improvement of library staff performance, taking into account the perspectives of users, the school as a whole, finances, available resources, and student learning. Even the best library staff require supervision in order to maintain high-quality service and to show support of that staff. You should keep in mind the staff's merit, their worth in terms of cost-effectiveness, and the significance of their contributions to the total library program. According to Powell and Brodsky (2004), "Supervision is a disciplined, tutorial process wherein principles are transformed into practical skills, with overlapping foci: administrative, evaluative, clinical, and supportive" (11). On a profound level, as a supervisor, you shape the library's atmosphere not only for its users but also to promote staff development, including building cohesive and high-functioning staff teams.

Evaluation is often a hot button for people. Somehow it connotes being scrutinized with the intent of criticizing a person and revealing an individual to be subpar. Even successful people get a bit uncomfortable being evaluated. A couple of factors may contribute to such stress, and can be ameliorated: the feeling of "us" versus "them," which can be replaced by the concept of coaching; and the use of the term "critical," which should be considered more as a juncture point or snapshot rather than a final judgment. In other words, performance evaluation should be considered a snapshot of workers' efforts and achievements, taken with the intention of helping to sustain and improve them as part of the library program's overall effectiveness.

Clinical supervision is an effective model of evaluation that builds on a positive supervisor-supervisee relationship. The clinical supervisor serves as (1) a teacher who identifies and addresses staff learning needs; (2) a consultant who oversees staff services to library users; (3) a coach who diagnoses performance and suggests best practices; and (4) a mentor who models and facilitates staff development (United States Department of Health and Human Services 2009). The goal is to build an effective school library program by making work manageable for the staff and helping them develop professionally.

The basic approach of clinical supervision is direct observation and specific feedback. Typically, you and staff build on existing work contracts, determine reasonable accountability, and create an individual development plan of knowledge and skills goals. Ideally, the plan should state the rewards for meeting goals and consequences for noncompliance. These goals are the basis for formative evaluation, a process that focuses on changeable behavior, which should not be confused with overall performance evaluation. In addition to direct observation, the supervisor can examine sample work, feedback from others, and self-assessment. Often the supervisor and supervisee agree ahead of time on the observation criteria to use and address. The supervisor takes notes during the observation (or videotapes it), and then immediately debriefs the supervisee privately with, sometimes including written documentation. The feedback should focus on the behavior and underlying issue, and state the impact of the behavior along with the desired results. Together the supervisor and worker identify what needs to be changed, and what support (e.g., resources or training) is needed to improve performance. Thus, clinical supervision is a collaborative effort that benefits the staff, the users, and the library program as a whole.

Performance improvement is a straightforward process when everyone agrees that change is required and the worker is willing to make the necessary changes. It is important to identify the reasons why performance is less than stellar.

If specific skills are weak, they can often be improved with training; however, occasionally a worker may have so much trouble improving that job reassignment may be a most cost-effective action. Sometimes the job is not challenging, in which case the worker can be taught new skills or given more responsibility. Other times a person feels unappreciated or overlooked, in which case you and the worker can discuss ways to acknowledge achievement. Occasionally, the worker doesn't get along with peers, in which case, you will need to determine the cause of the resentment. Alternatively, the worker may have a bad attitude and not admit to or recognize the problem, in which case you will have to isolate the specific behavior and its consequences, and then ask the worker to try a different approach and review the results. Temporary or situational personal problems can also negatively impact performance, so you might try to help the person get help or consider other job options. In any case, the intervention may be authoritative in nature by being direct and informative, or facilitative by helping the worker to self-reflect or gain self-confidence.

Coaching skills can help workers improve performance through motivated empowerment (McPheat 2010a). The coaching session sets the vision, clarifies expectations, identifies deliverables, and determines the resources needed to meet the goal. The coach listens to the worker, questions him or her to obtain clarification and deeper understanding, and rephrases the worker's ideas. Rather than telling the worker what to do, the coach advises the worker about opportunities, and helps him or her to feel comfortable taking on the responsibility for self-improvement. The coach models appropriate behavior, helps the worker identify performance goals with measurable outcomes and standards, provides feedback, and helps the worker record his performance. It should be noted that coaching is a professional, targeted partnership, in contrast to mentoring, which can be a personal and lifelong endeavor.

It's a different matter when the worker doesn't want to change or doesn't see any reason to change; then the key factor is usually motivation (Bagshawe, 2011). A worker may be motivated by several factors: staff relationships, intellectual stimulation, achievement, power or control, self-expression, independence, status or recognition, professional or personal development, sense of contributing, personal meaning, salary, and physical working conditions. Several of these motivating factors can contribute positively or sabotage results. For instance, with good performance often comes independence, but some people might balk at following directions because they want more independence, thus undermining their performance. For many tasks, negative self-expression can hinder positive human interactions. On the other hand, when people have *no* motivation, they see no reason to act, and so withdraw or become discontent. Thus, you need to identify and give attention to the worker's key motivator, and build a reward system that leverages the motivation; for example, the person might get public praise or more autonomy for work well done. Herzberg (1968) posited a dual-factor motivation theory of hygiene versus motivation factors; hygiene or maintenance factors include basic conditions of safety, job security, and adequate salary, without which a worker will be dissatisfied. However, once those maintenance factors are in place, they do not motivate the worker; instead, factors such as professional growth and enrichment are more motivating. In general, you should provide good working conditions, make tasks meaningful and interesting, and help people achieve and develop.

Another theory that shows how personal attitudes and beliefs impact job performance is expectancy theory (Vroom 1964). Expectancy is a person's subject assessment that effort leads to job performance, and with that a positive outcome. Effort-to-performance expectancy assumes that a person can do the job: perceived capacity. Performance-to-outcome expectancy assumes that hard work will be rewarded. The term "valence" refers to the value of the outcome as perceived by the worker such that desirable rewards encourage effort. Vroom asserted that motivational force depends on the degree of positive expectancy— the valence significance—and the degree that job performance leads to desired outcomes. For example, a temp worker tries hard to be on time because he thinks he will get a permanent job as a result. The trick is that each person has unique expectancies and valences, and resources might not be available for the worker to achieve his or her desired outcome. Furthermore, some people are unaware of their own expectancies and motivations. Certainly, you have your work cut out for yourself trying find and leverage workers' motivations as well as capabilities to perform well and contribute to the SLP's well-being and improvement.

Occasionally, poor performance requires discipline. Some of the reasons for disappointing work have already been discussed: inability, personal demands, and attitude problems. Similarly, individuals may break the rules to show off, "push the envelope," express negative feelings, or for the sheer "rush." In any case, the SLP manager has to address the problem when it affects the library program's effectiveness. Garner (2012a) suggested several steps that the SLP manager can take when disciplining a worker. Gather data about the behavior, and then meet with the person in private to clarify roles, discuss the problematic behavior and its impact on the library program, and discuss alternative actions and consequences. Sometimes the person being disciplined may think that they are being victimized or singled out because of this attention and treatment, so it is important to share the evidence and focus on actions rather than the person per se. The individual being disciplined must realize that he or she can control the choices, and that natural consequence will ensue. It is also important to state the parameters of the discipline, including the time frame, sanctions, and penalties, as well as nonnegotiable actions such as theft or violence. The SLP manager will likely have to take additional action when the worker is a student, such as making a referral to the school counselor. In fact, most schools have disciplinary procedures that must be followed, so be aware of these steps, and follow them carefully. With these school policies in mind, monitor and support worker performance regularly so that a trusting professional relationship can preclude disciplinary measures, and minor interventions can be done before problems escalate.

Interpersonal Issues

As an SLP manager, you have to oversee each library worker as both an individual and as a group member. Worker interaction involves both task-related and social issues, which you should facilitate and monitor in order to optimize the SLP's effectiveness.

TEAM BUILDING

It takes a team to run an effective school library program. Even if the SLP manager is the only staff person, volunteers or friends can sometimes complement the school librarian's efforts. Because each person provides a unique set of knowledge, skills, and experiences, together they can provide a richer library experience for its users.

Garner (2012b) described high performance teams. In the context of the SLP, these teams align their efforts to achieve the library program's goals, and respond effectively to the school community's needs. They are productive and interdependent. They share leadership and develop meaningful relationships. They enjoy their jobs yet continue to develop. In order to be effective, several team needs should be met: achievement, recognition, learning, security, freedom, and social. You have the responsibility of facilitating an effective team of library workers.

Teams do not string up whole but rather develop over time. They start as a collection of people with just nominal membership. Library workers have an advantage in that they have a common goal, similar values, and a unique role within the school community. Therefore, your first team-building task will be to help library workers become acquainted with each other professionally and personally. Fortunately, one of the best ways to start such acquaintances is through shared meaningful authentic activity, which is a daily occurrence in the library. Through successful interaction, the team can then build trust. Keep an eye on each person—if someone is undependable, it affects the entire team; work privately with that person quickly to rebuild trust and competency through targeted interventions.

After the team forms, it must work out its identity, clarifying roles and testing interdependence without stepping on one another's toes. Even though conflict may arise, it is better to address the issues rather than try to brush them off; help members to focus on the end game of program effectiveness, and encourage members to solve problems among themselves. By working through differences, the team can agree on effective means of communication and practices for mutual gain, a stage called "norming." Continued success then leads to a performing team that can focus on optimizing the library program, and celebrate their effectiveness. You can help teams develop in several ways (Garner 2012b).

- Provide members with opportunities to share information and feelings; food can serve as a concrete way to share and relax.
- Help the team and its members to set and monitor goals.
- Encourage members to ask one another for help and suggestions.
- Practice the three *A*s: appreciating, accepting, and acknowledging each other.
- Follow the model of geese in flight: take turns leading, and keep an eye on each other.
- Support positive and constructive feedback among the team.
- Provide opportunities to share good learning experiences.
- Encourage members to listen to one another, build on each other's ideas, and take calculated risks to improve library services.
- Provide opportunities to celebrate team achievements.

Within the team, group dynamics deal with social and task issues. Some of the informal roles include: encourager, listener, seeker, taskmaster, communications coordinator, problem solver, harmonizer, evaluator, and synthesizer. Usually, individuals self-select these roles, and the balance of these dynamics helps to make the team stable as seen from the outside.

It should be noted that team effectiveness can be jeopardized by divas, poor workers, cliques, cultural differences, gender differences, unresolved conflicts, and lack of rewards and recognitions. Coaching can also help to improve the team. As with individuals, the coach works with the team to identify its purpose and priorities, sets the tone for acknowledging and dealing with group problem performance, and builds a team development plan. Barriers to performance might include unclear vision and goals, ineffective leadership, poor decision making, insufficient feedback, issues about roles, poor procedures, or personality conflicts, among other possibilities. As with individuals, the coach helps the team generate options and build enthusiasm, so that the team can be supported in its efforts. For teams to grow strong, they must trust each other, understand their strengths and weaknesses, be interdependent, take positive risks, and identify the conditions for optimum collaboration.

As a matter of good management and another way to support teamwork, convene library team meetings regularly. Of course, each meeting should have a purpose and value to the staff. Some tips for running effective meetings follow (McPheat 2010b).

- Identify the purpose of the meeting: to brainstorm, plan, monitor, make decisions, or celebrate. Determine specific desirable outcomes.
- Schedule meetings that fit best with the anticipated attendees; link to other obligatory meetings. Use digital scheduling applications such as Doodle if necessary, particularly if you plan to meet with those who volunteer less frequently.
- Create an agenda with specific items, responsible members, and time frame; enable members to suggest agenda items.
- If possible, provide agenda information and materials to prepare or bring ahead of time.
- Prepare meetings by setting up the room, providing supplies, and arranging seating, preferably in a circle.
- Set ground rules for participation, including active listening, safe and confidential sharing, and mutual respect.
- Make sure that everyone has a chance to provide input; watch for people who dominate the conversation. Watch body language for unspoken opinions.
- Know and leverage the group's dynamics.
- At the end of the meeting, review the next steps and identify which individuals are responsible for specific actions. Thank everyone.
- After the meeting, follow up with identified tasks and decisions. Make sure that minutes are taken and disseminated in a timely manner.

INTERGENERATIONAL ISSUES

Increasingly, the team of library workers consists of several generations, not only because of student presence, but also because adult members may range from recent high school graduates to retirees. Each generation represents developmental differences and socially constructed experiential influences, which can lead to occasional conflicts. As the SLP manager, you should facilitate negotiations to find a mutual ground of understanding and cooperation. An atmosphere of inclusivity also results in richer library experiences for workers and the school community at large.

Levinson (1978) detailed three stages of life, which includes seasons of upheaval and change as well as seasons of stability and synthesis. Rick and Kathy Hicks (1999) identified unique characteristics of each generation as they grew up in different times. Implications for library worker interaction are provided in italics.

- Early adult: 22–28 years old entering the adult world, 28–33 transitioning between old life structures and new life challenges, 33–40 settling down. *These workers are likely to be tech-savvy or willing to explore new options. Millennials, in specific, are likely to be tolerant of differences, collaborative, and civic minded. Jobs should provide variety and flexibility, and staff development should emphasize the benefits of skill-building to optimize career options.*
- Middle adult: 40–45 midlife transition, 45–50 entering middle adulthood, 50–55 transitioning as in early adulthood, 55–60 culmination and peaking of middle adulthood. *Jobs should provide for balance in workers' lives, both by being more productive as well as leveraging the job for personal growth and social contributions. These workers usually seek autonomy and purpose, so should be given such opportunities in their jobs. Some workers may be experiencing a midlife crisis, which can lead to personal and professional renewal and retooling.*
- Late adult: 60–65 late adult transition, 65 onwards old age. *Older adults can mentor younger workers in terms of interpersonal skills with a range of ages. Their cognitive processes may be slower, but the self-pacing aspects of staff development and opportunities for socializing can comfort them.*

CULTURAL COMPETENCE

For library workers to work with multicultural resources and with people of different cultures, they need to be culturally competent. Culture may be defined as "the customary beliefs, social forms, and material traits of a racial, religious, or social group" and "the set of shared attitudes, values, goals, and practices that characterizes an institution or organization" (*Webster's Collegiate Dictionary,* 11th ed.). Therefore, soccer moms, gamers, individuals with hearing impairments might each be considered a cultural group. In librarianship, cultural issues apply to the clientele, the librarian, the setting, and the library program in general (e.g., resources and services). The 2012 diversity standards of the Association of College and Resource Libraries (ACRL) provide a useful guide to determine if the library program is culturally sensitive and relevant. The standards address issues of resources, service, and workplace climate. In sum, the standards call for librarians to be culturally knowledgeable and inclusive throughout their practice. SLP managers should model and lead efforts to develop and exercise cultural competence among library workers.

Hofstede's model of cultural dimensions (2001), which was introduced in chapter four, provides useful frameworks for examining culturally sensitive library worker implications (*noted in italics*).

- Power distance. What is the degree of equality between people? How equitable is the power distribution as defined from low-status people? In low-power societies, status is less important. *Power distance impacts interpersonal relations.*
- Individualism versus collectivism. People in individualistic societies tend to belong to several groups, each of which is loosely-knit, whereas collectivist societies tend to have a few, well-defined groups who are highly loyal. "In-group" refers to a collective in which members are highly interdependent and have a sense of common fate; groups to which they do not belong are "out-groups." *Individuals have preconceived attitudes about individual versus cooperative efforts.*
- Masculinity. To what degree are genders differentiated? Are traditional gendered roles supported in terms of achievement, control, and power? How are women valued relative to men? *Males might be more competitive or need more praise.*
- Uncertainty avoidance. How tolerant is society of uncertainty and ambiguity? Are different options acceptable or are strict rules the norm? *How structured should learning activities be? Does assessment ask for one right answer or does it encourage new answers? Do activities focus on accuracy or on different perspectives?*

DEALING WITH DIFFICULT PEOPLE

Sometimes library workers may have values or behaviors that do not fit together harmoniously. Library managers are responsible for worker esprit de corps. Benfari (1999) identified several personality types that can jeopardize group dynamics and the efficient functioning of the library program. He asserted that values should be expressed and assumptions examined in order to deal with dysfunctional behavior. To this end, Benfari identified several types of difficult people, and the ways to interact with them:

- *Sherman tanks,* who attack and threaten. Don't back down or let them go free. Remain calm. Give them time to run down. Get their attention, and keep eye contact. Focus on problem solving rather than arguments.

- *Negativists.* Be optimistic, and don't get drawn into their arguments. Focus on realistic steps, including addressing worst-case scenarios.
- *Bulldozers,* who require achievement and express dominance. Listen. Do your research, but avoid sounding more expert than they. Work around them.
- *Micromanagers.* Encourage people to self-regulate behaviors, and document their progress and problems. Be prepared and prevent problems.
- *Type A stress carriers.* Remain calm and relaxed. Don't placate them or try to change them. Distance yourself from them.
- *Snipers,* who attack indirectly. Ask them to share their thoughts with the group, and seek group confirmation of the covert attacks. Deal with the underlying problem privately.
- *Unpredictable exploders.* Give them time to calm down. Recognize their concerns and determine the reason or trigger for their explosions. If need be, walk away from the explosion.
- *Clams,* who are passive-aggressive or who want to avoid conflict or failure. Ask open-ended questions, let them talk and try not to respond until they open up.
- *Stone tablets,* who are rigid and rule-based. Gather and present facts rather than argue. Ask the reasons behind the rules. Emphasize the need for fairness.
- *Stallers,* who are indecisive and hope that problems will go away. Find out the reasons for their delays, and explore the problem. Suggest ways to do the task, including improving your part of the function.
- *Superagreeables,* who let the group down. Build personal relations with them, and interpret their humor. Look for opportunities to find out why they feel threatened or what they are avoiding.
- *Balloons,* who are pseudo-experts. Give facts as alternatives to their version. Let them save face in public, and deal with them privately.
- *"Ain't it awful" game players,* who suck you into their pitiful lives. Don't agree with their plights. Instead, help them solve problems with specific action steps.

Bringing It Down to You

In managing people, you are exercising your legitimate power: the power of your position. Other sources of power that can strengthen management's position include expertise, charisma, and networking. In addition, you have power to give (or take) rewards such as public recognition and perks. Of course, with power comes added responsibility—you are held accountable for the functioning of the library worker team, and must report to your own supervisors.

Power does not have to be a win-lose or zero-sum proposition. Your power also enables you to empower others. Library workers can gain more expertise and autonomy. They can serve as library liaisons in other parts of the school. They can network with people outside the school, and bring more resources and support to the library as a result. Through the empowerment of the library worker team, the library program as a whole becomes more powerful—and so do you.

Think about how you have gained power throughout your life. How have other people empowered you? How have you taking advantage of opportunities to gain expertise and learn networking techniques? How have you applied those new skills to your professional and personal life? How has your power helped improve your workplace? Have you thanked those people who have helped you along the way? Such reflections may inspire your own ideas for managing others as well as helping them manage themselves.

Ultimately, the library can be a powerhouse for good—and it is only as good as the people who power that library. Your management of people channels their energy into impactful action that results in a synergetic learning environment. Power to the people!

References

Association of College and Resource Libraries. 2012. *Diversity Standards.* Chicago, IL: Association of College and Resource Libraries.

Bagshawe, A. 2011. *Getting Motivation Right.* London, England: MTD Training and Ventus.

Benfari, R. 1999. *Understanding and Changing Your Management Style.* San Francisco, CA: Jossey-Bass.

Collins, R. 1993. *Effective Management.* Chicago, IL: Commerce Clearing House.

Emery, F., and E. Thorsrud. 1976. *Democracy at Work.* Leiden, The Netherlands: Martinius Nijhoff.

Feldman, D. 1976. "A Contingency Theory of Socialization." *Administrative Science Quarterly* 21 (3): 433–52.

Garner, E. 2012a. *Effective Discipline.* Casselberry, FL: Eric Garner and Ventus Publishing.

———. 2012b. *Team Building.* Casselberry, FL: Eric Garner and Ventus Publishing.

Herzberg, F. 1968. "One More Time: How Do You Motivate Employees?" *Harvard Business Review* 46 (1): 53–62.

Hicks, R., and K. Hicks. 1999. *Boomers, Xers and Other Strangers.* Wheaton, IL: Tyndale House.

Hofstede, G. 2001. *Culture's Consequences: Comparing Values, Behaviors, Institutions, and Organizations Across Nations*, 2nd ed. Thousand Oaks, CA: SAGE.

Levinson, D. 1978. *The Seasons of a Man's Life.* New York, NY: Knopf.

McPheat, S. 2010a. *Coaching and Mentoring.* London, England: MTD Training and Ventus Publishing.

———. 2010b. *Running Effective Meetings.* London, England: MTD Training and Ventus Publishing.

Nicholson, N. 1984. "A Theory of Work Role Transitions." *Administrative Science Quarterly* 29 (2): 172–91.

Powell, D., and A. Brodsky. 2004. *Clinical Supervision in Alcohol and Drug Abuse Counseling: Principles, Models, Methods*, rev. ed. San Francisco, CA: Jossey-Bass.

United States Department of Health and Human Services. 2009. *Clinical Supervision and Professional Development of the Substance Abuse Counselor.* Washington, DC: United States Department of Health and Human Services.

Vroom, V. 1964. *Work and Motivation.* New York, NY: Wiley.

10

Managing Services

PEOPLE BRING RESOURCES TO LIFE AND ADD VALUE TO THEM through effective service. First, you, as a manager of a school library program (SLP), can assess the available material and human resources (system "input products") and determine what actions can be achieved using those resources (system "input processes") that result in user activities and products (system "outputs") to support and advance the library's and school's mission (system "outcomes"). You should also identify those gaps in services that require added resources, and determine the need for such services. Because demand usually outpaces capacity, prioritizing existing and potential services is a necessary task. It is preferable to begin by offering a limited number of excellent services rather than a scattered variety of poorly implemented services. Strategic planning and ongoing assessment must drive services in order for the school library to influence the school most effectively. This chapter provides examples of service procedures and reference sheets.

A Systems Approach to Library Services

The library fulfills its mission through a planned system of resources and services. In collaboration with library staff and potentially a library advisory committee, you should examine the library's mission. If no mission exists, it will be necessary to develop a mission statement. Chapter five detailed how to plan strategically, based on the library's mission and statement of purpose in alignment with the school's mission. The American Association of School Librarians (AASL) 2009 guidelines for school library programs, *Empowering Learners,* also provides valuable advice.

THE NATURE OF SERVICE

Even if the library has many resources, the program's impact is minimal without high-quality service. Resources are "things," and services are what the library staff do with those things. Just as a sentence needs a noun and a verb, so libraries need resource products and action processes. Still another way to think of service is that it is intangible and transitory, in contrast to resources that can be stored.

Library services can be classified along several dimensions (Dumler and Skinner 2008):

- services that deal with resources, ranging from processing to facilitating intellectual access
- degree of labor intensity, ranging from checking out a paperback to providing reading advisory service
- degree of client contact, ranging from backroom cataloging to one-to-one reference guidance
- skill of the service provider, ranging from ten-minute training of a middle school volunteer to master's degree preparation for management skills

PRECONDITIONS FOR LIBRARY SERVICES

To determine library services, certain assumptions must be made and several preconditions must be in place. The most important assumption is that library services must support and align with both the school's mission and the SLP's mission. These missions are not limited to the official academic curriculum, but must also consider how to best serve the whole child and promote lifelong learning.

In terms of resources needed to provide services, the most important consideration is staffing. Many research studies highlight the need for a full-time team of at least one credentialed school librarian and one paraprofessional library worker. Although technically a library collection could be entirely digital, space would still be needed to enable the school community to view and use those resources. On a more profound level, the SLP must provide physical resources because knowledge is represented in many formats, and students must learn how to comprehend and manipulate those informational media. Thus, facilities are needed so that individuals can engage with resources, and people can engage with each other. Furthermore, those facilities need to be properly supervised and made accessible so that the resources can be used effectively. It should also be noted that those facilities and resources may require technical support—not only for the collection itself, but also for the administrative programs needed to provide services. Last, but not least, library services require funding in order to provide human and material resources.

As the SLP manager, you must identify the available and needed resources in order to determine what services are feasible to provide. First list baseline services, based on existing conditions, and then identify additional services that can be added when resources can be provided to support them.

WHAT SERVICES SHOULD THE LIBRARY PROGRAM PROVIDE?

Increasingly, schools are taking a systems approach to planning and implementation. That is, what inputs are necessary to result in desired outputs? If the ultimate outcome is student success, what does that look like in terms of the library program? The library team can start by observing users in action. What are concrete indicators of learning and achievement? Here is a starting list:

- engaged reading
- locating and using relevant resources in a variety of formats
- peer coaching and tutoring
- student groups editing a video
- teachers discussing curriculum while consulting professional periodicals
- students posting reviews onto the library web portal
- library aides creating learning stations

School community products such as newspapers, blogs, research papers, and debates might also be made possible because of library program efforts. The library team can also consult AASL standards and accreditation rubrics, "translating" them into behaviors and products evidenced in the library and elsewhere. The team should be sure to walk throughout the school site to capture evidence of library influence; taking photos is a good way to record these data.

Next, the library team can determine what library services lead to those concrete indicators of student success. Again, it should be noted that service impact can be direct or indirect. If the librarian suggests an online video tutorial that helps a student understand math, that would be a direct influence. If the librarian locates a local funding source for a science teacher so that chemistry equipment can be acquired, that would lead indirectly to student learning. In short, library services support the conditions for optimal learning and success.

An easy approach to identifying influential services is to examine school community products. For instance, you can review the bibliographies of students' research projects and read I-Search papers, which trace a student's research process. Did a student yearbook editor consult school archives maintained by the library? As an aid for a local production, did the French class critique a play provided by the library's video collection? Did the debate team's arguments depend on library resources procured in collaboration with the debate team advisor?

It should be noted that service may impact student success indirectly. For instance, when the school librarian conducts a faculty in-service on how to use subscription databases, teachers will be more likely to incorporate articles into their teaching and learning activities, which can in turn help students comprehend subject matter more deeply and perform better on tests. Therefore, it is important to trace back student achievement from the desired outcome to the experiences and people that lead to that result.

- What *competencies and dispositions* should students attain?
- What *curriculum* is offered? How closely does content align to academic content frameworks or industry standards? Does the curriculum incorporate technological skills, which may be aligned to national standards such as the International Society for Technology in Education (ISTE) (e.g., www.iste.org/standards)?
- What *organizational structures* are in place to facilitate instructional design: professional development, allocation of space, repositories to share lessons and best practice, ways to facilitate collaboration, scheduling for planning and learning?
- What *instructional strategies* are used? What kinds of learning activities do teachers provide students in order to ensure that there are sufficient opportunities to learn, practice, and demonstrate competence? How does the learning environment facilitate content knowledge and application?
- What *resources* are used to deliver the curriculum? Who determines which resources to incorporate? Do teachers have the skills to use those resources, and do they have the support to make sure resources are available and operational?
- What background, experiences, skills, and dispositions do *students* bring to the learning environment?

Thus, when determining services, deconstruct the actual design and implementation of learning activities into their composite elements to determine which actions lead to positive conditions for gaining competency. Does collaboration between the instructor and school librarians impact learning? Does the presence of a rich collection of current and relevant online resources correlate with content knowledge? In short, SLP managers should analyze the entire planning and implementation process, both for curricular and cocurricular experiences.

PRIORITIZING LIBRARY SERVICES

After listing possible library services, each service must be examined in terms of the materials, workload, and expertise needed to provide that service. In some cases, a service might not be worth the effort it requires, (e.g., cataloging websites), or might be not considered important by the rest of the school community (e.g., level 3 cataloging).

In chapter nine, table 9.1 illustrated a sample table of library services that noted the estimates for service time required, level of expertise, and priority. In most cases, you have the knowledge to complete this table, but it is wise to consult other library workers and peers at other libraries to ensure accurate, consistent, and reasonable expectations. The table can then serve as a database of information in order to develop a service "menu" when negotiating with administrators. Before those negotiations, you should work with the library staff and advisory group to develop some best-case service combinations that can optimize student and school outcomes.

Table 9.1 builds on the notion of cost-benefit analysis to determine which services to provide; another aspect that should be included in that table is who will be the beneficiary of each service. Another approach uses a marketing approach, which was introduced in chapter five, on communication. You can conduct a SWOT (strengths, weaknesses, opportunities, threats) analysis to determine what group is underrepresented in the library, such as mathematics teachers, or identify a niche service that no one else is providing, such as local referrals for teen recreational opportunities. In some cases, the SLP may provide a service, such as interlibrary loan, that has escaped the notice of the school community. Typically, marketing tries to leverage existing services, or provide services that use available resources, in order to attract more business.

Optimizing Services through Management

Prior chapters have discussed ways to manage material and human resources, so managing services combines those two entities. In a way, managing services resembles conducting an orchestra because services are usually interdependent at both the resource level and the action level. For instance, reserves service is only as good as collection development. Instruction is often impacted by technological expertise. Just as you can trace the influence of the library on student achievement by tracing back how student competence is based on learning experiences that depend on instructional design and available resources, so too can you track how one service builds on another. Such procedural sequencing is especially important when providing information services because materials may need to be ordered and processed before they can be used to answer informational needs.

Each library service must be monitored to make sure that adequate material and human resources can be allocated within a reasonable time frame for the service to be provided effectively. For example, whoever processes materials should notify you when supplies are running low. You need to keep track of software updates and upgrades, especially for integrated library management systems and school intranets. These upgrades may necessitate additional training for those library workers who deal with the software. When class assignments are given, make sure that resources are available; perhaps a pathfinder should be created, which involves dedicated time. In addition, unexpected situations such as paper jams and unscheduled class visits can impact service. In short, stable and dependable service depends on proactive efforts and timely responses to immediate needs.

As much as possible, maintain a weekly and monthly schedule for predictable service needs, such as system backups, supply inventory, display changes, budget review, and administrative reports. Also keep a binder or database of predictable class research assignments, noting the usual timing of class visits. In this way, resource needs can be anticipated, including when to update webliographies and tutorials. You might even list likely activities and deadlines throughout the year, such as orientation, peak research project months, and end-of-year functions.

Just as library services are interdependent, the library program's set of services are interdependent with the rest of the school's services. Therefore, keep the big picture in mind, and align services to the school's mission and optimize library service links with other services. For instance, the library can provide videotaping services for drama productions, or talk about digital citizenship when the school is set up as a polling station during an election. Library staff can help locate volunteer venues for students' community service requirements, which can strengthen library links with the community. In addition, keep in the school "loop" in order to discover when other services and resources may affect library services, such as budget cuts or the recruitment of technical support staff.

Service projects or initiatives, in particular, require careful coordination (Jessen 2010, 2012). Typically, a project tries to solve a problem or address a need, and may well be innovative. Projects are usually a break from the routine, and may be perceived as exhilarating or scary. A project may be small, requiring few resources and just a couple of volunteers, such as a community-based READ poster campaign. On the other hand, a project may be a complex endeavor that requires significant staff effort and time, such as establishing a library-based tutoring service. To develop the project master plan, identify tasks, responsible

Table 10.1

Gantt Chart

	Week 1	Week 2	Week 3	Week 4	Week 5	Week 6
Workshop program	Start		Speakers selected		Workshop materials done	Workshop held
Physical logistics		Room scheduled			Site and catering set	Site monitored
Registration		Target audience identified		Procedure set	Participants known	Registration confirmed
Publicity				Flyers made	Media contacted	Media monitored

persons, time frame, and milestones. In some cases, a project contract might be needed in order to specify jobs, budgets, and specifications. Table 10.1 is an example of a Gantt chart, which is a useful tool to organize this information.

Service quality depends on a number of factors: available resources, the service provider, and the client. For instance, a student might say, "The library doesn't have any books on my assignment topic," but that student might not have asked for assistance, or the library staff might not have taken steps to help. Perhaps the students didn't know how to use the OPAC or follow the shelving order. Perhaps the book was misshelved. And perhaps the library really doesn't have any print materials on that topic, which might indicate a lack of communication between the library staff and the classroom teacher. All along the way, a number of services are involved, and can be measured in terms of their effectiveness.

Service quality varies with each service provider. For instance, two different people might handle the circulation desk at some point, and their competence and personality may differ, so that a single assessment about circulation service may be insufficient; multiple measures are needed to take into account the perceptions of a variety of library users.

Therefore, in order to assess library service, you need to understand how users measure service quality. Particularly when the library staff think they are doing high-quality service and the users think that the service is poor, you have to reconcile those perceptual differences. In some cases, the user doesn't realize the limitations within which the library staff have to work, and in other cases the staff may be devoting valuable time to a detail that doesn't matter to the user. Nevertheless, basic criteria exist to judging service quality (Berry and Parsuraman 1991):

- reliability of performance and dependability
- tangible physical evidence of the service, such as the appearance of the library facility and equipment used
- responsiveness measured by staff willingness and readiness
- assurance that the staff is knowledgeable and able to elicit trust
- empathy and individual attention

According to Dumler and Skinner (2008), one of the main reasons for assessing service is to find ways to increase service productivity in terms of output per person per hour. To accomplish this goal, identify and measure those critical factors that must work properly in order to meet the service goals and objectives. For instance, to provide optimum physical access to print materials, resources have to be accurately and thoroughly catalogued, quickly and accurately shelved, and the shelving itself must be organized logically and well labeled. In addition, the OPAC needs to be easily accessible, and students have to be taught how to use it efficiently. Workflow charts can be an effective way to identify those key tasks and decision points.

In addition, solicit the input of the workers who perform each service: what helps them do their jobs, and what impediments stand in their way? Indeed, when workers are given discretion over their efforts, they are more likely to perform efficiently. Of course, that extra effort depends on the library worker's commitment to the library program, their colleagues, and the school community as a whole. In sum, show your commitment to the library workers by finding the best match between services and human resources.

Managing Specific Library Services

Chapter six, which dealt with managing resources, detailed services that ensure physical access to the library collection. Three other main library services address the intellectual access to resources: instruction, information services, and reading promotion. Each of these services involves specific management skills.

INSTRUCTIONAL SERVICES

SLP managers may design and deliver instruction independently or in collaboration with other teachers and support professionals. In either case, instructional services, from a single learning activity to an integrated information literacy curriculum that spans academic domains, must be managed. Instruction requires effective communication: from marketing to teaching and reinforcement and to assessment. As an SLP manager, you need to organize learning resources for handy retrieval, use, and assessment. You also must document processes and results. Instruction may also require technical or administrative support. Fundamentally, you should plan, implement, and assess instructional services as part of the overall management of the school library program.

Managing instructional services involves several dimensions:

- Preconditions: the learning environment (e.g., furniture, space configuration, power, Internet connectivity, lighting, sound levels, accessibility, operating hours), material resources including equipment, access to digital resources, staffing availability and expertise, school schedule and planning time
- Curriculum: student learning outcomes, knowledge of formal and informal curriculum, information literacy curriculum, curricular philosophy, school norms for multidisciplinary and cross-curricular learning activities
- Documentation: curriculum, lesson and learning activity plans, student handouts, learning objects, and knowledge management repositories
- Communication: publicity about instructional services, library orientation, scheduling, collaborative instructional design and delivery, and learning aids
- Use of resources: library collection, access to other resources, pathfinders and webliographies, print and digital reference guides, technology access and support
- Assessment: information-seeking behaviors, resources and their use, the learning environment, instructional design, teaching strategies, collaborative processes, and learning

In those cases where the library program includes an explicit curriculum, you will have to deal with the curricular issues of student learning outcomes, standards, curriculum development and approval, selection of instructional materials, equipment needs, scheduling class times and locations, instructional design and delivery, differentiated instruction and accommodations for students with special needs, assessment, grading, class management, and communication with families. In addition, curriculum may also need to be mapped to site graduation requirements, state standards, or national standards such as Common Core State Standards or ISTE's technology standards. Formal instructional time also impacts the availability of school librarians to provide services to the rest of the school community. In that respect, collaborative instruction at point of need may be a more effective use of professional school library expertise.

INFORMATION SERVICES

Information and reference services remains a core library function. Such services may take the form of static information services such as web portals and informational documents, as well as just-in-time interactions. The Reference and User Services Association (RUSA) of the American Library Association defines reference work as including "reference transactions and other activities that involve the creation, management, and assessment of information or research resources, tools, and services" (RUSA 2008, 1), and further defines reference transactions as "information consultations in which library staff recommend, interpret, evaluate, and/or use information resources to help others to meet particular information needs. Reference transactions do not include formal instruction or exchanges that provide assistance with locations, schedules, equipment, supplies, or policy statements" (RUSA 2008, 1).

Web portals can provide information services in several ways. Some school libraries merely link to a district, library system, or commercial web portal. Some websites address a number of objectives (e.g., library service, facilities, reference, reading, curriculum support, technology literacy), providing a few links for each area. Some web portals have very specific objectives, such as research steps, and may even focus on a few targeted subjects, such as science or social studies; this approach works best for magnet schools that can link to each other. Each objective and audience requires attention, so school librarians tend to link to a few high-quality resource directories such as Internet Public Library, KidsClick, and Kathy Shrock's website. The library portal can also serve as first-line reference help through links to pathfinders, web tutorials, and a customized FAQ page based on typical queries.

The library portal can also incorporate online interactive reference service, be it simply an e-mail address or a link to an existing information service, in order to provide just-in-time help. It should be noted that remote online reference service requires several management level decisions (Kasowitz, Bennett, and Lankes 2000): fees and fee structures, availability and accessibility, interface requirements, technical support, acceptable turnaround time, staff expertise (especially in communicating with children), quality control, and types of queries to be handled (e.g., reference, general homework, research projects).

The core of interactive information service, though, consists of face-to-face interaction (usually in the library, although it could occur via web conferencing to other areas of the school). RUSA has developed standards for reference and information services librarians and those in associated fields (www.ala.org/ rusa/resources/guidelines), which can be used to guide and assess practice. At the very least, information services should: anticipate user needs and encourage user awareness of potential resources; answer information queries competently; provide user information aids in appropriate formats; network with other libraries and make appropriate referrals; publicize information services; develop and make available its information service policy; and use community needs assessments to provide appropriate information services. Information service personnel should be knowledgeable, personable, and effective communicators. When dealing with young people's information needs, library workers should treat them respectfully and age-appropriately, paying special attention to youth's cognitive level and emotional state.

READING-PROMOTION SERVICES

As an SLP manager, you should have a strategic plan for developing reading-promotion services, with clearly defined objectives and coordination with other existing reading efforts. This plan should start by assessing current reading efforts and expectations in the school community, and then determining what resources and staffing are available to provide complementary reading-promotion services. At the very least, library services should highlight how reading can meet personal informational and recreational needs of the school community. You should also assess community assets and services that promote reading, such as public libraries, recreational centers, youth groups, and religious institutions. These venues can be publicized by the school library staff, and you can collaborate with these entities to optimize reading promotion.

As you identify gaps in reading-promotion efforts, research how other school libraries successfully promote reading. What resources and staffing were needed? What strategies did library staff employ? How was impact assessed? Based on the literature review and analysis of the local situation, plan and implement reading-promotion services. Throughout the process, document and assess the library workers' efforts to optimize service impact.

Farmer and Stricevic's 2011 synthesis of reading-promotion research identified several promising reading-promotion practices:

- Promotion communication methods: displays, posters, media announcements, social media, digital storytelling
- Reading-related products: bookmarks, reviews, bibliographies
- Programs: story hours, contests, speakers, workshops
- Reading-related services: readers' advisory, book clubs, tutoring, reference service, collection development, class instruction, professional development

They also identified library program preconditions needed to provide reading-promotion services: a high-quality accessible library collection that meets the interests and needs of the school community, an organized and welcoming learning environment, and competent approachable library workers.

Bringing It Down to You

What is your image of the school library in terms of services? What do you imagine that the school community could accomplish with the help of the library's services? Do you see these actions occurring in the library itself, in the classroom, at home?

What services can the library provide that no one else can? This may be a hard question to answer honestly. Theoretically, classroom teachers can promote reading, teach information literacy and research skills, and help students

Food for Thought

Managing Library Services without a Physical Library

Is it possible to provide library services without a physical library? Because a central physical collection is more effective, and a central learning commons optimizes intellectual interaction, it is possible to provide library services without a physical library.

These days, access to information can be more valuable than ownership of information. Increasingly, ebooks are complementing and supplementing print items. Library workers can also provide interlibrary loan services to expand access to needed information. The library catalog can serve as a federated repository of resources, located throughout the school campus as well as beyond. The library portal can include digital pathfinders and learning objects that support the curriculum. Indeed, SLP managers can serve as chief information officer, managing the school community's knowledge base, including curriculum, learning activities, and student products.

In terms of information services, including instruction, you can provide just-in-time help online through instant messaging and online conferencing. For routine information needs, you can create online FAQs, thus focusing on more in-depth reference help. On a more systematic basis, you can be embedded in courses using learning management systems and other online links. Without a physical library, you can schedule class visits easily, and coteach in various learning environments. At the faculty level, you can codevelop curriculum and provide in-service professional development.

Similarly, reading promotion can be conducted throughout the school using publications such as posters, bibliographies, bookmarks, newsletters, multimedia presentations, blogs, podcasts, and videos. Library workers can create displays in classrooms, halls, and other meeting places. You can also provide booktalks and other reading-promotion presentation and events throughout the school and online via conferencing tools. In effect, the entire school may be considered the library.

be effective producers of knowledge. Some classrooms have Internet-connected computers and in-house print collections that teachers can guide their students to use. Where librarians excel is in systematically collecting, organizing, and making widely available relevant resources for the school community. They are also experts in locating information within resources, and providing targeted instruction in the effective use of those resources. School librarians are also uniquely positioned to work with the entire school community across the curriculum, and so can make connections more than teachers.

What services do you need to do yourself? This is another hard question because even though you may like to do displays, for example, others can do that competently. You should train others and delegate service to them as much as possible, and devote yourself to those services that require professional expertise. Furthermore, even though you think that a particular library service, such as the book talk, is vital, the rest of the school community might not agree; so unless you can convince them of its importance, you may have to give that service a lower priority—or find a more cost-effective way to provide it.

As noted in chapter nine, you should encourage students not only to take advantage of library services but also lend a hand in providing those services. Just as community service helps students become more aware of their community's functions, achieve a greater sense of responsibility, and feel more connected to society, so too can encouraging and supporting students as they participate in library service offer those same societal benefits. Moreover, one of the main reasons that individuals become librarians and other information professionals is because of early service in the library. You might well grow your own eventual replacement!

References

American Association of School Librarians. 2009. *Empowering Learners: Guidelines for Library Media Programs.* Chicago, IL: American Library Association.

Berry, L., and A. Parsuraman. 1991. *Marketing Services: Competing through Quality.* New York, NY: Free Press.

Dumler, M., and S. Skinner. 2008. *A Primer on Management.* Mason, OH: South-Western.

Farmer, L., and I. Stricevic. 2011. *Using Research to Promote Literacy and Reading.* Hague: Intl. Federation of Library Associations.

Jessen, 2012. *Project Leadership Step by Step: Part I,* 2nd ed. London, England: Ventus Publishing.

———. 2010. *Project Leadership Step by Step: Part II.* London, England: Ventus Publishing.

Kasowitz, A., B. Bennett, and D. Lankes. 2000. "Quality Standards for Digital Reference Consortia." *Reference and User Services Quarterly* 39: 355–61.

Reference and Users Services Association. 2008. *Definitions of Reference.* Chicago, IL: American Library Association.

11

Managing Communication

S CHOOL LIBRARIANS CONSTANTLY LINK INFORMATION WITH people. As an intermediary, school librarians (SLs) aim to facilitate that connection through effective communication. In some cases, school librarians set up the communications channel, such as a library catalog or signage, to provide the conditions for direct resource-to-human interface. In other cases, school librarians actively engage in the communications process through instruction or interviews. In still other cases, school librarians have a message they want to communicate. Indeed, while a well-managed school library program (SLP) should speak for itself, it takes proactive public relations to get that story out so the entire school community can take advantage of what the library program has to offer. In any case, as an SLP manager, you impact the communication efforts; therefore, effective communication skills are essential.

What are those skills? Certainly, basic oral and written skills are needed, and active listening is a must. But in today's world, communication skills call for more sophisticated means of communications planning and assessment. Communication as a management function requires a planned set of objectives and strategies, careful assessment of available resources, and ongoing attention to ensure that the right message is sent to the right people in order to make the intended impact. Both one-way and two-way communication must be considered, depending on the desired outcome; certainly, the maturation of social media requires new management skills as well as technical expertise. Additionally, you need to identify the appropriate format for communication, leveraging the potential of different technologies—and their costs.

The impact of effective communication is obvious: increased user satisfaction, informed decisions, positive action, improved services, and greater professional fulfillment. Likewise, poor communication can result in lost users, lost revenues, and lost jobs. Because school librarianship is basically a service profession, effective communication is a core activity. This chapter provides tools to help you manage the communication function for the best outcome.

A Communication Model

Understanding how communication works will help you manage the process and results. Fundamentally, communication deals with two parties, and reflects a dynamic between the internal and external life. In purposeful communication, a person's goal or intent drives the process. That inner drive is externalized because the goal requires another person's response. The internal message or content frames the goal, which is externalized via some kind of medium. That shaped message is sent within a context of time and space with the aim of being received by an identified audience. Hopefully, that audience accepts, comprehends, and acts on the message as the sender intended. Only when the originator gets some kind of feedback can it truly be said that communication has occurred. All along the way, interference can occur, from expressing an idea inarticulately to distracting the audience so they are totally unaware of the incoming message. As an SLP manager, you need to evaluate each step of the communications process in order to predict possible glitches and strategize for optimum outcomes. Evaluating a completed communication cycle enables you to modify SLP goals and efforts for the next time.

The following example shows how the communication model guides communication planning.

1. Goal: persuade middle school teachers to incorporate fiction when teaching history
2. Target audience: middle school teachers
3. Message: historical fiction provides a rich reading experience for students that helps them to connect with history on an emotional level, and presents a research-based context for history
4. Medium: faculty in-service, including presentation of sample booktalks, display of sample books, sample lessons for teachers to analyze, bibliography handout

5. Context (time, money, space, environment, culture, situation): forty-five minutes during a department faculty meeting, ideally in the library; printing costs for handouts (also available online on the library web portal)
6. Response and action: distribute teacher exam books, discuss learning activities, and design at least one learning activity that includes historical fiction
7. Evaluation: degree and quality of participation, lesson analysis quality, book-borrowing statistics, follow-up learning activities that incorporate historical fiction
8. Modification: depends on evaluation results

ISSUES OF CONTENT

What's the idea? Ideas are internal; information is external. In a way, "naked" ideas are "dressed" in some kind of container or package. Marshall McLuhan asserted that the "medium is the message": that the packaging, the format, shapes the information. For instance, the movie version of a story differs from its written original, and a graphic novel differs from a verbal narrative of the same story. Each format has its unique characteristics, which express information uniquely. It is important to understand how to translate an idea in light of its communication channel, and to decide what architecture or interface is the most effective way to structure and communicate information. Translating a brilliant concept into a compelling documented message can be daunting today because so many tools are available. Here are some critical features of different communication formats, noting how to apply them most appropriately.

Written communication can vary widely: from memos to reports, from flyers to manuals, from periodicals to grants. For directions, "dense" information, and permanent records, written documents are hard to beat. Written communication remains the mainstay of digital communication as well, even in interactive reference sessions.

Visual communication ranges from posters to displays, from pictures to photos, from signage to charts, from icons to diagrams. Particularly in pluralistic societies, visual communication is key. Because numerical data can be difficult to interpret, providing data analysis using visuals can optimize understanding. It should be noted that some visual principles are universal but other elements may be culturally defined. For example, photos have an instantaneous, lifelike quality. Diagrams can simplify concepts or processes.

Audio-based communication is surprisingly varied and robust, thanks to technological advances. Speaking remains the principal method of interaction, yet people still will require training on how to convey their messages effectively.

Several stand-alone products capture and preserve audio communication: cassettes, radio, and podcasting. One of the benefits of these tools is that they can be edited and recombined to fit different communication goals.

Multimedia products offer the most nuanced and realistic kind of communication because they can combine text, visual, and sound elements. At this point, authoring tools such as PowerPoint have become ubiquitous, yet more attention should be given to ways to create convincing slides. Video, too, has become highly democratized so that many people can simply point a camcorder or webcam and record actions, and then quickly post the results online. On the other hand, a well-planned video session and careful post-production editing can result in effective communication. The Internet offers an open-ended environment in which to communicate a wide variety of messages in different ways, from e-mail broadcasts and screencasts to interactive social media. One of the most challenging aspects of Internet communication is choosing the best technique to create a specific message.

COMMUNICATION INTENT

What is the intent of the communication? Is it to inform someone, either in response to a query or as a self-initiated desire to share ideas? Does the originator want to start a communications loop in order to garner information? Is the originator trying to persuade the targeted audience—either to accept the originator's goal or to influence the audience's own intentions? It is also important to determine the basis for communicating information: to attain the originator's objective, or to *respond* to an audience's need. While you may develop SLP goals based on others' initiatives, the locus of intent makes a difference in content formation. Deciding what to say, in short, needs to examine the dynamic of the private originator and the potential audience.

The content itself can dictate the communication channel. For example, if the intent is to explain a process, a graphic or audiovisual communications channel may be the best choice. For instance, because video combines sound and moving image instantaneously, it would be a good choice to record and convey current events. A dialogue might be best conveyed using audio-recording. Some types of writing are more formal than others, so even within a format there may be variations. The subject matter can also influence the communications channel chosen; for example, if consumerism is the theme, then a mass media channel such as television might be appropriate. If the message conveys emotion, then the channel should facilitate an emotional response (e.g., images that convey compelling stories).

If the message is part of a larger communication enterprise, such as site or school district, then the communication channel might be predetermined, such as a newsletter for families. In some cases, the same channel should be used to provide consistency; in other cases, a variety of communications channels can enrich the intended message and appeal to the wider audience.

AUDIENCE FACTOR

As an SLP manager, you must identify the intended audience to determine how best to communicate. In general, use the same communication channel, or medium, as preferred by the intended audience. For instance, on a very pragmatic level, if the principal prefers to exchange information while talking in the hall, rather than via virtual or written memo, then use that method of communication (but remember to document the conversation as soon as possible for future reference). The choices have widened at the same time that mass media has been able to narrowly target their audience; likewise, you will need to analyze how specific groups use media—do they get their information from a poster or a Twitter feed, a weekly school newspaper or a viral YouTube video? The current digital media scene emphasizes interaction, immediacy, and instant gratification. Fortunately, digital media can often be easily repurposed to facilitate both variety and consistency in message making. In choosing communication channels, do not limit yourself to one medium, but rather "a variety of coordinated communications [media that] will send the same message to a target audience" (Marsh, Guth, and Short 2008, 16).

The audience factor is also crucial because the human element is needed in order to get the receiver to *act* on the information. During this interface, body language and unconscious communication may facilitate or hinder the communications cycle, so you should know how to identify those human interface factors and to optimize their impact. In an online environment, interface encompasses both the technical connection as well as the virtual human behind the screen; online reference service, for instance, has to compensate for lack of most senses by questioning and coaching in clear, unambiguous, and accepting ways.

In analyzing the audience, first consider their role: as a decision maker, as an influencer of other people, or as a user or consumer. In school settings, those roles are typically designated as administrator, decider, teacher and parent influencer, and student user. Next, gather relevant demographic data, noting the degree of homogeneity of the groups: socioeconomic status, gender, and race. What are the audience's interests, values, experiences, and networks? SLP managers gather much of this information through observations and interaction in the library and elsewhere in the school and community. School publications and displays also reveal characteristics of each audience.

In gathering such information about the audience, also identify the medium and communication patterns of each targeted audience (Plevyak and Heaston 2001). If the school allows cell phones (and even if it doesn't), students are likely to be seen texting and checking social media throughout the day, so you should incorporate such media in communicating with students. What media channels do administrators use to communicate with teachers? Probably e-mail, flyers, and face-to-face meetings, so incorporate those communication strategies. However, teachers are likely to use additional media in communicating with each other, such as wikis and informal break times, so try to get access to those more informal mechanisms as well.

How does this audience analysis impact communication strategies? Consider promoting a culture of reading. For the student audience, you might booktalk in classes or create podcast, blog about new books, have students create public service announcements about reading, hold read-ins or poetry slams, advise lunchtime or virtual book clubs, invite authors to speak in person or online, or have character costume contests. For the parent audience, you might hold an evening family workshop, speak at a parent-teacher organization meeting, write articles for the parent newsletter, start a parent reading corner, or hold a book fair during open house. For the teacher audience, you might bring new books to a faculty meeting, hold a kaffeeklatch about professional reading, collaboratively design learning activities that foster reading, collaborate with reading specialists on an in-service workshop, or set up a book request process to facilitate teacher participation in collection development. For the administrator audience, you might help write a grant to acquire more reading materials, provide research findings about effective reading strategies, or help plan a schoolwide reading initiative. The underlying message is to promote a reading culture, but the specific communication—and associated actions—may differ by audience.

It should be noted that internal communication differs from external communication for several reasons: extent of shared knowledge, frequency of interaction, political and organizational implications, and so on. For instance, among the library's own workers, communication is likely to be more informal and at point-of-need. However, written policies and procedures are still needed in order to provide consistent high-quality service. Additionally, if library worker hours vary, then regular meetings and posted announcements and memos should be used to ensure that everyone gets the same message. Additionally, internal messages themselves may be unique within the group, such as setting and reviewing short-term group goals, praising efforts and accomplishments, socializing, and quelling rumors and gossip (Reid 1999). In contrast, in examining the school's external communication process, you are likely to find more formal messages, mechanisms and procedures, which may require administrative preapproval.

PLANNING

In planning a communication effort, you must contextualize the SLP message. Assess SLP needs as well as the needs of related organizations and those who will receive the communication. Know how to market SLP communication by determining what factors will hook the audience and get ideas across effectively. In short, planning should mirror the communications model. Additionally, consider developing campaigns as a series of communication cycles. In this way, the intended messages can be reinforced and supplemented for more substantial goals. Here is a simple template for planning a communication piece.

- What: state the purpose of the message and its role within the library's communication plan.
- Why: justify the choice of communications channel.
- Who: describe the audience.
- When: set the time line for dissemination.
- Where: identify specific locations for its dissemination.
- How: determine how to measure the communication's effectiveness.

The message should capture the audience's attention, hold its interest, arouse desire, and inspire action (i.e., close the deal). Whenever possible, test the drafted message on a member of the target audience, ideally an associated library worker (e.g., a student or a parent).

Consider developing a "media kit" which can serve as an orientation for incoming teachers, potential workers, school boards, organizations, or media outlets. Media kits typically include a news release about a timely event or accomplishment such as Tech Week, a new database, a staff award, or a major donation. In addition, these kits include:

- A backgrounder (similar to an encyclopedia entry) gives the history and overview of the library and its program.
- Fact sheets can be written like news stories or they can present specific facts about the library program, such as mission statement, list of services, statistics, and staff information.
- Photo opportunity sheets resemble news releases in that they promote an event that has visual appeal, such as a Read Across America library event with a local politician or entertainer serving as the guest reader. Although not a photo opportunity sheet, the media kit might include a few high-quality images that tell a compelling story about the library, such as a student teaching a senior citizen how to use social media.
- Sample library publications such as the current newsletter or pathfinder; showcase value-added products.
- A library bookmark might be appropriate, especially if student-created.
- The SLP manager's business card adds a professional touch.

These kits may be packaged in a folder with internal pockets, as a tabbed folder that the teacher can put into a file cabinet, burned onto a DVD, or uploaded onto a thumb drive. The media kit should also be included on the library web portal.

Unlike a single communications piece or media kit, a communications campaign is a strategic coordinated plan that involves a collection of communication activities to achieve a specific goal. The time frame might be short, such as promoting a library contest, or longer-term to promote digital citizenship. As with other communication efforts, a communications campaign has to identify its stakeholders, and craft its message with each type of stakeholder in mind. However, the overarching message should be clear, consistent, and memorable. Here are the steps of a communication campaign (Movement Advancement Project 2008).

1. Clearly state the specific campaign objective or goal: what are you trying to accomplish?
2. Determine the time frame and approach.
3. Identify your target audience: whom should you target to reach your goal?
4. Determine your key message: what will attract, engage, and move your audience to act?
5. Identify your media tools: how will you reach your audience?
6. Identify your spokespeople: who will your audience trust and like?
7. Create a budget.
8. Identify specific tasks, associated people to do the tasks, and a timetable for tasks. Note how one task may impact another.
9. Decide how to evaluate the campaign.

Some useful communication plan templates are found at:

- Microsoft Office (http://office.microsoft.com/en-us/word-help/ creating-a-marketing-communications-plan-HA001168402.aspx)
- The W. K. Kellogg Foundation (www.wkkf.org/knowledge-center/ resources/2006/01/template-for-strategic-communications-plan .aspx)
- The World Wildlife Fund (http://assets.panda.org/downloads/wwf _communications_strategy_template_t_.doc)
- You Gotta Be Kidding Campaign (www.gacampaigncentral.org/ PlanYourCampaign/TemplatesSamples/tabid/72/Default.aspx)

CULTURAL ISSUES
As noted in chapter nine on managing people, cultural differences should be acknowledged and appreciated. As societies become increasingly diverse, you must make sure that all communication is respectful of different cultures and is sensitive to English learners. Here are a few factors to remember when producing and conveying information, based on Sarkodie-Manash (2000).

- Get to know the audience; obtain and share demographic information with library workers.
- In all communication, use plain English and short sentences, and avoid idioms. Rephrase and simplify statements. Define new terms. Use meaningful gestures.
- If using audio files or online speech, speak clearly, slowly, and without an accent.
- Use repetition, paraphrasing, and summaries.
- Focus attention on essential vocabulary needed for the subject matter. Provide bilingual glossaries and visual references.
- Use visual aids and graphic organizers to help the audience understand content organization and relationships.
- If you can't understand someone, don't pretend you do.
- If possible, communicate in the learner's primary language. Pair students linguistically. Consider providing resources in primary languages and using translators for presentations to groups whose first language is not English.

Check the readability of written sources, and locate materials that include visual or aural cues. It should be noted that some images may be unrecognizable, demeaning, or have different meanings to difference cultures.

COMMUNICATION CONFRONTATIONS
Hopefully, the library workers have a productive and professional relationship. However, those workers may well interact with people who may be difficult in specific circumstances. At the very least, workers should feel comfortable speaking with you about any such instances, and describing the situation and how it was handled. Over time, you can document trends and effective ways to deal with troublesome users. In some cases, the problem stems from library practices that should be examined and improved. In other cases, personality clashes occur, which may be situation-specific or because one or both of the participants are having an off day. An isolated incident can be ignored, but repeated confrontations require intervention. In any case, difficult interactions can serve as opportunities for improving user perceptions and library services.

Some preventative measures lower the likelihood of confrontations.

- Treat each person fairly and with respect. Validate each one as an individual, and be sympathetic.
- Provide a safe, trusting, positive, and open library atmosphere.
- Establish and communicate clear, consistent expectations. Enforce expectations consistently.
- Differentiate between attitudes and actions, between anger and confrontation.
- Know when to pick battles and when to ignore behaviors.

Rhea Rubin's 2010 book *Defusing the Angry Patron* provides excellent advice for dealing with angry individuals and stressful situations.

- Listen actively. Don't interrupt, but wait until the person is done with his or her complaint.
- Focus on the problem, not the person. Define the problem in terms of need. Address each problem separately.
- Try not to argue or feed into their anger.
- Stay calm and professional. Take your time to respond.
- Know yourself, and your "buttons." Pay attention to personal signs of stress, such as a higher pitched voice, tightened muscles, and other paralanguage. Breathe deeply and try to relax. Sometimes it is better to take a breather than confront the patron immediately.
- Don't be afraid to apologize. Showing that you are on the patron's side can help reach a solution.
- Translate accusations into a request for a service that you can provide.
- Be assertive. If you have to disagree, be diplomatic. One useful tactic is "fogging": accepting criticism whether it is accurate or not by repeating the phrase back to the complainer (e.g., "Yes, I just don't understand.").
- Give the patron personal space, and walk away if you sense danger.
- On the phone, speak slowly and in a deeper voice. Hold the phone an inch away from your mouth to avoid sounding loud or slurred. Avoid transferring the patron or putting him or her on hold. Give the caller two warnings before hanging up.
- In virtual communications, use short sentences and quick responses. Don't use ALL CAPS.

Here is Rubin's step-by-step formula for dealing with unacceptable behavior (73).

1. Give a good faith statement that indicates that you are in control and are giving the patron the benefit of the doubt: "This is very frustrating, isn't it?"
2. Quickly define the problem behavior. Reprove the behavior, not the person. "Ripping up a magazine. . ."
3. Briefly explain how the behavior impacts your ability to provide library service before allowing the patron to respond.
4. Suggest ways to address the anger, such as moving to a separate quiet room, calling in another person, or waiting until the patron is calm enough to listen.
5. Work towards a solution that addresses the patron's need within the library's parameters.
6. Be assertive, using "I" statements.
7. If a solution is not found, let the patron choose whether to stop the disruptive behavior or leave.

Dealing with difficult people can take its toll on anyone. It can be hard to focus on the problem rather than on emotions. Remember this reality as it impacts your own library staff. While it can be hard to control another person, the library worker can try to control his or her own responses to personal emotions. Being aware of one's own body and changing its position can diffuse stress. For instance, raised shoulders limit blood to the brain, which decreases the ability to think, so even lowering the shoulders can help sharpen problem-solving ability. After a difficult situation, the worker might go for a short walk, or do a little journal writing. When workers keep calm, and successfully resolve the situation, they should feel proud of themselves. You can also praise their coping behavior. With continued success in dealing with stressful situations, library workers become more professional, and confrontations are likely to decline in number and degree.

MEASURING THE IMPACT

Communication is used to accomplish some goal, be it to inform or to persuade. In some cases, it is easy to determine the impact of communication: the goal is reached. Yet there may be various reasons for that success. Perhaps more importantly, when communication is *not* effective, you need to determine the reason. One of the best methods is to work backwards from the ideal response or action all the way back to the original idea. It should be noted, though, that the entire communications cycle has greater impact than any one of its steps because of the *relationships* between each step. In any case, gather relevant data throughout the communication cycle, and analyze each factor in order to maximize the end results. By measuring the impact of communication, you can systemize the program's communication efforts to optimize the entire process. Remember that you do not have to produce all the communication; you should manage those efforts.

Here are some criteria for evaluating the effectiveness of different types of communication products, relative to their format.

Presentation Criteria
- There is clear evidence of connection to the target message, and the presentation includes frequent references to facts, concepts, and properly documented resources.
- The sequence of information is logical and intuitive, menus and/or paths to all information are clear and direct, and information is well presented and accurate.
- Subject matter knowledge is evident throughout. All information is relevant and correct.
- The combination of multimedia elements with words and ideas enhances communication and persuasion. Navigation from slide to slide is consistently easy and logical.
- The flow provides a logical sequence of ideas.
- The presenter engages the audience in interesting and thoughtful ways, prompting the audience to think critically and respond appropriately.

Newsletter Criteria
- Each article establishes a clear purpose in its lead paragraph and demonstrates a clear understanding of the topic.
- The details in the articles are clear, effective, and vivid.
- The newsletter looks professional. Columns are justified and separated by consistent gutters. There is adequate space between articles. All articles have headlines and captions that capture the reader's attention and accurately describe the content.
- Graphics are attractive, well-cropped, and clearly related to the articles they illustrate.
- No spelling errors remain after one or more people (in addition to the typist) have read and corrected the newsletter.

Video Criteria
- Information is well presented, clear, and accurate throughout.
- Images are relevant and complement the text. Each image is cited in the text and identified. The number of images is appropriate.
- Effects are varied, yet cohesive, and significantly enrich the presentation.
- Grammar and spelling are flawless, and the flow provides a logical pathway of ideas.

- The style is consistent and engaging throughout.

Multimedia Criteria
- The presentation is clearly connected to the library program, and includes frequent references to facts, concepts, and properly documented resources.
- The sequence of information is logical and intuitive, and menus and/or paths to information are clear and direct. Information is well presented, clear, and correct throughout.
- Subject matter knowledge is evident throughout. All information is relevant and accurate.
- The combination of multimedia elements with words and ideas takes communication and persuasion to a very high level.
- Grammar and spelling are flawless.
- The flow provides a logical pathway of ideas.

Website Criteria
- All necessary content is included, and is accurate and cohesive.
- The site presents an exciting and engaging view of the library's purpose.
- The web portal is easy to use.
- Site implementation demonstrates an understanding of the purpose and use of a library web portal.
- The website has an inviting, logical page and portal structure and is easy to navigate.
- Visual elements and layout work well together esthetically.
- All technical elements work correctly.
- Links have been checked.
- The site complies with ADA.

Face-to-Face Workshop Criteria
- All content is communicated at the appropriate level of complexity, well organized, and logically sequenced.
- All resources for the attendees are useful and professional.
- Concepts and practice are well balanced.
- The workshop facilitator is well prepared and knowledgeable.
- The facilitator engages and interacts well with all attendees.
- The workshop climate is conducive to learning and interaction.
- All attendees participate actively and appropriately.
- Pacing and length are appropriate for the attendees.
- The physical site is comfortable.

Webinar Criteria

- All content is communicated at the appropriate level of complexity, well organized, and logically sequenced.
- All content is useful.
- Concepts and applications are well balanced.
- The webinar facilitator is articulate, well prepared, and knowledgeable.
- The webinar facilitator introduces him- or herself and encourages group socialization.
- The webinar facilitator engages and interacts well with all attendees.
- The workshop climate is conducive to learning and interaction.
- All attendees participate actively and appropriately.
- The webinar's pacing and length are appropriate for the attendees.
- All technical aspects have been resolved before the webinar.

In addition to assessing the message, you will also need to evaluate the communicator, who could be any of the library's workers.

Communication Instrument   (by permission of Jennifer Bello)

Please rate the library worker's performance on each of the three communication types (oral, written, and graphical/visual communication).

ORAL COMMUNICATION

Please rate the person's communication skills over the course of the semester/year during public speaking opportunities (to inform or to persuade). Use the scale below to assess the person's ability to perform the selected oral communication criteria:

Poor		Average		Superior	No Opportunity to Evaluate
1	2	3	4	5	N/A

1. Organizes content concisely and logically.
2. Presents a professional demeanor appropriate to the audience and situation.
3. Speaks clearly and loudly as appropriate to the condition.
4. Achieves rapport with the audience.
5. Varies vocal tone and pattern.
6. Uses appropriate audiovisual materials and other technology to support the presentation.

7. Effectively responds to questions and comments.

8. Uses audience-appropriate vocabulary, content, and style.

WRITTEN COMMUNICATION

Please rate the person's communication skills over the course of the semester/year during writing opportunities. Use the scale below to assess the person's ability to perform the selected written communication criteria:

1. Synthesizes materials into appropriate presentational types.

2. Organizes research material to support an original thesis.

3. Presents ideas and arguments clearly, logically, and with an appropriate balance of textual and graphical materials.

4. Uses appropriate grammar, style, and form.

GRAPHICAL/VISUAL COMMUNICATION

Please rate the person's communication skills over the course of the semester/year during opportunities to present ideas through the use of data-rich graphics. Use scale below to assess the person's ability to perform the selected graphical/visual communication criteria:

Poor   Average   Superior   No Opportunity to Evaluate

(1)——(2)——(3)——(4)——(5)   (N/A)

1. Expresses ideas by means of appropriate visual and graphical representations.

2. Uses graphical and visual techniques to appropriately display data.

3. Uses appropriate symbolism when presenting graphical and visual concepts.

4. Selects presentation methods that are appropriate to the concepts or data being presented.

5. Uses graphical and visual techniques to properly present multi-dimensional data or concepts.

Marketing

What is marketing? How does it differ from public relations (PR) or advocacy? PR focuses on long-term interaction between an organization and its publics, while marketing is a management function that focuses on more immediate products and services that respond to consumer wants and needs; the core is economic exchange. In 2007, the American Marketing Association defined marketing as "the activity, set of institutions, and processes for creating, communicating, delivering, and exchanging offerings that have value for customers, clients, partners, and society at large" (1). Marketing is often confused with the idea of sales or selling. *Selling* focuses on the needs of the *seller; marketing* on the needs of the *client* or *stakeholder. Advocacy* seeks to change attitudes, policies, positions or practices by particular groups or persons.

Why do SLPs need marketing? The public has so many information choices that it may be unaware of potentially well-matched options. Because the role of the school library is sometimes unclear, school librarians need to define their value. In so doing, they should examine their potential client market, or their "publics." In addition, as the local school site, education in general, and the public expectations change, school librarians should respond in a timely manner in order to remain relevant. Marketing provides a systematic process for identifying and delivering optimal products and services. This process also improves the profession as a whole and increases its value.

Before you can market school libraries, you must conduct market research: gathering and analyzing data about the SLP, its publics, the school organization, and the current set of circumstances facing the library program.

PUBLICS AND MARKETS

In order for SLPs to add value to their publics, you first must identify their publics, or market. At the school site level, the primary public is the school community, which is internal. It may be subdivided by function, age, and interest. Secondary publics for school libraries typically include local schools, libraries, and other youth-serving agencies. Intervening or influencing publics, those entities that can help send a message to another public, should also be identified; typical members of that public include administrators, parents, other librarians, local bookstores, and media. It should be noted that in today's digital society, anyone using social media can assume that role, including students. According to Guth and Marsh (2012), for each public or market segment you must determine:

- how each influences the organization's ability to achieve its goals
- its opinion of the organization
- what its stake or value is relative to the organization

- who its opinion leaders and decision-makers are
- its demographics
- its psychographics (e.g., their political leanings, religion, attitudes, values)

Because you know what the school library program can offer, you can determine which market to target. A SWOT analysis (detailed in chapter five) provides useful information about needs and opportunities. If you want to reach the widest audience—an approach called mass marketing—try to find an issue or value that is the common denominator for everyone. Alternatively, you can focus on a few key market segments to provide more specific products or services. In general, SLP managers should segment markets (i.e., potential users) by age or type of use: parents who want to volunteer at the library, reluctant readers, techies, manga fans. Typically, an organization has resources or services that are underused or undervalued that it wants to promote. Perhaps it sees a target user market potential that has previously ignored it. In general, you should try to go to the biggest bang for the buck, to get the best return for the effort.

MARKETING STRATEGY

Why do marketing? To get results! Most libraries focus on managing key relationships and activities, but they might also have social responsibility goals (e.g., providing positive reading experiences to students with special needs).

Marketing objectives are based on clear priorities of the school library program and its goals—those deemed critical for the success of the program. Objectives set should be specific, measurable and realistic.

- Strategy: The chosen strategy should position marketing efforts in relation to the target audience. SLP managers will then need to determine the relevant mixture of resources to achieve objectives.
- Budget: What financial resources does the library have? How are they allocated?
- Time frame and evaluation: SLP managers should be clear about the amount of time required to execute a marketing initiative. They must establish from the outset how to assess the initiative's success.

The marketing mix is sometimes referred to as the "five *P*s" of marketing. This suite of resources should be applied in the correct proportions to deliver positive marketing outcomes. The components of the mix are: products, price, place, promotion, and personnel (Guth and Marsh 2012). In chapter five, the focus of marketing was to gather facts; in this chapter the focus is action.

Product Strategy. Products are more than boxes. Wood (2012) states that a product can be goods, services, places, ideas, and people, noting "when planning services, marketers must focus on delivering benefits through the appropriate combination of activities, people, facilities, and information" (82). Services need to go through development processes to ensure success. And what constitutes a good product or service? Think about performance, features, reliability, durability, esthetics, and perceived quality.

Pricing. Normally, SLPs don't think about pricing per se. However, each resource costs money; when users borrow items from the library, they save the cost and inconvenience of purchasing them, which can be substantial. Additionally, each service requires labor time, and may involve using resources such as Internet connectivity and equipment. This is one situation where time *is* money. For instance, a certificated librarian's time could be used to check out materials or instruct students; could a volunteer do the check-out work instead? Does it make more sense for the librarian or a clerk to handle textbooks? Might it be most cost-effective for the librarian to do an in-service for teachers on how to use databases rather than meet with random faculty one at a time?

Place. The third part of the marketing mix addresses when, and where to make library products and services available to the target market. To do that well requires knowing how that target market accesses goods and services and understanding the external environment (including competitors) as well as the product itself and its life cycle. What value accrues along the way from its inception to its delivery? What is the flow, or the logistics? Although the library facility is the traditional place of service, school librarians might do booktalks in classrooms or provide information services online. Convenience is a big factor in terms of place, so virtual communication may be highly valued.

Promotion. Yes, finally you get to talk about great school library programs! The key drivers of promotion are attracting attention, stimulating interest, and creating a desire for the product or service. Promotion calls upon the advertising "front line" and PR tools as well as other techniques. Know what you're talking about and to whom, and have the product ready, and a good communication strategy should do the trick. Wood (2012) emphasizes integrated marketing communication built on analyzing the audience, clarifying objectives and budget, identifying issues, and doing background research. Note that communication will change over the life cycle of the product; for instance, a flyer might be used to announce a new database, direct instruction provided to demonstrate how to use the database, and reference guide sheets made available to provide reminders.

Part of promotion may involve branding, which distinguishes the product and builds connotations that lead to users perceiving value and establishing loyalty. Good examples include the Library of Congress's American Memory collections, the Folger Library, or Girl Scouts. That's why ALA had its @yourlibrary campaign: to help libraries around the world by providing an easily recognizable brand that libraries can adopt and leverage at the local level (see www.ala.org/ala/issuesadvocacy/advocacy/publicawareness/campaign@yourlibrary/index.cfm).

Food for Thought

Library web portals can serve as a cost-effective marketing strategy to showcase the library's benefits and engage publics to use both the website and the library itself. Examining the library's web portal from a marketing perspective highlights some considerations, as enumerated by Infusionsoft (2011, 4–6).

1. What first draws your attention? Where do your eyes go first?
2. Can you tell immediately what the website is about?
3. Can you view important information without scrolling down?
4. Can you easily see the benefits of the school library program?
5. Is there a clear call to action, such as promoting learning?
6. Is the website visually and esthetically appealing?
7. Is the font easy to read?
8. Are there bulky chunks of text that could be broken up for easier reading?
9. What is the tone of the writing? Is it appropriate to the audience?
10. Does it include multimedia or social media?
11. Is the menu clear? Is the website easy to navigate?
12. Is contact information easy to find?
13. Does the user feel personally connected?

You might ask a few stakeholders to answer these questions; sit beside them as they view the library portal and give their personal feedback as they respond to the prompts.

With this information, it is easier to improve the library web presence so that it more effectively tells the library's story and provides online services. In the process, you might want to make the portal more interactive by incorporating social media elements such as blogs, polls, tutorials, student reviews, RSS feeds, and Twitter links.

As noted above, the communication arena has changed dramatically because of social media. You can even incorporate viral marketing, enlisting the help of the target market to identify the desired product as well as to communicate about it. One traditional example is the READ or library poster contest. The California School Library Association sponsors an annual student @yourlibrary poster contest (www.csla.net/index.php/pr-media/student-poster-contest). Be aware that when you use viral marketing you are sharing control of the message and communication channels. so be prepared for feedback. For instance, will library workers be happy with what people tweet about the library?

Personnel. None of the preceding components of the marketing mix can occur without people. Staff, whether paid or volunteer, who understand the marketing approach are vital for achieving success. These people are the internal marketing support. Additionally, user support is required to ensure that goals are reached. For instance, if the library program wants its readers to be happy, library workers need to provide them with good service (e.g., readers' advisory, good reading material in stock) to attain the goal.

MARKETING EVALUATION

The best marketing plan is the one that sells efficiently and gets optimum results. Did the marketing plan work? Assess your marketing plan's effectiveness along the way and make any necessary adjustments. The type of assessment measures and instruments should be determined from the start. The concept of metrics refers to numerical measures of specific performance-related activities and outcomes, which can be applied to marketing evaluation. The most obvious results are personnel impact and student success.

Focusing on assessing the marketing performance: examine the marketing strategy, operation, and relations with the target market. An effective approach to assessment is a systems approach that identifies each input and output factor. The following critical questions can help you assess marketing efforts at benchmark points, for example, when researching, strategizing, implementing, reflecting, and debriefing (Wood 2012):

- Did the goal focus on the publics' needs and interests?
- Was the target market appropriate and impactful?
- Did the library program differentiate itself from competitors, and capitalize on that uniqueness?
- Did the marketing mix reflect the results of the market research?
- Did the library workers understand the marketing plan, and have the skills and resources to implement it?
- How did the librarian manage the marketing mix?
- Did the library brand itself? How could it have been done better?
- How were marketing problems analyzed and addressed?
- Did the school library program achieve its intended program and meet the marketing goals?
- Did the marketing plan and results address SWOT findings?
- Were the channels for delivering products and services convenient for the target market?
- Does the school library have good relationships with its publics?
- How was feedback from the publics gathered, analyzed, and incorporated into marketing plans?

- How do publics perceive the school library program's marketing goal, and have those perceptions changed over time?

Advocacy

People are often generally supportive of what libraries do but not engage actively. Unlike PR, which has a more general objective of building and sustaining positive relationships with the public, or marketing, which is more of a two-way street, advocacy is a conscious, concerted effort to promote positive change. The American Library Association (ALA) focuses on the need to emphasize active support in its definition of advocacy. To that end, ALA has defined advocacy as "turning passive support into educated action by stakeholders" (www.ala.org/offices/ola/gettingstarted). Thus, advocacy seeks to change the attitudes, policies, positions and/or practices of particular groups or persons. The Canadian Association for Public Libraries (CAPL) takes a more proactive approach, defining advocacy as: "a planned, deliberate, sustained effort to raise awareness of an issue or issues. Advocacy is thus an ongoing process where support and understanding are built incrementally" (www.cla.ca/divisions/capl/advocacy/workbook.htm).

In sum, the key elements of advocacy include action orientation, planned effort, sustainability, and evaluation. Each advocacy plan has to identify the goals, the audience, the key messages, the advocacy team, and which strategies to use.

As an SLP manager, you might advocate for lifelong reading habits, responsible use of technology (digital citizenship), equitable access to information, and collaboration. In addition to focusing on their own schools, SLP managers tend to advocate for stronger school library programs in the face of inadequate school library support and sliced library budgets. A key in advocacy is to find allies with similar goals and values, and to make sure to align advocacy goals with the school community's priorities, such as student success.

Just as many advocacy issues exist, so too can advocacy activities vary; they include researching an issue, writing a white paper or position statement, contacting decision makers, making presentations, creating and disseminating leaflets and other fact sheets, staffing a booth, wearing campaign clothes or badges, conducting trainings, and raising funds. The choice of activities depends on the advocacy goal, the targeted audience, the time frame, available resources, budget, and capable willing personnel.

Schuckett (2004) provided several tips for communicating effectively as an advocate:

- Be prepared, professional, and passionate.
- Be brief, but get your key message out early and often.

- Aim to be understood, but don't try to impress: the focus should be on the message, not you.
- Personalize your message.
- Know your audience. Tell stories that are either factual, anecdotal, or emotionally inspiring.
- Present a call to action: choose three key actions you want the audience to take.
- Use visuals if possible, but do not hand out materials until after the presentation.
- Invite, and be prepared for, questions. If you don't know the answer, say that you will find out, and then follow up later with that answer.

Increasingly, professional library associations at different levels are developing advocacy resources like toolkits to provide information ammunition for school library communities. A few of these toolkits include:

- IFLA School Libraries and Resource Section (www.ifla.org/en/publications/school-library-advocacy-kit)
- InfoLit Global (www.infolitglobal.info/directory/en/browse/category/products/advocacy_toolkits)
- American Library Association (www.ala.org/advocacy/sites/ala.org.advocacy/files/content/advleg/publicawareness/campaign@your library/prtools/schoollibrary/FINAL_toolkit.pdf)
- American Association of School Librarians (www.ala.org/ala/mgrps/divs/aasl/aaslissues/toolkits/toolkits.cfm)
- Resources for School Librarians (www.sldirectory.com/libsf/resf/promote.html)
- California School Library Association (www.csla.net/res/sip_toolkit.htm)
- School Library Systems Association of New York State (www.crbsls.org/slsa)

Several videos are being produced and disseminated by school librarians and partners. Here is a sampling:

- ALA Library Advocacy Video Contest (www.ala.org/ala/issues advocacy/advocacy/libraryadvocacyday/videocontest/index.cfm)
- ALA I Love Libraries—check out "Love Your Library" (www.ilove libraries.org)
- Australian Teacher Librarians (www.youtube.com/watch?v = E4HY 700RQWc)
- Taiwanese High School (www.youtube.com/watch?v = 9zeL1ncRF18)

Sample Advocacy Letter

Dear Assemblywoman Brown:

As a secondary school librarian—and a parent—I urge you to support and pass Database Legislation AB2540.

Only four states in the United States do not provide statewide subscription databases of articles for libraries. These databases are extremely important in education because they select and index age-appropriate educational articles that support public school curriculum. Particularly in an Internet-intensive world, being able to channel students' interests into acceptable and useful resources is certainly comforting for schools, families, and communities. Typically, these databases can be accessed from home, reinforcing positive computer use and facilitating homework completion.

In terms of cost to the taxpayers, funding a statewide database would actually save money. The scale of use would result in deep discounts from vendors, which more than compensate for the existing costs that individual schools and districts have to bear. Funding can switch from one line to another. As magazine subscriptions rise, these databases continue to be a cost-effective method of disseminating information—without fear of document decay or theft.

The most compelling reason is one of equity: *all* children in California deserve equal access to resources so they can succeed academically to become prepared, contributing citizens.

I regularly teach information literacy and digital literacy skills in collaboration with classroom teachers. In faculty in-services, I have teachers evaluate and use these important databases so they can incorporate these vetted resources into their learning activities and better instruct students how to use them. I also provide reference and information services throughout the day on an individual basis, where one of the most often-asked questions is "How do I find an article for my class assignment?" Helping K–12 students learn these skills will improve their likelihood for success in their academic and professional world.

Your attention to this bill is most appreciated—for the sake of California's future.

Sincerely,

Joan Smith

- Los Angeles (www.youtube.com/watch?v=cPF12jD6F-s and www
  .teachertube.com/viewVideo.php?video_id=183895)
- Mansfield University (www.youtube.com/watch?v=cdv1Jwci31A)
- Joyce Valenza (http://joycevalenza.edublogs.org)
- Denver Public Schools (www.youtube.com/watch?v=RB-JuBZYfQc)
- University of Washington (www.youtube.com/watch?v=a_uzUh
  1VT98 and www.youtube.com/watch?v=a_uzUh1VT98)

From Communication to Relationships

Communication can be a one-shot event, but a series of successful communication cycles can lead to positive relationships between the communicator and the audience, which adds up to good public relations. Be it within the organization or external, ongoing and effective communication makes the working environment more productive and more satisfying. Public relations exemplifies purposeful, long-term communication and partnership between school librarians and other entities. Communication facilitates change; through effective and purposeful communication, school librarians can change mindsets and create new relationships.

DEGREES OF INTERACTION

School librarians tend to talk about collaboration, and valuable work with others can be accomplished at various levels of interaction, as identified by Montiel-Overall (2005).

1. Networking: informal social connections that can lead to joint efforts
2. Coordination: formal relations between equal partners; "management processes that ensure that events are synchronic and work harmoniously" (Montiel-Overall 2005, 30)
3. Partnership: working relationship of parties who share a common goal and agree on joint roles
4. Cooperation: working relationships that are characterized by give and take; parties help each other further their individual goals and see their part relative to the whole (see also Denise 1999)
5. Collaboration: symbiotic relationship with shared vision, thinking, planning, creation, and evaluation
6. Integrated instruction
7. Integrated curriculum: principal creates an environment that facilitates collaboration; time and resources are provided to support collaboration

Montiel-Overall also recognized several issues that affect these working relationships: trust, congeniality, reciprocity, equity, mutual recognition of expertise, and effective communication.

Interaction can occur at the group level as well. Coalitions are goal-specific agreements between or among groups that draw upon mutual values and issues. After a goal is reached, the coalition might disappear, but it can also continue and evolve into a long-term relationship with equal status.

DETAILING PARTNERSHIPS

Partnerships take time and effort, but they are worth the investment because they enable each person or group to achieve what they could not do alone.to be implemented effectively. Essentially, partners determine common goals, and identify which of their unique talents and resources can help accomplish those goals. Successful activities can build upon each other, leading to long-term sustainable partnerships. Partnerships can help develop collections, promote information and digital literacies, foster a culture of reading, facilitate active and deep learning, provide engaging programs and events, encourage research, garner more funding, and optimize the school's implementation of its mission.

If partnership benefits sound so great, why don't more partnerships exist? Several factors account for such reluctance: professed lack of time, a fear of losing control, discomfort in self-disclosure or negotiating, lack of training in collaboration, and a lack of awareness of the benefits of partnering.

To be fair, much work needs to be done before such partnerships can be effective, particularly in terms of social interaction and interdependence. Ultimately, partnerships are one-to-one relationships. People have to get to know each other on a personal level, and get along with each other. Engaging in positive school activities together, such as sharing meals, attending student events, and participating in faculty in-services are simple ways to get started. Working together for a back-to-school event, site self-study, or fund-raising campaign offers opportunities to see how each partner operates in support of positive goals. How effectively does the person communicate? Is the degree of personal space compatible? Is the degree of self-disclosure compatible? Does the person carry a fair share of the workload? Is the person open and honest? Is the person trustworthy and dependable? Does the person know how to give and receive constructive criticism? All of these questions can help determine the nature of the potential partnership. It is fine to have different types of partnerships—though deep and enduring partnerships are valuable, in some cases occasional short-term partnerships may work better.

Partnerships, like other group dynamics, develop and change over time. At the beginning, partners usually try to get along and are fairly accommodating, if a little shallow. They usually need time to explicitly state their expectations and clarify their roles. As they feel more comfortable sharing, they may also feel ready to risk conflict. If partnerships can deal with differences—at least on a professional level—they are more apt to build a mature relationship that can be productive and sustainable. Personal issues can also change the nature of the partnership; family status and demands, other career opportunities, changing leisure patterns, and health all affect partnerships. For instance, two single professionals might socialize after school, but that would change if one got married and started a family.

Partnerships can also exist between an individual, such as the SLP manager, and a group, such as an academic department or grade level. Usually, one person in the group acts as the liaison and extends an invitation. In such situations, the individual has to figure out group norms and dynamics as well as personal characteristics, so such partnerships tend to be more formal and less personal.

In any case, cultivate and assess partnerships in order to optimize their posi-

Circles of Influence

Potential partners include anyone in the school community and several entities in the larger community such as libraries, educational institutions, public agencies, service groups, and local enterprises. The school community is full of partners, some formal and some informal, and they come in all degrees of interaction, depth, and sustainability.

One useful activity is to make a sociogram of the school community, including both individuals and groups (e.g., departments).

1. Start by drawing a target (as in archery) with yourself in the middle circle.

2. Draw a circle for each person or group, with the size of the circle symbolizing that entity's power. Alternatively, create different shapes for different kinds of entities.

3. Indicate the relative closeness of each entity by their distance from each other.

4. Draw lines between circles, with arrows indicating the usual communication direction. The thickness of the line can indicate the frequency or importance of the communication. Intermittent communication can be symbolized by dotted or dashed lines. Antagonistic relationships can be indicated by jagged lines or contrasting colors.

5. Analyze the sociogram. Which people or groups emerge as leaders and influencers? You should probably strengthen professional relationships with those entities. Do some people have the ear of people in power? Those people should also be inculcated or at least acknowledged. Is there someone that you could empower?

tive impact. Both the professional goals and activities and the social interaction should be examined, always taking into consideration the results and the impact of that partnership. At the very least, ask yourself: "Could I have attained the same results as effectively if I had done it by myself?" Even though it sometimes feels like working solo might be more time-efficient, the long-term benefits of partnerships can make those first endeavors worth the extra work. Partnerships between you and classroom teachers can be assessed along several dimensions:

- Assessment: Partners use a variety of strategies to assess students, resources, and services. Assessment is used to improve practice and positively impact student success.
- Planning: The SLP manager is a full partner throughout the curricular planning process, including instructional design and implementation. Information and digital literacies are integrated throughout the curric-

By creating and analyzing the sociogram, you can more easily discern the areas of power, build your own power base, and align your efforts accordingly. You might also find that you have more power than you anticipated, which you can leverage to improve the school library program. Here is a sample sociogram.

Sociogram Showing the Relationship between the Librarian and Stakeholders

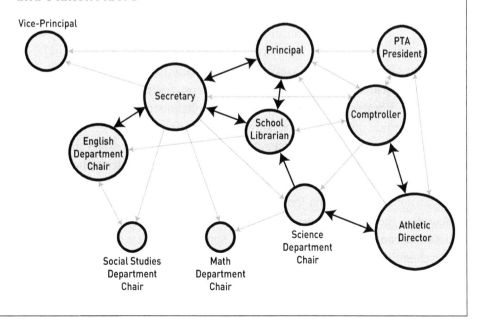

ulum. All activities involving the library program are planned coopera-
tively. Partners modify plans in response to changing needs.

- Implementation: Partners team-teach and team-assess. Partners use and share a variety of resources and strategies.
- Commitment: Partners communicate regularly with each other and the school community. Partners coach each other naturally as needed. Partners depend on each other for support. Partnerships are long-term and sustainable.

Policies and Procedures

Policies explain what is the right thing to do, and procedures explain how to do things right. Both types of documents provide a systematic approved basis for decision making. They clarify expectations, provide guidelines, and help make people accountable. Procedures are useful for standardizing and stream-lining tasks, especially when several workers execute them. Both policies and procedures are usually developed by library workers, and approved by the SLP manager; often other stakeholders such as a library advisory group and site administrators provide input into these documents. As a rule, policies must also be approved by the school board because they serve as legal documents that can protect the school. Policies are usually general statements, and are infrequently changed. In contrast, procedures are usually very detailed, but can be easily modified as situations change or improved methods are found.

SLPs need a variety of policies. Some may be subsumed by the school or district, such as student discipline, acceptable use policies, copyright, hiring processes, facility use, communication relations, finances, disaster planning, confidentiality, and ethical behavior. As an SLP manager, you must understand and follow these policies, as well as communicate them to library workers and users. Some school districts have a library service office, which may generate districtwide library policies such as selection, acquisitions and donations, chal-lenged materials, intellectual freedom, confidentiality of records, bibliographic control, resource sharing, conservation, and discarding materials. With the advent of social media and personal electronic devices, district and library pol-icies that deal with technology use probably need updating. Finding these pol-icies can sometimes be challenging, but as public documents (at least in public education), they must be accessible. Here is a list of additional school library policies to consider: mission statement, special collections, archiving, circula-tion, scheduling, instruction, student aides, handling difficult users, programs, production and duplication services, storage, inventory, and reporting.

LOCATING DOCUMENTS

Whenever possible, try to find existing policies and procedures rather than creating them from scratch. Generally, state departments of education or library services have laws and regulations that pertain to school libraries. Districts and school sites may also have relevant policies, which should align with state documents. In addition, national and state school library professional associations often list applicable policies and procedures. Even if existing documents are not perfect, they can serve as a starting point to develop relevant practice. In addition, most schools have a mandatory procedure for developing policies. Whatever the basis for the policy, the final version should contain the following elements: its purpose, explanation of the policy, a scope and applicability statement that explains whom it impacts, a responsibilities section, how the policy is to be enforced, and effective date. Some policies require background statements that justify or contextualize the policy, and some policies should include definitions for clarity. Elizabeth Downs's 2010 book *Media Specialist's Policy and Procedure Writer* is an excellent source of practical documentation. Other valuable sources of information follow.

- Florida Atlantic University Libraries (http://libguides.fau.edu/content .php?pid = 102626&sid = 1030593)
- Clarion University Institute of the Study and Development of School Library Information Centers (http://jupiter.clarion.edu/~amiller/state resources.htm)
- Resources for School Librarians (www.sldirectory.com/libsf/resf/manage .html#manuals)

It is a good idea to keep a virtual folder and physical binder of all policies and procedures for handy reference.

WRITING DOCUMENTS

As noted above, procedures guide library workers in their tasks. Those procedures may be communicated in written form (print or digital), screencast, or podcast. However, at least one format should be archived in print format. Here are some tips for writing procedures.

- Use simple, step-by-step directions.
- Ideally, write one concept or task per page.
- Number each step.
- Write all the possible actions at steps where decisions are made.
- Incorporate images (e.g., photos, diagrams, screen dumps) as needed to clarify processes.

- Define all technical terms.
- Explain what to do in case of errors.
- Create FAQs for complex tasks or tools, such as library management systems.

Draft procedures should be pilot-tested by affected library workers, and could even be drafted by them in the first place.

In addition, ready-to-use standardized forms and templates can streamline work and provide a consistent look for library communications. Some word processing programs have a good starting collection of templates, and the library's logo can be added in order to brand the communication. For instance, a library certificate template is easy to develop and use routinely. Other potential forms or templates include other awards or recognition; pathfinders; flyers; library passes; collaboration-planning, volunteer-application, and complaint forms as well as forms for fines or replacement cost form. Forms and templates should be kept in a central digital folder for quick retrieval and use.

ETHICAL ISSUES

Librarians have a professional code of ethics, the most notable being the American Library Association's Code of Ethics, which is available at www.ala.org/advocacy/proethics/codeofethics/codeethics. Its strongest principle is the commitment to intellectual freedom and the freedom of access to information. As an SLP manager, you are responsible for modeling and teaching the school community about the responsible use of information, including such points as copyright compliance and netiquette. You also must defend citizens' information rights, which can be jeopardized in a social climate of fear. In this digital age, ethical issues have expanded in variety and complexity. Distortion of information, cyberbullying, sexting, security leaks, and identity theft all present dire life-changing consequences, especially with the advent of ubiquitous global broadcasting.

You also must ensure that all library workers model ethical behavior and protect the school community's information rights. Explain that just because someone is within his or her legal rights, that does not mean that the action is acceptable ethically. Some of the simple activities that model ethical behavior include checking student ID cards, requiring acceptable use policies, explaining the need to keep personal information (including passwords) private, setting up computers for easy supervision, keeping circulation records and computer usage confidential, ensuring that all software and database licenses are in compliance and on file, sharing resources and displaying posters about digital citizenship, promoting media literacy, sharing broadcast download permission guidelines with teachers, and promoting Creative Commons.

On an administrative level, you must ensure that infrastructures and policies are in place and enforced to support ethical practices such as providing equitable, open, and safe access to information; making provisions to ensure that the educational community is digitally safe; having a plan to secure and protect educational data in case of crime or disaster; maintaining privacy and confidentiality of individual records; creating and enforcing policies that protect the information and digital rights of everyone; and training staff about these ethical issues Having these documents handy helps library staff when individuals challenge reading materials or other library practices. Such preventative measures also ease the concerns of school administrators.

Bringing It Down to You

Everyone has a preferred communication style. So how do you like to communicate?

- What format do you prefer: talking, e-mails, memos?
- In what formats can you competently create documents (e.g., video, web pages, etc.)?
- Are you a one-to-one communicator, or do you prefer communicating to groups?
- Do you prefer informal or formal communication: on the fly or at scheduled meetings?
- Do you tend to communicate in talking points with facts, or are you more of a storyteller?
- Are you a straight-shooter, or do you contextualize your message?
- How well—and how often—do you document your work?
- Do you prefer to write documents by yourself or collaboratively, or do you encourage others to craft them?

In analyzing your answers, you are clarifying your preferred communication style. It's a good idea to let your library workers know your preferences so they can at least understand your style, even if they do not mirror it. You should also have your library workers go through this exercise and share their preferences so everyone can be sensitive to their communication differences. This information can also help you by identifying library workers who may be more expert in creating documents in different formats.

References

American Library Association. 2009. *The Advocacy Action Plan Workbook.* Chicago, IL: American Library Association.

American Marketing Association. 2007. "AMA Definition of Marketing." Chicago, IL: American Marketing Association. www.marketingpower .com/Community/ARC/Pages/Additional/Definition/default.aspx.

Denise, L. 1999. "Collaboration vs. C-3 (Cooperation, Coordination, and Communication)." *Innovating* 7 (3): 1–6.

Downs, E. 2010. *Media Specialist's Policy and Procedure Writer.* New York, NY: Neal-Schuman.

Guth, D., and C. Marsh. 2012. *Public Relations: A Values-Driven Approach,* 5th ed. Boston, MA: Allyn and Bacon.

Infusionsoft. 2011. *Internet Marketing.* Chandler, AZ: Infusionsoft.

Marsh, C., D. Guth, and B. Short. 2008. *Strategic Writing,* 2nd ed. Boston: Pearson.

Montiel-Overall, P. 2005. "A Theoretical Understanding of TLC." *School Libraries Worldwide* 11 (2): 24–48.

Movement Advancement Project. 2008. *Communications Campaign Best Practices.* Denver, CO: Movement Advancement Project.

Plevyak, L., and A. Heaston. 2001. "The Communications Triangle of Parents, School Administrators, and Teachers: A Workshop Model." *Education* 121 (4): 768–72.

Reid, R. 1999. *MBWA: A Checklist for Managers.* San Diego, CA: Reid and Associates.

Rubin, R. 2010. *Defusing the Angry Patron.* New York, NY: Neal-Schuman.

Sarkodie-Manash, K., ed. 2000. *Reference Services for the Adult Learner.* New York, NY: Haworth Press.

Schuckett, S. 2004. *Political Advocacy for School Librarians: You Have the Power!* Worthington, OH: Linworth.

Wood, D. 2012. *The Marketing Plan Handbook.* 4th ed. Upper Saddle River, NJ: Prentice Hall.

12

From Manager to Leader

SOMETIMES MANAGING CONNOTES A SENSE OF COPING AND endurance rather than proactivity and improvement. The extra "oomph" usually requires leadership: a clear and articulate vision, and the skills to make that vision a reality through masterful resource allocation, delegation, and facilitation. This chapter defines leadership, and discusses the conditions for leadership that transcend management skills—and transcend the school library program (SLP). The chapter also provides guidelines for helping you transition from competent manager to inspiring leader.

First of all, it's okay to be an SLP manager. Good managers are needed to make sure that the school library runs hummingly. Nor should they abandon management if they become a leader. Rather, a school librarian leader can motivate and facilitate library workers and stakeholders to carry out a compelling vision of the SLP as Information Central and the heart of education. A school librarian leader transcends the library facility and program to embrace librarianship as a whole, and realize its potential within the school and greater community.

Who Are Leaders?

At the most basic level, leaders have the ability to lead people. Leaders have a vision for the SLP, and know how to articulate that vision clearly and compelling, and they are able to influence and motivate others to make that vision a reality. Leaders should have technical expertise and creativity. To achieve this, leaders self-manage effectively, especially under stress. In his book on principle-centered leadership, Covey (1991, 28) stated that leaders perform on four levels: personal trustworthiness, interpersonal trust, managerial empowerment, and organizational alignment.

In describing effective leadership, Adair (2010) focused on action-centered leadership that operates at the team level, operational leadership, management level, and strategic level. According to Adair, leaders must satisfy three sets of needs:

- Task needs: The group should be able to achieve objectives. Leaders must plan and allocate resources, identify group tasks, organize work functions, and monitor efforts.
- Individual needs: Leaders must make sure workers are trained and praised as appropriate. Leaders must also help individuals resolve their personal problems.
- Team maintenance needs: Leaders must establish and maintain an effective communication system, maintain cohesiveness and keep morale high, maintain high standards, and discipline when necessary.

Focusing specifically on instructional leadership, Weber (1989) identified five main functions that can be applied to SLPs:

- Define the school—and library program—mission.
- Manage curriculum and instruction.
- Promote a possible learning environment.
- Observe and give feedback to library workers.
- Assess the program.

The 2010 ALA/AASL standards for school librarian specialists include one standard that explicitly identifies leadership functions:

Candidates are able to articulate the role and relationship of the school library program's impact on student academic achievement within the context of current educational initiatives. Utilizing evidence-based practice and information from education and library research, candidates communicate ways in which the library program can enhance school improvement efforts. (National Council for Accreditation of Teacher Education 2010, 14)

Leadership Skills and Characteristics

Leadership requires both dispositions and skills. Although some people have a predilection for leadership, skills and behaviors can be learned and practiced. Covey (1991, 106) identified the following characteristics of principle-centered leaders: they are lifelong learners, service oriented, positive, synergistic, believe in others, strive for balance, see life as an adventure, and are self-renewing. In terms of traits, McPheat (2010) asserted that successful leaders must have a desire to lead, a commitment to the library program's and school's mission and vision, and integrity. In delineating integrity, McPheat included the elements of sincerity, authenticity, consistency, and substance.

Datar, Garvin, and Krop (2008) clustered leadership abilities as follows:

- Meeting job challenges: resourcefulness, decisiveness, ability to learn quickly, use of various strategies to do job
- Leading people: participatory management, change management, ability to confront and deal with problem employees
- Respecting self and others: self-awareness, ability to balance work and personal life, ability to put people at ease, relationship management, compassion and sensitivity, confidence and composure

Harvard (2001) developed a survey used to assess leadership, which lists the following sets of skills:
- Communication: oral and written, negotiation and conflict resolution, facilitation and influencing
- Technology: technology and computer skills
- Finances: budgeting, analysis, planning
- Supervision: planning, hiring, training, directing, assessing
- Management: strategic and tactical planning, implementation management, managing customers, marketing, networking, management of innovation and change
- Teamwork: leading a team, collaboration, working with virtual teams
- Self-management: self-awareness, goal-setting, emotional intelligence, time management, stress management, ability to balance work and personal life, using power and authority positively
- Physical skills: operating equipment, building and repairing, training others in physical skills

Patterson, Patterson, and Collins (2002) identified functions of teacher leaders.

- Establish a supportive learning environment.
- Maintain high expectations.

- Remain focused on identified priorities.
- Facilitate participatory management.
- Remain flexible and hopeful.
- Take charge.

Conditions for Leadership

A person can be a leader no matter his or her position. Whenever one is committed to—and communicates—a clear vision, works effectively with others, has relevant expertise, and uses the will and power to make that vision real, that person can lead.

BUILDING LEADERSHIP POWER

As noted earlier in the book, the power to lead can come from several sources (French and Raven 1959): legitimate position, expertise, ability to reward or punish people, via association with others in power, information use, charisma, and coercion. As a librarian leader, you can build your power base on several of these foundations, and empower others as well. In the process, you will contribute even more to library and school improvement.

The SLP manager usually demonstrates effective leadership in improving the SLP. Even then, the beginning SLP manager must earn the leadership role, especially if existing library workers are competent and have been working well together for a significant number of years. The new SLP manager has to get to know the library program in terms of material resources, services, and workers. Furthermore, the new manager has to get acquainted with the school community as a whole: its mission and operations, its organizational and power structures, and its culture. As noted earlier, a sociogram can facilitate this process. The new SLP manager has to conduct a personal needs assessment as well as determine the library program's needs in order to develop action plans for professional development and program improvement. Success in implementing those plans can then affirm the SLP manager's power base as a librarian leader.

As you take the lead in collaborating with other school community members, you extend your influence. Your colleagues' knowledge of resources and efficient use of information can help classroom teachers incorporate a wide variety of resources that can differentiate and enrich students' learning experiences, and librarians' research skills can provide valuable research-based practices to guide administration and curriculum development. Your technological expertise can help others increase their work proficiency through the effective use of technology, and help teachers incorporate technology into the curriculum.

Food for Thought

Leadership Self-Assessment

You have the potential to be a leader, but do you want to be one? Take a look at the functions and qualities above. Ask yourself:

- What is your vision of the school library program?
- How committed are you to seeing that vision become a reality?
- Do others follow your lead? Why?
- Do you feel competent, confident, and comfortable with yourself?
- What leadership functions resonate for you, and which seem like drudgery?

Go through the list of skills and traits, and rate your current level of competence from zero to ten (with ten being excellent). Think back to a decade ago. What was your level then? What actions did you take to improve? Identify some traits and skills that you would like to strengthen, then jot down a couple of actions you can take to improve yourself as a leader. As you have probably guessed, leadership is a lifetime journey.

Your instructional expertise can contribute significantly to instructional design and delivery, including co-teaching and co-assessing student learning. With the power within in the library program, your schoolwide power and leadership grows with evidence-based success.

PARAMETERS OF LEADERSHIP

The perception of the limits of power can vary. School administrators are expected to serve as the main site leaders. Their leadership philosophy and style may reflect a highly hierarchical structure and autocratic approach that precludes sharing power; such leaders tend to think of power as finite, and believe that if power is shared or given, less remains for them. In such environments, bestowed leadership probably is bound by loyalty, and independent leaders may well be perceived as rivals. At the other end of the leadership spectrum, some leaders believe in an open-ended model of leadership where power is shared and expanded through use, which facilitates the rise of more leaders. In short, leadership styles reflect differences in human interactions and interaction with environmental forces (Tannenbaum and Schmidt 2008), which impacts how others in the organization can become leaders.

Schools are generally considered as complex, loosely-coupled organizations where subgroups act relatively independently. In such organizations, several leadership opportunities exist, and leadership overall is decentralized. An overarching shared vision and mission, supported by common goals, pulls disparate parts together. Therefore, site administrators serve more as coordinators. In any case, job satisfaction and leadership blossoms in settings that model and support participatory governance (Zhang 2006). An organizational culture of openness with a focus on continuous improvement also fosters distributed leadership.

Increasingly, schools are adopting a distributed collaborative leadership model that leverages collective intelligence. Nissen, Merrigan, and Kraft (2005) posited four approaches in implementing collaborative leadership: acknowledging existing community leaders, identifying collaborative leadership tasks and functions, planning for collaboration, and balancing short-term and long-term outcomes. Collaborative leadership poses great advantages for SLP managers, who tend to lead from the middle, and know how to collaborate effectively.

Student-Centered Leadership

Increasingly, school communities are implementing student-centered practices. In school settings, student success is most easily framed in terms of the school's mission and its list of target student outcomes. The mission statement provides a philosophical stance, and the outcomes define broad goals that are then operationalized into measurable objectives and indicators. The school culture also plays a role in identifying student success. Indeed, what are the school's measures of success: grades, standardized test scores, sports championships, beauty contest winners, literary awards, service to the community, or college acceptances and scholarships? These markers reflect the school community's values, which are influenced by leaders, including you as the librarian leader. With effective leadership, the SLP can contribute to student success through:

- a shared vision to support students
- shared beliefs and norms about student achievement
- partnerships with the school and greater community to promote consistent work with students and explicit development of personal assets
- a sense of community to provide students with opportunities for service and leadership among themselves (Benson, Scales, and Leffert 1999)

In examining the school-level factors that lead to student achievement, Marzano (2003) listed five components: curriculum, goals and feedback, parent and community involvement, a safe and orderly environment, and collegiality and professionalism. The Association for Supervision and Curriculum Development (ASCD) (2009) developed a whole-student approach to student achievement: making sure students are healthy, safe, engaged, supported, challenged, and sustained. You can serve in a leadership capacity to ensure that these factors are in place via the library program.

- Health: Promote healthy habits through resources and programs.
- Safety: Communicate and enforce behavior rules. Foster a climate of high expectations. Help students be responsible for their own behavior. Promote and model positive values.
- Engagement: Let students help make decisions. Show students the relevance and application of learning, such as lifelong reading.
- Support: Provide appropriate resources. Assess student learning, and then provide appropriate scaffolding and other interventions.
- Challenge: Provide a range of resources so students can increase knowledge and skills. Provide healthy competition and contests such as poetry slams and debates. Show connections between school and life. Seek opportunities for cross-curricular learning. Facilitate global awareness. Teach information literacy, which promotes critical thinking.
- Sustainability: Align school efforts and the library's program. Conduct relevant professional development. Identify school community needs and create interventions. Share data and resources in order to optimize student success.

In short, SLP management promotes the aim of preparing and supporting student success and managing a learning environment fosters intellectual and psychological engagement. On a larger scale, library program leadership can contribute substantially to schoolwide improvement in student success.

Representative Leadership Styles

As mentioned above, leaders have preferred ways of interacting with people and forces. No one leadership style is perfect, partly because individuals vary in personality and competencies. Because different environments and situations call upon different leadership skills, librarian leaders should learn about different approaches to leadership so they can adapt those styles that seem more comfortable and personally effective. In some ways, trying on leadership styles is analogous to finding one's fashion style (e.g., classic, romantic, casual, glam, punk, etc.) and choosing how to dress for different occasions.

DIRECTIONAL LEADERSHIP

A couple of leadership styles reflect a sense of direction and growth. As an example, path-goal leadership identifies a specific direction. Such leaders are results-oriented, and aim for improved worker performance. To that end, they encourage participatory decision making and are supportive of workers' efforts to meet organizational goals.

In his book *Good to Great* (2001), Collins posited a three-stage disciplined approach to leadership. First, leaders must have a disciplined staff, which requires hiring the right person for the right job. Next, the organization should be disciplined in thought and focus with single-minded commitment on what it does best. At the third stage, the leader has to instill a discipline of action, which involves a culture that ensures that continued effort will make a significant difference. The underlying leadership concept is to build greatness that lasts, preserving the organization's core identity and instituting stimulating programs that leverage the organization's strength.

TRANSACTIONAL VERSUS TRANSFORMATIONAL LEADERSHIP

Transactional leadership focuses on ways that leaders interact with others. Such leaders use contingency rewards based on performance or other criteria. They tend to manage by exception, either actively urging people to perform according to an established norm, or more generally paying attention to performance only when it falls outside the norm. In some cases, such leaders have a laissez-faire, hands-off attitude.

In contrast, transformational leadership has a more value-added approach, and pursues continuous improvement. Such leaders motivate workers by inspiring vision and idealized influence. These leaders provide intellectual stimulation, and give individualized consideration to workers. Both the people and the organization as an entity transform themselves through stimulating and supportive leadership (Simpson 2012).

SERVICE LEADERSHIP

Libraries are basically service organizations. As such, they add value through resources and actions that support the public good. In school settings, service supports the school's mission and its constituency. Financial gain and self-aggrandizement are not goals. VanDuinkerken and Kaspar (2015) provide a good overview of service leadership. As a service leader, the SL must be committed to service, communicate that value and vision of service, and ensure that vison becomes a reality through transformational practice. The service leader models a commitment to service, and expects staff to share that commitment. The service leader balances encouragement and accountability of the staff. Indicators of effective service leadership include a desire to do the right thing, motivation and commitment to serve, collaboration, minimal power distance among staff, and a trusting and respectful environment. To foster these workplace behaviors, the service leader should be self-aware, demonstrate integrity, build rapport with both staff and the school community, provide leadership in developing a service-oriented SLP, foster proactive innovation to stay relevant, and serve as a steward to ensure sustainability of the SLP.

Within this context, service leadership "is a cultural mindset that empowers all library employees to extend their customer service philosophy so that it can develop, becoming an organizational practice and cultural value" (VanDuinkerken and Kaspar 2015, 16).

VanDuinkerken and Kaspar (2015, 16) explain it this way:

> The modeling of service as a value should manifest in all activities and in all roles within the organization. While any individual can be a service leader or practice principles of service leadership, this service orientation is most effective when modeled by those with managerial responsibilities or supervisory authority.

Making the Change

Education is closely linked to change. It exists in a world of change, and should prepare students to deal with the change that they experience. Education itself is changing more quickly than ever due to internal and external forces; as technology's role in education expands, the issue of change becomes paramount. Educational leaders in particular should help the school community deal with change by communicating and collaborating, staying focused on the goal, and facilitating change through patience and support.

Change involves internal and external factors, and leads to negotiated modifications at some level: personal, group, or organizational. A person's job function may change because of layoffs, emerging technologies may require changes in teaching or administrative actions, new state or federal educational regulations may impact school policies and budgets, or shifting population demographics will require instructional reexamination. In chapter five, change was addressed in terms of planning. Now you can look at change from the perspective of an organizational leader and change agent.

Kotter (1996) argued that change failures were due to ineffective behavior on the part of leadership, which act as change agents. He posited an eight-step process to lead organizational change.

1. Create urgency. This step requires leadership and honest discussion about threats and opportunities.
2. Form a powerful coalition by identifying key players.
3. Create a vision for change and a strategy to achieve it.

4. Communicate the vision, and model the change.
5. Overcome obstacles.
6. Create short-term wins to provide early success that motivates further change.
7. Build on change, making adjustments as needed. Anchor change in the organization's culture, publicly recognizing models of change.

Heck and Hallinger (2010) analyzed unidirectional and reciprocal-effects models of change in elementary schools. They found that change is more successful when leadership is conceptualized as a collaborative, mutually reinforcing system of organizational relationships and interdependent processes that lead to decisions, which should be assessed continuously. Change is also a spiraling phenomenon in that enacted change usually results in adjustments in other parts of the system, which invoke further change. Therefore, in order to lead effectively, educational leaders need to understand change and its processes. They must define their own roles within the change process, particularly as change agents and managers of change.

One of the most effective ways that you can lead is by functioning as a change agent. Change agents have specialized technical and communication skills that provide positive forces that can overcome resistance to change. They can optimize the conditions for change through helping relationships. Change agents can help people's sense of efficacy by providing clear instructions, modeling behavior, providing opportunities for practice, and reinforcing changed behavior. As a leader, you may serve in that role as workers implement change strategies that frame and support conditions for change: sharing curriculum and instruction, modeling and facilitating reflective teaching, developing policy, and helping to develop a shared vision (Henderson, Finkelstein, and Beach 2010).

Leadership for Results

In the final analysis, leadership is only as effective as the result it achieves. As an SLP manager and leader, you must assess your leadership effectiveness along with your management skill in order to optimize your impact—and the impact of the SLP.

The Partnership for 21st Century Skills (2009) asserted that school districts are responsible for student knowledge and skills, education support systems, educational leadership, policymaking, partnering, and continuous improvement. Its MILE guide includes an assessment tool that can be used to generate a shared educational vision, and to develop a comprehensive, aligned action plan that can be implemented successfully. Its educational leadership dimension states that leaders should communicate and develop consensus on a vision of student learning that encompasses academic content and twenty-first century skills; model and foster integration of these skills throughout education; establish yearly measurable goals around equitable educational opportunities and staff performance to actualize the school's vision; and ensure that those goals are achieved.

The ultimate basis for assessing leadership and management is student success. Although students' standardized test scores can serve as one data point, several other student-centric data should be considered: sample student work, retention and graduation rates, post-secondary placements, student awards and recognitions from outside the school, frequency and nature of discipline referrals, and student and family satisfaction. In addition, adult members of the school community's outputs and outcomes should also be used to measure leadership effectiveness: presentations and publications, retention rates and promotions, productivity, mentoring, public awards and recognitions, community engagement and service, and staff morale. With these data, leaders can then determine how well they have allocated resources and supported efforts to fulfill the school's mission.

As an SLP manager and leader, you can also identify your own impact on the school library program—and the program's impact on the school overall and on student success in particular. The same outputs and outcomes can be used, focusing on how library resources and services have added value to the lives of teachers, other support personnel, administrators, and parents as well as students; in short, providing the conditions for optimal learning and success.

Bringing It Down to You

If you were to choose a clothing style to fit your leadership style, what would it look like: a Superman cape, a military uniform, a waitress, a three-piece suit, denim shirt and jeans? What styles sound new and intriguing? What leadership styles do you practice? What might you do to gain confidence when using that appealing leadership style? Do you always use the same style, or do you adjust your leadership style to the conditions that you face? Do you find yourself reverting to a specific style under stress, and is it effective? Perhaps you should monitor your stress, and think of other ways to lead under those circumstances.

As you think about yourself as a leader, also look at those around you. Which leaders seem effective? Why? Are they effective with one group but not another, or good in some situations but not in others? Why? Analyzing the basis for effective leadership helps you determine what factors you already possess—or want to adopt. In the process, you may find that you have all the qualities of the leader, and that you have been acting as a leader without even realizing that fact. Now that you are aware of your effect and effectiveness as a leader, you can influence even more people to make the library and the site a better place to learn and grow. Congratulations!

References

Adair, J. 2010. *Effective Strategic Leadership,* rev. ed. New York, NY: Pan Macmillan.

Association for Supervision and Curriculum Development. 2009. *Educating the Whole Child.* Alexandria, VA: Association for Supervision and Curriculum Development.

Benson, P., P. Scales, and N. Leffert. 1999. *A Fragile Foundation: The State of Development Assets among American Youth.* Minneapolis, MN: Search Institute.

Collins, J. 2001. *Good to Great.* New York, NY: Harper.

Covey, S. 1991. *Principle-Centered Leadership.* New York, NY: Simon and Schuster.

Datar, S., D. Garvin, D., and C. Krop. 2008. *The Center for Creative Leadership.* Cambridge, MA: Harvard University Press.

French, J., and B. Raven. 1959. "The Bases of Power." In *Studies in Social Power,* edited by D. Cartwright, 259–69. Ann Arbor, MI: Institute for Social Research.

Harvard College 2001. *Harvard ManageMentor: Managing Your Career Tools.* Boston, MA: Harvard University Press.

Heck, R., and P. Hallinger. 2010. "Collaborative Leadership Effects on School Improvement: Integrating Unidirectional- and Reciprocal-Effects Models." *Elementary School Journal* 111 (2): 226–52.

Henderson, J., J. Finkelstein, and A. Beach. 2010. "Beyond Dissemination in College Science Teaching: An Introduction to Four Core Change Strategies." *Journal of College Science Teaching* 39 (5): 18–25.

Kotter, J. 1996. *Leading Change.* Cambridge, MA: Harvard University Press.

Marzano, R. 2003. *What Works in Schools.* Alexandria, VA: Association for Supervision and Curriculum Development.

McPheat, S. 2010. *Leadership Skills.* London, England: MTD Training and Ventus Publishing.

National Council for Accreditation of Teacher Education. 2010. *ALA/AASL Standards for Initial Preparation of School Librarians.* Washington, DC: National Council for Accreditation of Teacher Education.

Nissen, L., D. Merrigan, and M. Kraft. 2005. "Moving Mountains Together: Strategic Community Leadership and Systems Change." *Child Welfare* 54 (2): 123–40.

Partnership for 21st Century Skills. 2009. *The MILE Guide.* Tucson, AZ: Partnership for 21st Century Skills.

Patterson, J., J. Patterson, and L. Collins. 2002. *Bouncing Back! How Your School Can Succeed in the Face of Adversity.* Larchmont, NY: Eye on Education.

Simpson, S. 2012. *The Styles, Models and Philosophy of Leadership.* London, England: MTD Training and Ventus Publishing.

Tannenbaum, R., and W. Schmidt. 2008. *How to Choose a Leadership Pattern.* Cambridge, MA: Harvard University Press.

VanDuinkerken, W., and W. Kaspar. 2015. *Leading Libraries: How to Create a Service Culture.* Chicago, IL: American Library Association.

Weber, J. 1989. "Leading the Instructional Program. In *School Leadership: Handbook for Excellence,*" 2nd ed., edited by S. Smith and P. Piele, 191–224. Eugene, OR: ERIC Clearinghouse on Educational Management. (ED 309 504).

Zhang, Z. 2006. *Retaining K–12 Teachers in Education.* Charlottesville, VA: University of Virginia.

BIBLIOGRAPHY

Adair, J. *Effective Strategic Leadership.* Rev. ed. New York, NY: Pan Macmillan, 2010.

Albrecht, K. *Organizational Development.* Englewood Cliffs, NJ: Prentice Hall, 1983.

American Association of School Administrators. *School Budgets 101.* Alexandria, VA: American Association of School Administrators, 2012.

American Association of School Librarians. *Empowering Learners.* Chicago, IL: American Library Association, 2009.

———. *A Planning Guide to Information Power.* Chicago, IL: American Library Association, 1999.

———. *Standards for the 21st Century Learner.* Chicago, IL: American Library Association, 2007.

———. *A 21st-Century Approach to School Library Evaluation.* Chicago, IL: American Library Association, 2012.

American Association of School Librarians and Association of Educational Communications and Technology. *Information Power.* Chicago, IL: American Library Association, 1988.

American Library Association. *The Advocacy Action Plan Workbook.* Chicago, IL: American Library Association, 2009.

American Marketing Association. "AMA Definition of Marketing." Chicago, IL: American Marketing Association, 2007. www.marketingpower.com/ Community/ARC/Pages/Additional/Definition/default.aspx.

Association for Supervision and Curriculum Development. *Educating the Whole Child.* Alexandria, VA: Association for Supervision and Curriculum Development, 2009.

Association of College and Resource Libraries. *Diversity Standards.* Chicago, IL: Association of College and Resource Libraries, 2012.

Bagshawe, A. *Getting Motivation Right.* London, England: MTD Training and Ventus, 2011.

Bailey, C., Jr., K. Coombs, J. Emery, A. Mitchell, C. Morris, S. Simons, and R. Wright. *Institutional Repositories.* SPEC Kit 292. Washington, DC: Association of Research Libraries, 2006.

Barbour, J. "Management Theories." In *Encyclopedia of Educational Leadership and Administration,* edited by K. English, 635–39. Thousand Oaks, CA: SAGE, 2006.

Benfari, R. *Understanding and Changing Your Management Style.* San Francisco, CA: Jossey-Bass, 1999.

Benson, P., P. Scales, and N. Leffert. *A Fragile Foundation: The State of Development Assets among American Youth.* Minneapolis: Search Institute, 1999.

Berry, L., and A. Parsuraman. *Marketing Services: Competing through Quality.* New York, NY: Free Press, 1991.

Blake, R., and J. Mouton. *The Managerial Grid.* Houston, TX: Gulf Publishing, 1964.

Burgoyne, J., and R. Stuart. "Managerial Skills." *Personnel Review* 5, no. 4 (1976): 19–29.

Cannon, R. "Learning Environment." In *Encyclopedia of Educational Media Communications and Technology,* edited by D. Unwin and R. McAlees, 342–58. New York, NY: Greenwood Press, 1988.

Carr-Ruffino, N. *The Promotable Woman.* 4th ed. Pompton Plains, NJ: Career Press, 2004.

Collins, J. *Good to Great.* New York, NY: Harper Business, 2001.

Collins, R. *Effective Management.* Chicago, IL: Commerce Clearing House, 1993.

Common Core State Standards for English Language Arts and Literacy in History/Social Studies, Science, and Technical Subjects. Washington, DC: Council of Chief State School Officers, 2010.

Common Core State Standards for Mathematics. Washington, DC: Council of Chief State School Officers, 2010.

Covey, S. *Principle-Centered Leadership.* New York, NY: Simon and Schuster, 1991.

Dall'Alba, G., and J. Sandberg. "Unveiling Professional Development: A Critical Review of Stage Models." *Review of Educational Research* 76, no. 3 (2006): 383–412.

Datar, S., D. Garvin, and C. Krop. *The Center for Creative Leadership.* Cambridge, MA: Harvard University Press, 2008.

Denise, L. "Collaboration vs. C-3 (Cooperation, Coordination, and Communication)." *Innovating* 7, no. 3 (1999): 1–6.

Dewey, J. *How We Think.* New York, NY: D. C. Heath, 1933.

Downs, E. *Media Specialist's Policy and Procedure Writer.* New York, NY: Neal-Schuman, 2001.

Dumler, M., and S. Skinner. *A Primer for Management.* Mason, OH: South-Western, 2005.

Ely, D. *New Perspectives on the Implementation of Educational Technology Innovation* (ED 427775), Syracuse, NY: ERIC, 1999.

Emery, F., and E. Thorsrud. *Democracy at Work*. Leiden, The Netherlands: Martinius Nijhoff, 1976.

Erickson, R., and C. Maruson. *Designing a School Library Media Center for the Future*. Chicago, IL: American Library Association, 2007.

Farmer, L. "Brace Yourself." *School Library Journal* 58, no. 3 (2012): 38–43.

———. "Predictors for Success: Experiences of Beginning and Expert Teacher Librarians." In *Educational Media and Technology Annual*, edited by V. J. McClendon, 157–84. Westport, CT: Libraries Unlimited, 2008.

———. *Student Success and Library Media Programs*. Westport, CT: Libraries Unlimited, 2003.

Farmer, L., and I. Stricevic. *Using Research to Promote Literacy and Reading*. Hague: International Federation of Library Associations, 2011.

Fayol, H. *Administration industrielle et general*. Paris, France: Dunod, 1916.

Feldman, D. "A Contingency Theory of Socialization." *Administrative Science Quarterly* 21, no. 3 (1976): 433–52.

Fiedler, F. *Leader Attitudes and Group Effectiveness*. Westport, CT: Greenwood, 1981.

French, J., and B. Raven. "The Bases of Power." In *Studies in Social Power*, edited by D. Cartwright, 259–69. Ann Arbor, MI: Institute for Social Research, 1959.

Furnham, A. *Management Intelligence*. New York, NY: Palgrave Macmillan, 2008.

Gale Encyclopedia of Small Business. 3rd ed. Farmington Hills, MI: Gale, 2006.

Garner, E. *Effective Discipline*. Casselberry, FL: Eric Garner and Ventus Publishing, 2012.

———. *Team Building*. Casselberry, FL: Eric Garner and Ventus Publishing, 2012.

Guth, D., and C. Marsh. *Public Relations: A Values-Driven Approach*. 5th ed. Boston: Allyn and Bacon, 2012.

Halsted, D., S. Clifton, and D. Wilson. *Library as Safe Haven*. New York, NY: Neal-Schuman, 2013.

Harvard College. *Harvard ManageMentor: Managing Your Career Tools*. Cambridge, MA: Harvard University Press, 2001.

Heck, R., and P. Hallinger. "Collaborative Leadership Effects on School Improvement: Integrating Unidirectional- and Reciprocal-Effects Models." *Elementary School Journal* 111, no. 2 (2010): 226–252.

Hempel, J. "Space Matters." *Business Week*. July 2016. www.businessweek.com/innovate/NussbaumOnDesign/archives/2006/07/jumps_new_space.html.

Henderson, J., J. Finkelstein, and A. Beach. "Beyond Dissemination in College Science Teaching: An Introduction to Four Core Change Strategies." *Journal of College Science Teaching* 39, no. 5 (2010): 18–25.

Herzberg, F. "One More Time: How Do You Motivate Employees?" *Harvard Business Review* 46, no. 1 (1968): 53–62.

Hicks, R., and K. Hicks. *Boomers, Xers and Other Strangers*. Wheaton, IL: Tyndale House, 1999.

Hofstede, G. *Culture's Consequences: Comparing Values, Behaviors, Institutions, and Organizations across Nations*. 2nd ed. Thousand Oaks, CA: SAGE, 2001.

———. *Culture's Consequences: International Differences in Work-Related Values.* Newbury Park, CA: SAGE, 1980.

Huber, J., and S. Potter. *The Purpose-Based Library.* Chicago, IL: American Library Association, 2015.

Infusionsoft. *Internet Marketing.* Chandler, AZ: Infusionsoft, 2011.

Institute of Education Statistics. *Fiscal Year 2005 Data Element Definitions.* Washington, DC: Institute of Education Statistics, 2005. http://nces.ed.gov/surveys/libraries/Pdf/PLS_Defs_FY05.pdf.

Jessen, S. *Project Leadership Step by Step: Part I.* 2nd ed. London, England: Ventus Publishing, 2012.

———. *Project Leadership Step by Step: Part II.* London, England: Ventus Publishing, 2010.

Johnson, P. *Fundamentals of Collection Development and Management.* 2nd ed. Chicago, IL: American Library Association, 2009.

Kalyanpur, M., and Harry, B. *Culture in Special Education.* Baltimore, MD: Paul Brookes, 1999.

Kasowitz, A., B. Bennett, and D. Lankes. "Quality Standards for Digital Reference Consortia." *Reference and User Services Quarterly* 39 (2000): 355–61.

Kotter, J. *Leading Change.* Cambridge, MA: Harvard University Press, 1996.

Lawrence, B. *Effects of State Policies on Facilities Planning and Construction* (ED 459970). Charleston, WV: ERIC, 2001.

Levinson, D. *The Seasons of a Man's Life.* New York, NY: Knopf, 1978.

Loertscher, D., B. Woolls, and J. Felker. *Building a School Library Collection Plan.* San Jose, CA: Hi Willow, 1998.

Lombardi, M. *Standing on the Plateau Looking Forward: The Croquet Project.* Durham, NC: The Croquet Consortium, 2005.

Marakas, G. *Decision Support Systems in the 21st Century.* 2nd ed. Upper Saddle River, NJ: Prentice Hall, 2002.

Marsh, C., D. Guth, and B. Short. *Strategic Writing.* 2nd ed. Boston: Pearson, 2008.

Marzano, R. *What Works in Schools.* Alexandria, VA: Association for Supervision and Curriculum Development, 2003.

Maslow, A. *Motivation and Personality.* New York, NY: Harper, 1954.

McPheat, S. *Coaching and Mentoring.* London, England: MTD Training and Ventus Publishing, 2010.

———. *Leadership Skills.* London, England: MTD Training and Ventus Publishing, 2010.

———. *Managing Budgets.* Warwickshire, England: MTD Training and Venus Publishing, 2012.

———. *Running Effective Meetings.* London, England: MTD Training and Ventus Publishing, 2010.

Montiel-Overall, P. "A Theoretical Understanding of TLC." *School Libraries Worldwide* 11, no. 2 (2005): 24–48.

Moos, R. *The Human Context: Environmental Determinants of Behavior*. Malabar, FL: Krieger, 1986.

Movement Advancement Project. *Communications Campaign Best Practices*. Denver, CO: Movement Advancement Project, 2008.

Mowl, G. *Innovative Assessment*. Newcastle on Tyne, England: University of Northumbria, 1996.

National Board for Professional Teaching Standards. *Library Media Standards*, 2nd ed. Arlington, VA: National Board for Professional Teaching Standards, 2012.

National Center for Education Statistics. *Evaluation of Definitions and Analysis of Comparative Data for the School Library Statistics Program*. Washington, DC: National Center for Education Statistics, 1998.

National Council for Accreditation of Teacher Education. *ALA/AASL Standards for Initial Preparation of School Librarians*. Washington, DC: National Council for Accreditation of Teacher Education, 2010.

Nicholson, N. "A Theory of Work Role Transitions." *Administrative Science Quarterly* 29, no. 2 (1984): 172–91.

Nissen, L., D. Merrigan, and M. Kraft. "Moving Mountains Together: Strategic Community Leadership and Systems Change." *Child Welfare* 54, no. 2 (2005): 123–40.

Northeast Document Conservation Center. *Preservation Education Curriculum*. Andover, MA: Northeast Document Conservation Center, 2008.

Oblinger, D. *Learning Spaces*. Washington, DC: EDUCAUSE, 2006.

OCLC. *Environmental Scan: Pattern Recognition*. Dublin, OH: OCLC, 2003.

Partnership for 21st Century Skills. *The MILE Guide*. Tucson, AZ: Partnership for 21st Century Skills, 2009.

Patterson, J., J. Patterson, and L. Collins. *Bouncing Back! How Your School Can Succeed in the Face of Adversity*. Larchmont, NY: Eye on Education, 2002.

Plevyak, L., and A. Heaston. "The Communications Triangle of Parents, School Administrators, and Teachers: A Workshop Model." *Education* 121, no. 4 (2001): 768–72.

Powell, D., and A. Brodsky. *Clinical Supervision in Alcohol and Drug Abuse Counseling: Principles, Models, Methods*. Rev. ed. San Francisco, CA: Jossey-Bass, 2004.

Reference and Users Services Association. *Definitions of Reference*. Chicago, IL: American Library Association, 2008.

Reid, R. *MBWA, A Checklist for Managers*. San Diego, CA: Reid and Associates, 1999.

Rounds, R. *Basic Budgeting Practices for Librarians*. 2nd ed. Chicago, IL: American Library Association, 1994.

Rubin, R. *Defusing the Angry Patron*. New York, NY: Neal-Schuman, 2010.

Sarkodie-Manash, K., ed. *Reference Services for the Adult Learner*. New York, NY: Haworth Press, 2000.

Schuckett, S. *Political Advocacy for School Librarians: You Have the Power!* Worthington, OH: Linworth, 2004.

Simpson, S. *The Styles, Models and Philosophy of Leadership*. London, England: MTD Training and Ventus Publishing, 2012.

"SLJ's Average Book Prices for 2016." *School Library Journal* 62, no. 3 (2016). www.slj.com/2016/03/research/sljs-average-book-prices-for-2016/.

Stuart, R., and B. Moran. *Library and Information Center Management*. Westport, CT: Libraries Unlimited, 2007.

Tannenbaum, R., and W. Schmidt. *How to Choose a Leadership Pattern*. Cambridge, MA: Harvard University Press, 2008.

Turkle, S., and S. Papert. "Epistemological Pluralism: Styles and Voices within the Computer Culture." *Signs: Journal of Women in Culture and Society* 16, no. 1 (1990): 128–65.

United States Department of Health and Human Services. *Clinical Supervision and Professional Development of the Substance Abuse Counselor*. Washington, DC: United States Department of Health and Human Services, 2009.

VanDuinkerken, W., and W. Kaspar. *Leading Libraries: How to Create a Service Culture*. Chicago, IL: American Library Association, 2015.

Velasquez, D., ed. *Library Management 101*. Chicago, IL: American Library Association, 2013.

Vroom, V. *Work and Motivation*. New York, NY: Wiley, 1964.

Vygotsky, L. *Mind in Society*. Cambridge, MA: Harvard University Press, 1978.

Weber, J. "Leading the Instructional Program." In *School Leadership: Handbook for Excellence*. 2nd ed., edited by S. Smith and P. Piele, 191–224. Eugene, OR: ERIC Clearinghouse on Educational Management, 1989.

Wiles, J. *Curriculum Essentials*. New York, NY: Pearson, 2005.

Wood, D. *The Marketing Plan Handbook*. 4th ed. Upper Saddle River, NJ: Prentice Hall, 2012.

Young Adult Library Services Association. *National Teen Space Guidelines*. Chicago, IL: American Library Association, 2012.

Zaltman, G., and R. Duncan. *Strategies for Planned Change*. New York, NY: Wiley Inter-Science Publications, 1977.

Zhang, Z. *Retaining K–12 Teachers in Education*. Charlottesville, VA: University of Virginia, 2006.

INDEX

A

access, 1, 2, 3, 35, 36, 37, 83, 91, 96–97, 100–101, 117–118, 120, 129
acquisitions. *See* collection development
Adair, J., 228
Addams Elementary School, 115
administration, 6
administrators, 2, 64, 148, 200, 231–232
advocacy, 210, 215–218 *See also* communication
Albrecht, K., 54
American Association of School Administrators, 34
American Association of School Librarians, ix, 5, 15–16, 18, 21, 31, 33, 74, 90, 124, 132, 156, 182, 228
American Libraries, 126
American Library Association, 15–16, 58, 94, 215, 224, 228
American Marketing Association, 210
assessment, 31–32, 64–65, 75, 83–87, 129, 149, 156, 183, 187–188, 189, 191, 199, 214–215, 221, 230, 231, 237 *See also* evaluation
Association for Supervision and Curriculum Development, 232–233
Association of College and Resource Libraries, 175–176
Association of Educational Communications and Technology, 23
audience. *See* communities
audio, 197–198

B

Bagshawe, A., 170–171
Bailey, C., Jr., 106, 132
Barbour, J., 8–9
Beach, A., 236
Bello, J., 165–168, 208–209
Benfari, R., 176–177
Bennett, B., 190
Benson, P., 232
Berry, L., 187–188
Bertalanffy, L., 9
Blake, R., 53–54
book fairs, 144
bookstores, 118, 128
Bringing It Down to You, 11, 22, 42, 77–78, 109, 133, 149, 177–178, 192–193, 225, 237–238
Brodsky, A., 168–169
budgets, 139–140
    library, 73, 88, 140–141
    reports, 137–139
    school, 34, 136–137
Burgoyne, J., 48

C

California Education Code, 4
California School Library Association, 18
Canadian Association for Public Libraries, 215
Cannon, R., 112
Carr-Ruffino, N., 56–57

cataloging, 97, 98, 99–100
    See also processing, collection
    development
change, 9, 75–76, 235–236
circulation, 37, 87, 101–104
Clifton, S., 131
coaching, 170, 173–174
    See also staffing, professional
    development
collaboration, 32, 42, 70, 73, 116, 143,
    146, 148–149, 218–219, 232, 236
    See also planning
collection development, 32, 36, 82, 86
    acquisitions, 36–37, 88–89, 96–98
    analysis, 87–90
    deselection, 88–90, 107–108
    organization, 117–118
    policies, 92–3, 95–96
    processing, 98–99
    selection, 3, 92–95
    See also resources
Collins, J., 75, 234
Collins, R., 10, 47, 155–156, 229–230
Common Core State Standards, 31, 32,
    81–82, 189
communication, 18, 189, 195–196, 212,
    218
    advocacy, 16
    branding, 212
    campaigns, 202
    documents, 159, 197, 206, 223–224
    evaluation, 205–209
    format, 197–198, 199–200, 206–208
    model, 196–197
    procedures, 201, 202, 215–216,
    223–224
    public relations, 39–40, 48, 50, 73,
    142, 144, 210
    skills, 51, 140–141, 146, 195–196
    See also displays, marketing, media
    kits, signage
communities, 66, 83, 91–92, 199, 210,
    larger, 39–40, 146–147, 191
    school, 19–20, 23, 30, 119, 143, 146,
    183–184, 220–221, 237
Coombs, K., 106, 133
copyright, 3, 224
    See also ethics, legislation
Covey, S., 228, 220
culture, 57–58, 84, 203
    competence, 40, 175–176
    library, 159
    school, 25, 37–38, 40, 57, 232
curriculum
    development, 30–32
    library, 31, 189

    school, 29–30, 184
cyberbullying, 68

D
Dall'Alba, G., 46
databases, 14, 91, 93, 97–98
Datar, S., 229
decision making, 52–53, 72, 152–154
Denise, L., 218
Dewey, J., 111–112
disabilities, 3, 120, 125, 129–130
disasters, 106–107, 131–132
displays, 117, 118–119
donations, 143–145
Doshisha Secondary Girls School, 125
Downs, E., 223
Dumler, M., 52, 62, 73, 75, 182, 188
Duncan, R., 76

E
Ely, D., 76
Emery, F., 155
Emery, J., 106, 132
environmental scan, 38–39, 65–66
    See also SWOT analysis
equipment. *See* technology
Erickson, R., 121
ethics, 224–225
evaluation, 31, 165–168, 169, 205–209,
    214–215
    See also assessment
Every Student Succeeds Act, 141–142, 157
expectations, 161, 171, 204, 210

F
facilities, 34–35, 111, 123–124, 131,
    182–183
    renovations, 128–129
    See also furniture, space
Farmer, L., 11, 14–15, 140, 191
Fayol, H., 6, 7–8
Feldman, D., 159
Felker, J., 84–85
Fiedler, F., 54–55
finances
    funding, 130, 141–142, 143–144, 146
    See also budgets, donations, grants
Finkelstein, J., 236
focus groups, 88
Follett, 90
food for thought, 2, 20, 33, 38–39, 49, 66,
    69, 124–125, 142, 161, 192, 213, 231
French, J., 230
Furnham, A., 55
furniture, 36, 120–124, 126, 127–128
    See also facilities

G

Gale Encyclopedia of Small Business, 128
Gantt chart, 187
Garner, E., 171, 173
Garvin, D., 229
gender issues, 56–57, 176
goals, 26, 31, 70, 146, 169, 196, 198, 219, 233–234
grants, 146–149
    See also finances
green ecological management, 108–109, 127–128
groups, 26, 48, 173
    See also communities, organizations
Guth, D., 66, 199, 210–211

H

H. W. Wilson, 90
Hallinger, P., 236
Halsted, D., 131
Harry, B., 40
Harvard College, 229
Heaston, A., 199–200
Heck, R., 236
Hempel, J. , 114
Henderson, J., 236
Herzberg, F., 9, 171
Hicks, K., 175
Hicks, R., 175
Hofstede, G., 57, 176
Huber, J., 66, 69

I

infographics, 91
    See also visuals
information, 1, 16, 197, 198
Infusionsoft, 213
Institute of Education Statistics, 4, 90
instruction, 67, 184, 207, 228
    in libraries, 16, 68, 188–189
integrated library management system, 88, 99, 101, 144, 192
interlibrary loan, 87
International Association of School Librarianship, 132
International Literacy Association, 94
International Society for Technology in Education, 184, 189
interviews, 87
inventory, 104, 105, 107, 131, 132

J

Jessen, S., 186–187
jobbers, 97, 98, 100
Johnson, P., 87–90, 95–96

K

Kalyanpur, M., 40
Kasowitz, A., 190
Kaspar, W., 234–235
Kitty Hawk Elementary School, 28
Kotter, J., 235–236
Kraft, M., 232
Krop, C., 229

L

Lankes, D., 190
Lawrence, B., 130
leadership, 16, 227–228
    and management, 227
    conditions for, 230–233
    functions, 228
    skills, 229
    styles, 231–232, 233–235
    See also change
learning, 184
    environment, 21–22, 112–114, 189
    skills, 33
    theories, 112–113
Leffert, N., 232
legislation, 15, 141–142
Levinson, D., 175
librarians, 157–158
    See also school librarians
libraries, 6, 146
    benefits, 1–2
    definition, 4–5
    See public libraries, school libraries
Library Research Services, 18
lighting, 117
literacy, 16, 81–82, 118, 142
    See also reading
Loertscher, D., 84–85
Lombardi, M., 134, 244
Lyrasis, 133

M

magazines. *See* periodicals
maintenance, 83, 104–106, 123, 131–132, 145
maker spaces, 115–116
management, 6–7
    functions, 22–23, 41–42
    of school libraries, 6–7, 42, 64, 73, 81, 101, 108, 128–129, 142–143, 188–189, 195–196, 233
    of self, 47–48, 56–58
    principles, 7–8
    qualities, 48
    roles, 10,
    skills, 21, 48, 50, 51

management *(cont'd)*
    styles, 53–56
    theories, 8–10
Marakas, G., 52
marketing, 66, 117, 185, 210–213
Marsh, C., 66, 199, 210–211
Maruson, C., 121
Marzano, R., 232
Maslow, A., 8, 69
McGregor, D., 9
McLuhan, M., 197
McPheat, S., 137–138, 140, 170, 174, 229
media kits, 201–202
meetings, 116, 174
Merrigan, D., 232
mission
    library, 5, 6, 85
    school, 26, 28–29, 38, 182
Mitchell, A., 106, 132
Mölnlycke Bibliotek, 115
Montiel-Overall, P., 218–219
Moos, R., 112
Moran, B., 8–9
Morris, C., 106, 132
motivation, 170–171
Mouton, J., 53–54
Movement Advancement Project, 202
Mowl, G., 65
multimedia, 198, 199, 206, 207

N

National Association of State Educational Media Professionals, 15
National Board for Professional Teaching Standards, 16–17
National Center for Education Statistics, 5
National Council for Accreditation of Teacher Education, 15, 2010
Nicholson, N., 160
Nissen, L., 232
Northeast Document Conservation Center, 131, 132

O

objectives, 31, 55, 62, 70, 74, 139, 146, 190, 211
Oblinger, D., 112, 113
OCLC, 86, 91, 92
Ohio State University, The, 133
organizations, 26, 231–232
    as systems, 7, 26–27, 181, 183, 236
    definition, 7
    professional, 94–95, 132, 142, 148, 216

P

Papert, S., 112–113
parents, 143–144, 200
    See also communities
Parsuraman, A., 187–188
Partnership for 21ˢᵗ Century Skills, 236–237
partnerships, 148–149, 219–220
    See also collaboration, communities, teachers
Patterson, J., 229
periodicals, 94–95, 99, 101–102, 107
personal growth, 46, 51, 160, 231
personnel, 27, 136, 154–156, 214
    human resource officer, 158, 159
    intergenerational, 174–175
    socialization, 164
    See also staffing of libraries
philosophy of education, 30–31, 34, 112
planning, 50, 61–62, 200–201, 202, 221–222
    action plans, 70–72
    goal-setting, 68–69
    steps, 63–75
    team, 63–64, 70
    types of plans, 62
    See also change
Plevyak, L., 199–200
policies, 73, 92–93, 95–96, 222–223
post-secondary, 19
Potter, S., 66, 69
Powell, D., 168–169
power, 50–51, 177–178, 221, 230–231
Princeton Academy of the Sacred Heart, 28
principals. *See* administrators
procedures, 96, 102, 222–223
professional development, 16, 46, 162, 207
    See also staffing of libraries
programs. *See* school libraries, programs
projects, 186–187
public libraries, 2, 3, 4, 5, 94, 105
publishers, 94–95, 97

R

Raven, B., 230
reading, 16, 19, 118–119, 191, 192, 200
reference
    services, 190–191, 192
    sources, 117
Reference and Users Services Association, 190
reflection, 77–78
Reid, R., 200
repairs. *See* maintenance
research, 8, 16–17, 18, 112–113, 114, 182, 191

resources
   allocation, 72–73, 136–137
   library, 2, 3, 27, 82, 189
   school, 34, 184
     See also collection development,
      maintenance, reference
Resources for School Librarians, 15, 156
reviews, 94–95
Rio Branco School, 119
Rounds, R., 139–140
Rubin, R., 204–205
rural libraries, 130

S

safety, 120
Sandberg, J., 46
Sarkodie-Manash, K., 203
Scales, P., 232
scheduling, 186
Schmidt, W., 231
school librarians, 5–6, 15–17
See also librarians, school libraries
school libraries
   assets, 41
   benefits, 1–4, 7, 112, 230
   functions, 6, 152–154, 156–157, 188,
   189
   ideal, 13, 17–18, 20
   naming, 5
   products, 27
   programs, 5
   standards, 14–15
School Library Journal, 18, 90, 140
schools, 26–27
   districts, 96, 98, 136, 141, 144, 222, 236
   impactful factors, 41–42
Schuckett, S., 215–216
security, 108, 120, 122, 123
Senge, P., 9
service, 234–235
   library, 182, 212
   school, 186
   See also instruction, reading, reference
Short, B., 199
signage, 119–120
Simons, S., 106, 132
Simpson, S., 234
Skinner, S., 52, 62, 73, 75, 182, 188
socialization, 39, 159–160, 164, 175
sound, 125
space, 3, 111–114
   impact, 111–113
   offices, 116
   physical, 114–117, 121
   virtual, 35, 112, 113, 130, 192
   See also facilities

staffing of libraries, 4, 5, 157–162, 182,
   188, 200
   communication, 208–209
   disciplining, 171–172
   functions, 63, 156
   hiring, 158–159
   interpersonal issues, 48, 50, 156,
   159–160, 172–177, 203–205
   recruitment, 157–158
   training, 155–156, 160–162, 164
   See also personnel
stakeholders, 63, 76–77, 143, 148–149
   See also communities
statistics, 18–19, 90
storage, 116, 123, 127
stress, 47, 55
Stricevic, I., 191
Stuart, R., 8–9, 48
students, 163–168, 172, 193, 200
   success, 183–184, 232, 237
supervision, 50, 168–172
   See also professional development,
   staffing of libraries, students,
   volunteers
supplies, 37
surveys, 88
SWOT analysis, 67–68, 185, 211
   See also environmental scan
systems. *See* organizations

T

Tamalpais Union High School District,
   28
Tannenbaum, R., 231
teachers, 3, 20, 82, 143, 146, 183–184,
   200, 220, 221–222, 229–230
technology, 3, 35–37, 91–94, 95, 97, 98,
   100, 105–106, 108, 109, 113, 119,
   128, 132, 144–145, 148, 222, 224–225
   hardware, 37, 107, 117, 120, 121,
   122–123, 124
   online resources, 87, 96–97
   software, 37, 132
   space, 116
   See also technology, by format
textbooks, 36–37, 103–104
Thorsrud, E., 155
time management, 47, 167
training. *See* professional development,
   staffing of libraries
Turkle, S., 112–113

U

United States Department of Health and
   Human Services, 169
United States Department of Labor, 157

V

values, 47, 57, 212, 232, 234, 235
VanDuinkerken, S., 234–235
Velasquez, D., 38
vendors, 97–98, 105, 120–121, 144
videos, 91, 198, 206–207, 216, 218
vision, 22–23
    library, 45–46
    school, 27
visuals, 197
    See also infographics
volunteers, 143–144, 155, 158, 162–163
    See also staffing of libraries,
    supervision, training
Vroom, V., 171
Vygotsky, L., 113

W

Weber, J., 228
webinars, 208
websites, 190, 192, 207, 213
weeding. *See* collection development
Wiles, J., 30–32
Wilson, D., 131
Wood, D., 211–212, 214–215
Woolls, B., 84–85
Wright, R., 106, 132

Y

Young Adult Library Services Association,
    130

Z

Zaltman, G., 76
Zhang, Z., 232